NEW SWAN SHAKESPEARE

GENERAL EDITOR
BERNARD LOTT M.A., PH.D.

Romeo and Juliet

NEW SWAN SHAKESPEARE

WILLIAM SHAKESPEARE

Romeo and Juliet

EDITED BY

JOHN INGLEDEW, M.A.

LONGMAN

LONGMAN GROUP LIMITED
Longman House
Burnt Mill, Harlow, Essex. U.K.

This edition © Longman Group Ltd 1965

First published *1965
New impression *1981

ISBN 0 582 52729 5

Illustrations by Clyde Pearson

We are indebted to the University of Cambridge
Local Examinations Syndicate for permission to
reproduce questions from past examination papers.

Printed in Hong Kong by
Sheck Wah Tong Printing Press Ltd

INTRODUCTION

The purpose of this book is to give and explain, in the simplest way, the text of one of Shakespeare's plays. The text itself is complete; spelling and punctuation have been modernised and notes and a glossary have been added; a section giving hints to examination candidates has been included at the end of the book (page 205).

All explanations have been given within the range of a specially-chosen list of 3,000 most commonly used English root-words. Every word in the book which falls outside this list is explained. This is done in the following way:

words which are not used in everyday Modern English as Shakespeare used them, or which are not now used at all, will be found explained in notes on the pages facing the text;

words which are still used in ordinary modern English with their meaning unchanged, but which are not among the 3,000 root-words of the chosen list, will be found explained in the glossary at the back of the book.

References to one or other of these places, and a study of section 3 of this introduction, should be sufficient to remove all difficulty in the understanding of the text. Explanations of longer passages are also given within the range of the word-list.

The rest of this introduction is arranged under the following headings:

1 *The Story*

A street fight breaks out in the Italian city of Verona between the members and servants of two noble families which have long been enemies, the Capulets and the Montagues. It rages until Prince Escalus, the ruler, arrives to stop it.

Lord and Lady Montague, worried by the strange behaviour of their son, Romeo, ask his cousin Benvolio to discover the reason for it. Romeo tells Benvolio that he is in despair because his love for Rosaline is not returned. When they discover that Rosaline will be at the Capulets' feast that evening, Romeo and Benvolio go along in disguise. Romeo, forgetting his love for Rosaline, is captivated by Juliet's beauty and confesses his love to her. He is later shocked to learn that she is a Capulet. Juliet, in her turn, has fallen in love with Romeo, and is similarly upset to discover that he is a Montague. Later that night Romeo climbs the wall of Juliet's garden and hears her talking to herself and revealing her love for him. He promises to prove his love by marrying her, and at day-break visits Friar Lawrence, who is persuaded to agree to marry them that afternoon, in the hope that this link between the two families will end their quarrel.

Juliet's cousin, the hot-tempered Tybalt, has recognised Romeo despite his disguise at the feast. He considers Romeo's presence there, uninvited, an insult to his family and is determined to revenge it. Tybalt meets Romeo just after his secret marriage, but Romeo, who wants to be on friendly terms with the Capulets, refuses to fight him. Romeo's friend, Mercutio, annoyed by what he thinks is Romeo's cowardice, fights Tybalt himself and is killed. His death angers Romeo, who fights and kills Tybalt. He is banished from Verona and sets out for exile in Mantua.

Lord Capulet tries to force Juliet to marry Count Paris. She refuses and seeks advice from Friar Lawrence, who gives her a drug which will make her unconscious for forty-two hours. On the morning fixed for the marriage she is found apparently dead, and her body is laid in the family tomb. Friar Lawrence sends a message to summon Romeo secretly to Verona to assist Juliet's escape, but because of a plague in Verona the message never reaches him.

Meanwhile, Romeo's servant Balthasar, believing Juliet to be dead, hurries to Mantua to inform Romeo, who buys some poison and hastens back to Verona. At the tomb Paris tries to prevent Romeo from entering. Romeo kills him and enters the tomb; he drinks the poison and dies beside Juliet. Friar Lawrence now arrives and finds Juliet waking up, but he is frightened by the sound of approaching voices and runs away. When she discovers Romeo dead by her side, Juliet in despair kills herself with his dagger. A crowd from the city reaches the tomb, and Friar Lawrence unfolds to them the whole tragic story of the two lovers. The two families are at last reconciled.

2 *The Language*

The words listed below, which have either changed in meaning since Shakespeare's time, or are shortened forms which he uses for some special effect (e.g. to fit in with the metre of the verse), or are no longer used to-day, occur so often in the play that it would be a waste of space to explain them on each occasion in the notes. (No attempt should be made to learn this list by heart; it is to be consulted when difficulties occur which are not explained in the notes.)

'a – "he".

alack – exclamation of sorrow or regret.

anon – "at once".

ay – "yes".

ay em – an exclamation of grief, or regret.

but – "only".

cousin, coz – any close relative (not necessarily the child of an uncle or aunt).

do, does, did are often used with another verb without adding any separate meaning, e.g. ". . . ere I did approach" (I.i.100).

e'en – "even".

e'er – "ever".

ere – "before".

fain – (as an adjective) "glad, willing"; (as an adverb) "gladly, willingly".

faith, i' faith, by my fay – "in faith, by my faith, indeed", an exclamation.

fie – an expression of disgust.

forth – "forward, out".

hence – "from this place".

hie – "go quickly".

hither – "to this place".

hold! – "stop, wait".

vii

marry – "indeed, to be sure" (originally an oath, "by the Virgin Mary").

methinks – "it seems to me".

mine – (sometimes) "my".

nay – "no, indeed, now then".

needs – "necessarily".

ne'er – "never".

o' – a shortened form of "of" or "on".

o'er – "over".

presently – "at once".

quoth – "said".

's – "is".

sirrah – a form of address (usually used to social inferiors).

soft! – "stop! wait a moment!" An exclamation.

still – (sometimes) "always".

straight – (sometimes) "immediately".

't – "it".

th' – "the".

thence – "from that place".

thither – "to that place".

thou (as subject) and *thee* (as object), the second person singular pronouns, were often used instead of "you". Most verbs used with *thou* end in *-est* or *-st*, e.g. ". . . thou canst not teach me" (I.i.230). The verb *to be* and a few others are irregular, e.g. *thou art, thou wilt, thou shalt*.

thy, thine – "your, yours" (singular).

whence – "from which place".

wherefore – "for which reason".

whither – "to which place".

withal – "with, besides".

ye – "you" (plural).

yea – "yes, indeed".

yon, yond – "that" or "those (over there)".

Two-thirds of the play is written in blank verse, that is, verse without rhyme having five stressed and five unstressed syllables in each line with the stress falling on those syllables which are accented in speaking:

> This búd of lóve, by súmmer's rípening bréath,
> May próve a beáuteous flówer when néxt we méet.
>
> (II.i.163).

The dramatist writing blank verse has greater freedom of expression than if he were writing rhymed verse, since he is not limited by the need to find rhyming words to end his lines. He can therefore come nearer to the patterns and forms of everyday speech and avoid the dullness which a play written wholly in rhyme tends to produce.

To introduce variety, or to draw our attention to words or ideas of importance, Shakespeare often varies this regular rhythmical pattern by arranging the stressed and unstressed syllables in a different order:

Dóst thou lóve me? I knów thou wílt say "Áy". (II.i.132).

Here the stress is placed on the first word of the line, *Dost*, and this impresses on us how anxious Juliet is to hear Romeo's answer to her question; it suggests the strength of her love for Romeo and the earnestness of her desire that he should return it. Variations in the rhythmical pattern can be used in this way to reveal a character's thoughts and feelings.

In his early plays (and *Romeo and Juliet* is one of these) Shakespeare makes extensive use of the couplet, in which each pair of lines has a rhyme of its own:

For nought so vile that on the earth doth live
But to the earth some special good doth give:
Nor aught so good but, strained from that fair use,
Revolts from true birth, stumbling on abuse. (II.ii.17–20).

You will notice that the whole of this scene of 94 lines is in rhyming couplets. Elsewhere couplets are commonly used to end a long speech and to close a scene, as in I.i, I.iii, and I.v.

Occasionally alternating rhyme is used, that is, rhyme in which, in a group of four lines, the first rhymes with the third and the second with the fourth, as when Juliet excuses Romeo's touch:

Good pilgrim, you do wrong your hand too much,
Which mannerly devotion shows in this;
For saints have hands that pilgrims' hands do touch,
And palm to palm is holy palmers' kiss. (I.v.96–99).

This highly formal kind of verse is often found in love-scenes where it is well-suited to the courtly declarations of lovers.

There is a good deal of prose in the play, most of it spoken by comic characters and those of low rank, like Sampson, Gregory, the Clown and other servants, to whom everyday language is most fitting. Blank verse, which is more elegant and less direct, is reserved for characters of higher rank, though sometimes, usually in scenes of minor importance, these speak prose, as in II.iv, where Mercutio and Romeo have a good-natured battle of words.

3 Imagery

A writer's or speaker's words can give us an understanding of one thing (a person, or idea, or experience, for example) by presenting our minds with a picture, an *image*, of something else with which it has some connection or similarity. Romeo suggests the richness and brightness of Juliet's beauty by saying that it shines out in the night:

> As a rich jewel in an Ethiop's ear. (I.v.45).

This kind of image, which makes a comparison, introduced by the words "as" or "like", between two different things, is called a *simile*. The particular quality of skilful poetic imagery is that it tells us more than a prose statement of fact could ever do. Romeo's words make a deeper impression on us than the simple statement, "She is very beautiful", would have done. We experience pleasure in following the working of the poet's imagination, and seeing with his eyes a likeness in unlike things and a unity in variety which we have never seen before and would never have seen for ourselves.

When a comparison is not made directly, but only suggested, the image is known as a *metaphor*. We have an example in Lady Capulet's description of Paris:

> Read o'er the volume of young Paris' face,
> And find delight writ there with beauty's pen;
> Examine every married lineament,
> And see how one another lends content;

And what obscured in this fair volume lies,
Find written in the margent of his eyes.
This precious book of love, this unbound lover,
To beautify him, only lacks a cover. (I.iii.75-82).

She speaks of Paris's face as a book, and extends the metaphor so that the various parts of a book – the words, the subject matter ("content") and the margin or edge of the page ("margent") – correspond to various parts of the face. Just as the marginal notes in a book tell us in a few words what the full text says, so Paris's eyes reveal at once his whole character. Juliet is the "cover" which will show the qualities of this "unbound lover" to the best advantage by marriage. The word "unbound" contains many meanings: the book without an outer cover, Paris not yet tied by the bonds of marriage, and the unlimited nature of his love, which helps to make it "precious". The closer we examine Shakespeare's use of metaphor and language the better we see how rich in suggestion it is, and how cleverly ideas are linked by the pattern of the imagery.

Imagery which speaks of an object, idea, or quality, as if it were a living being, is called *personification*:

The grey-eyed morn smiles on the frowning night. (II.ii.1).

By personifying day and night Shakespeare is able to tell us more than just the fact that it is now day. The word "grey-eyed" suggests the beauty of the half-light of early morning, and the contrast between "smiles" and "frowning" tells us that day is a happier time than night.

Shakespeare often repeats throughout a play images drawn from the same area of experience, so that they form a pattern which helps to make clear the meaning of the play, and the way he regards the story and its characters and wants us to regard them. This is one of the ways in which he imposes an artistic unity on the whole work. For example, he makes us see the beauty and purity of the love between Romeo and Juliet by repeating images taken from what is good and beautiful in nature – opening buds, flowers, trees, bird song, the heavenly bodies and so on – when he is describing this love. Their use of language associated with religion, as in I.v.92f, where words like "holy shrine", "pilgrims", "palm", "saints", "devotion", "prayer" and "sin" form the basis of the imagery, suggests that their love is virtuous and sacred, coming from the spirit. At the same time, the air of tragedy which hangs over and threatens this joyousness and beauty is created from the beginning by repeated images of violence, corruption and death. Shakespeare also frequently draws our attention to the passage of time by images of light and darkness, and these are closely linked to the changing fortunes of the lovers.

The use of poetic imagery, then, by its power of suggestion, of combining several ideas within one word or phrase, and of creating memorable pictures and comparisons, greatly enriches the substance of the play. The quality of poetry is largely determined by the quality of its imagery, and there is no greater master of imagery than Shakespeare, who enables us to see things and the connections between them with a fresh understanding.

4 *The Play as Drama*

Romeo and Juliet was probably written a year or two before its first appearance in print in 1597. A second and more complete text of the play was printed in 1599. Although Shakespeare's plays are to-day more commonly read than acted, we should remember that Shakespeare was chiefly concerned with stage performance and showed little interest in having his works printed and read. Our understanding of his plays will depend largely on the degree to which we can re-create them in our imagination as stage performances, and to do this we need some knowledge of the stage conditions of his time.

Romeo and Juliet was written for the public theatre of Shakespeare's time, which differed in many ways from our theatres to-day. It was smaller, and most of the area occupied by the stage and by the audience was unroofed. The "apron" stage, as it was called, stretched out into the centre of the theatre, with the audience sitting or standing round three sides of it. Doors opened on to each end of the back or fourth side, and between them was a recess, the inner stage, which could be shut off from the main stage by a curtain or screen. The roof above the inner stage formed the floor of a room or platform known as the upper stage. The inner stage would be used, for example, to represent Friar Lawrence's study (III.iii), Juliet's bedroom (IV.iii and IV.v), and her tomb (V.iii), while the upper stage would be used in III.v. where Romeo bids farewell to Juliet and descends by the rope ladder to the garden. The main stage was used for crowd scenes and street scenes (I.i and I.ii) and for Capulet's feast (I.v). When an actor was alone on-stage and wished to take the audience into his confidence, or wished to comment on what others were doing and saying in the background, he would come to the front of the stage in order to create that close relationship with the audience which was necessary.

The play was performed in daylight, in the afternoon. Although flaming torches might be carried, as in I.iv to create the impression that it was night time, the dramatist depended mainly on his descriptive powers to aid the imagination of the audience into accepting his changes of time. An example of this is Romeo's fine description of approaching dawn:

> Look, love, what envious streaks
> Do lace the severing clouds in yonder east.
> Night's candles are burnt out, and jocund day
> Stands tiptoe on the misty mountain tops. (III.v.7–10).

There was no front curtain to hide the stage while painted scenery and backcloths, such as we have to-day, were changed, or while "dead bodies" were removed. All the Elizabethans had was a few simple, easily-moved pieces of stage furniture, such as "trees" used for such scenes as V.iii, where we are told that Paris's Page and Balthasar hide behind yew trees. The general absence of stage scenery led Shakespeare and many other dramatists to paint their scenes poetically, a habit which has given us some of the finest poetry in the drama of the time.

xiii

If we keep in mind, then, that *Romeo and Juliet* was not a book, but words to be spoken and acted on a stage, we will not be worried, as some have been, by minor contradictions, such as the fact that Lady Capulet, who is less than thirty years old, speaks of her "old age", or that Juliet remains unconscious for only half the time that Friar Lawrence says she will. During performance of the play, which in Shakespeare's time was swift and uninterrupted, such details are unnoticed, and so have no dramatic importance.

5 Construction and Ideas

Romeo and Juliet is simple and complete in structure, with one main plot – the story of the lovers – and no secondary plot. Each event is linked to the next with considerable dramatic skill and economy. For example, Romeo goes to the feast in order to see Rosaline. His intrusion leads to his meeting with Juliet and so to his marriage, and also to the enmity of Tybalt. It is his marriage to Juliet which makes him refuse to quarrel with Tybalt, and it is this refusal which leads his friend Mercutio to fight Tybalt. This same friendship causes Romeo to revenge Mercutio's death, and so leads to his banishment. Events proceed in this logical way right down to the great climax of the last scene, and we see that very careful planning and construction lie behind the apparently simple structure.

Shakespeare based his play on a long poem, *The Tragical History of Romeus and Juliet*, a translation by Arthur Brooke in 1562 of a French account of this well-known Italian story. Shakespeare made many changes in the story which reveal his dramatic purposes. Brooke's poem covers a period of over nine months; by confining events to a period of less than five days, Shakespeare gives speed and excitement to the story. In Brooke the lovers live together for several weeks, but Shakespeare allows them only one night together, and so increases our sympathy for them and our sense of the harshness of their fate. He also gives much greater prominence to the quarrel between the two families and opens his play with a fight between them. He wants us to see that the personal tragedy of his hero and heroine

xiv

springs directly from this social evil, the "ancient grudge" which makes it impossible for their love to take an ordinary, happy course. Shakespeare shows how hatred poisons human relations in society, affecting almost everyone like a disease. It causes the violent deaths of Mercutio and Tybalt, Lady Montague's death through grief, the slaying of Paris and the suicides of Romeo and Juliet. At first even the lovers are influenced by it. Romeo speaks of Juliet as "my foe", and Juliet describes Romeo as "a loathéd enemy", and later they are forced into a course of lying and deception. It corrupts the good and peace-loving Benvolio into giving a false account to Prince Escalus of the fight between Mercutio and Tybalt. As Lady Capulet says, "Affection makes him false; he speaks not true" (III.i.173), but she too is led by the family hatred into giving an untrue account of the fight. In the face of these lies it is difficult for Prince Escalus to learn the truth and rule the city with justice, and social life is threatened by the brawls in which citizens defy the law and attack their neighbours. Lady Capulet, who at first tried to prevent her husband from fighting in the streets, plans to revenge Tybalt by having Romeo poisoned. Romeo and Juliet learn that love can only flourish where hatred is absent, and so have to cast off their names and family loyalties.

Despite the prevailing mood of tragedy, there is plenty of humour in the play. It is skilfully controlled, however, so that it does not weaken the tragic effect, but often heightens it, and always carries the story one step further by linking one event naturally with the next. We notice, for example, that all the joking of Sampson and Gregory is centred on violence and the family feud. Their unthinking acceptance of the quarrel as if it were their own, helps to keep it alive and breeds further trouble. Another comic figure, the Clown, is used as the means by which Romeo learns that Rosaline will be at the feast, and so leads to his meeting with Juliet. Mercutio's energy of mind and body and his careless gaiety, which bring so much laughter to the play, are the very qualities which lead him to quarrel with Tybalt and so hasten the tragedy. The Nurse, another source of amusement, plays an essential part in the action as the messenger between the lovers. In these ways, then, Shakespeare cleverly combines plot structure with character, using comic effects dramatically, and not just for their own sakes.

Shakespeare creates an atmosphere of tragedy through the dreams and forebodings experienced by his characters, so that we feel that events are directed by supernatural forces outside their power. The lovers are "star-crossed". As Romeo goes to the Capulets' feast he senses "Some consequence, yet hanging in the stars" (I.iv.108) which will bring about his early death, and after Tybalt's death he feels that he is "Fortune's fool" and that

> This day's black fate on more days doth depend;
> This but begins the woe others must end (III.i.115).

Juliet has an "ill-divining soul" which foresees evil, and there are many more examples in the course of the play.

Shakespeare makes considerable use of dramatic irony, the device in which characters speak and act in ignorance of the true significance of what they or other characters are saying, while sometimes the audience are aware of this because they know facts unknown to the speakers. Sometimes they do not, and only later see the irony of previous speeches and actions. For example, Mercutio's dying curse, "A plague o' both your houses" (III.i.102), is fulfilled in a way he would never have expected or wanted. Juliet sees Romeo in the garden "As one dead in the bottom of a tomb" (III.v.55); Capulet tells Juliet, after her refusal to marry Paris, that she will inherit nothing of his, while Lady Capulet rejects her daughter with the words "I have done with thee" (III.v.203), and all these statements are later seen to be truer than their speakers intended. There is irony, too, in the way events produce results which are the reverse of what is expected. The preparations for Juliet's wedding are used for her funeral:

> Our bridal flowers serve for a buried corse,
> And all things change them to the contrary (IV.v.89),

and this last line is an apt description of much that happens in the play. The coming of light makes things darker for Romeo and Juliet (III.v.36); Romeo's dreams "presage some joyful news at hand" (V.i.2), which, with cruel irony, turns out to be news of Juliet's death, and so on. All these methods stress that events are being controlled, as Friar Lawrence puts it, "by a power greater than we can contradict". Nevertheless, Shakespeare's hero and heroine have free will to act as they choose. It is impossible to state the exact degree to which supernatural power, the family feud, and their own actions are responsible for their fate; what is certain is that our sympathies are wholly with them, and that in their deaths we experience that sense of waste which is present in all great tragedy. The innocent are destroyed by the guilty, but the guilty do not escape. As the Prince tells Montague and Capulet, a scourge is laid upon their hatred, and "All are punished". Just as hatred begets only more hatred, so the love of Romeo and Juliet begets love, and through it the families are reconciled. The peace which results is "glooming", but it is nevertheless peace, and there seems more hope for the future than before; "grace" can conquer "rude will" as the Friar believes. Romeo, before his marriage, had declared:

> But come what sorrow can
> It cannot countervail the exchange of joy
> That one short minute gives me in her sight (II.v.3).

The lovers had their "one short minute" of joy, which we remember, despite their suffering, so that in the end love seems stronger than death itself. It is possibly this underlying sense of joy and hope which has made *Romeo and Juliet* one of Shakespeare's best-loved plays.

6 The Characters

Interest is centred on the hero and heroine whose names suggest, even to many who have not read the play, the perfect types of young lovers – noble, passionate and beautiful. But if they were no more than this they would be rather dull. Shakespeare makes them real and interesting individuals by mixing faults with their virtues (though he is careful not to make their failings so serious that they destroy our sympathy) and also by making them change and mature with experience.

At first *Romeo* is in a mood of deep melancholy. His behaviour in shutting himself off from his family and friends, avoiding the light of day, and spending his time weeping and sighing, follows the conventional pattern of the despairing lover. His suffering is real, but not deep; his mood is largely self-pity and his love exists only in his imagination. The fact that we never see Rosaline makes his passion seem all the more lacking in substance, and we see its shallowness in the speed with which he forgets all about it when he meets Juliet. Because of this we are at first in some doubt about the depth of his second love. His feeling for Rosaline had been built on "the devout religion of mine eye", as he called it (I.ii.90) rather than on any true knowledge of her, and again, with Juliet, he is "bewitchéd by the charm of looks" (II.Prologue,6), so that we suspect, as Friar Lawrence does, that he is a "waverer", and that

Young men's love then lies
Not truly in their hearts, but in their eyes (II.ii.67).

As his new love is tested in various ways we see that it is sincere, and as the lovers increase in knowledge of each other so their love deepens and matures. This growth, however, takes time. Romeo is certainly behaving selfishly and childishly when he throws himself on the floor of Friar Lawrence's cell, threatening to kill himself (III.iii). We applaud both the Nurse, who tells him to stand up and behave like a man, and Friar Lawrence, who tells him that his tears are womanish and his "wild acts denote/The unreasonable fury of a beast" (III.iii.109) and not the "valour of a man".

Romeo is essentially peace-loving. He will have nothing to do with the family feud and tries to prevent Mercutio and Tybalt from fighting, reminding them that it is against the law. His action in killing Tybalt, however, breaks the same law, and employs the same violent methods which he has criticised in others. He is wrong in arguing that he must clear the stain on his honour caused by Tybalt's slander, since slander cannot stain honour, and cannot be a sufficient motive for manslaughter. Prince Escalus describes those who raise their hands against their neighbours as "beasts", and the inhumanity of Romeo's action is underlined by Juliet's words when she hears what he has done; she calls him "serpent heart", "dragon", "fiend", "raven", "wolf". Since Tybalt would have been punished by law for his killing of Mercutio, as Lord Montague points out (III.i.181), Romeo's action in taking the law into his own hands and calling upon "fire-eyed fury" to take possession of him, is inexcusable. This is the kind of action which has perpetuated the feud, and Lady Capulet is no worse when she demands that the Prince should "For blood of ours, shed blood of Montague" (III.i.145). It is a sign of Romeo's growth in love and wisdom that he later refers to his killing of Tybalt as a sin, and begs forgiveness of Tybalt's corpse, and that by contrast he is most unwilling to fight Paris, and does so only in self-defence. There is a new calm and self-control in Romeo after his exile, and his first thought is now for Juliet. The final scene shows him at his best. His gentleness and courtesy to Paris, in the midst of all his own suffering, is admirable. The high opinion which other characters have of Romeo makes us more aware of his attractiveness; apart from the love of Juliet and his parents, we notice the affection which Friar Lawrence, Mercutio and Benvolio have for him, and the fact that "Verona brags of him/To be a virtuous and well-governed youth" (I.v.66).

Juliet, too, matures with experience, and her feeling for Romeo develops from a rather girlish affection to a deep womanly love. Her youth and inexperience are touchingly seen when she tries to hide her feeling for Romeo by first asking the names of other men in order to discover his (I.v.127f). This innocent trick reveals her love more clearly than any formal declaration could have done. Her love teaches her the wicked stupidity of the feud, and that it is character not name that matters. The generosity and selflessness of her love is seen in her fears for Romeo's safety when he appears in her orchard (II.i), and again when Romeo is about to leave for Mantua and Juliet argues that it is the nightingale and not the lark that they hear; as soon as Romeo hints that he will be in danger if he stays, she insists that he must go at once (III.v.17f).

Juliet's sufferings are greater than Romeo's. After Romeo's banishment she is rejected first by her father, then by her mother, and after this discovers that she can no longer trust her Nurse. Except for Friar Lawrence's friendship, she is completely alone, and so terrified that she even doubts his honesty for a moment, as she faces the thought of the potion and waking up in the vault. It is true to Juliet's nature that what gives her courage to take the potion is the threat to Romeo's safety which she sees in her vision (IV.iii.55). Her direct and practical nature lends strength and inspiration to her lover.

Many think that *Friar Lawrence*, who is a voice of peace and wisdom in the troubled world of Verona, is a mouthpiece for Shakespeare's own view of life. All his speeches have weight and authority, and all his actions are directed towards the spiritual welfare of Verona's citizens. As Capulet says, "All our whole city is much bound to him" (IV.ii.32). His deep knowledge of man and nature has convinced him that there is nothing wholly evil in the universe, and the entire play is an illustration of his belief that when "rude will" or passion overcomes "grace" or virtue in man, then spiritual death and all sorts of social evils follow. He is a practical man, quick in thought and action, and it is not his fault that his plans do not succeed. He admits that he was misguided in assisting at the secret marriage of Romeo and Juliet, but his motive was the admirable one of trying to bring peace to Verona. He is grateful for good fortune and makes the best of every situation, and teaches others to do the same. His moment of weakness, when he runs away in fear from the tomb (V.iii) in no way lessens his holiness and wisdom, but places him squarely in the world of real human beings.

The character of *Mercutio* is Shakespeare's own addition to the story and one of his most attractive and lively creations. He has great energy, wit, and a rough common sense which makes him impatient with affectation of any kind, whether it is

Romeo's "groaning for love", or the foreign manners of "antic, lisping, affecting fantasticoes" like Tybalt. But Mercutio has his limitations. He has no understanding of love; as Romeo says, "He jests at scars that never felt a wound" (II.i.43). In picking a fight with Tybalt, although he does so out of friendship for Romeo, he is resorting to the violence and misplaced sense of honour which is the cause of the family feud. All his courage and humour, however, are seen in his dying reply to Romeo who tries to comfort him by saying that his wound cannot be serious:

> No, 't is not so deep as a well, nor so wide as a church door,
> but 't is enough, 't will serve (III.i.92).

When Mercutio dies we feel that a bright light has gone out.

Benvolio, by contrast, is quiet, cautious, and peace-loving. Mercutio's assertion that Benvolio's head "is as full of quarrels as an egg is full of meat" is just the reverse of true. It is truer of Mercutio himself, as Benvolio mildly remarks. In this world of violence, Benvolio is almost helpless. He is assaulted by Tybalt when he tries to stop the servants from quarrelling (I.i). Mercutio pays no attention to his appeal to go home because of the danger of a fight with the Capulets (III.i), and when it does break out no one pays any attention to his request that they should retire to some private place to "reason coldly of your grievances" (III.i.49). Benvolio lives up to his name, which means in Italian, "I wish well". He is a type of the good friend, selfless and loyal, helping the Montagues to discover the cause of Romeo's melancholy, then trying to remove it, and in the end assisting him to escape.

Tybalt's character is briefly but brilliantly outlined. Every word of the 35 lines he speaks helps to reveal him. His first words are an expression of contempt for the servants (I.i.58), and these are at once followed by his threat to kill Benvolio for no apparent reason except a love of violence. He hates the word "peace", he tells Benvolio, who rightly describes him as "furious" and "fiery". As soon as he suspects Romeo's presence at his uncle's feast, he orders his servant to fetch his rapier, and determines to kill him with no attempt to discover why he is there, and no thought for the fact that it is not his house or his feast. When Capulet scolds him he goes off muttering angry threats. His twisted sense of honour is reflected in his reference to the "injuries" Romeo has done him (III.i.65). Tybalt is an unpleasant character, but we should notice that he is dearly loved by Juliet, and that he was not responsible for the fight in which Mercutio was killed.

The *Nurse* is a thoroughly human mixture of good and bad. She is coarse, vain and talkative, and too ready for an excuse to have a drink of her "aqua-vitae", yet she is warm-hearted and truly fond of Juliet, as we see from her memories of Juliet's childhood (I.iii), her playful attempt to increase Juliet's impatience (II.iv), and her attack on Capulet for his cruelty to his daughter (III.v.168). Her admission that Susan was "too good for me" and her obvious affection for her husband, also dead, are attractive qualities in her, but her advice that Juliet should forget about Romeo and marry Paris underlines the contrast between her coarseness and shallowness of nature and the fineness and purity of Juliet.

Paris, who cannot be allowed to engage too much of our attention and draw sympathy away from his rival Romeo, remains throughout a rather colourless and indistinct figure. His behaviour at the tomb makes it clear that he sincerely loved Juliet, and so strengthens our awareness that she is a lovable person, but we can hardly admire him when he addresses her as "my lady and my wife" (IV.i.18) before obtaining her consent, or for his inability to see that she does not care for him.

In Shakespeare's time it was believed that the ruler was God's deputy, a man chosen by God to be his representative on earth, with the duty of maintaining law and justice among his subjects. This is why Prince *Escalus* is respected and obeyed. His speeches and actions are firm and dignified, but he has difficulty in controlling the fiery passions of his lawless citizens.

Lord and *Lady Montague* are little more than voices, but Shakespeare draws more complete portraits of the Capulets.

Lady Capulet scolds her husband for fighting in the street, and later for the violence of his speech to Juliet, but she loses our sympathy in her threat to have Romeo poisoned, and for her failure in love when she rejects Juliet who turns to her for comfort after Capulet has threatened to turn her out of his house. *Capulet*, however, has his good points. He is a merry and generous host, quick to praise Romeo's good qualities and to put a stop to Tybalt's quarrelsomeness at the feast, but he is bad-tempered at times, boastful and fond of show. Capulet usually knows what is right, but fails to live up to this knowledge. Having told Paris that he must wait for two years until Juliet is old enough to marry, and must then gain her consent, he almost immediately attempts to force her to marry him within a few days, and in this he exceeds his parental authority. It is typical of his changeable nature that the one or two guests he plans to invite to the wedding, soon grow to half a dozen, and it is no time before he is ordering "twenty cunning cooks". While the Montagues are really upset by Romeo's unhappiness, the Capulets show no pity for Juliet and no respect for her feelings, but always put their own will before hers. None of the parents on either side takes any steps to heal their enmity until it is too late.

SHORT READING LIST FOR MORE
SENIOR STUDENTS

For details of Shakespearian word-meaning, students may consult:

A Shakespeare Glossary, by C. T. Onions, Oxford University Press, 1911, repr. 1958.

Explorations in Shakespeare's Language, by Hilda M. Hulme, Longmans, 1962.

Shakespeare-Lexicon, by A. Schmidt, de Gruyter, Berlin, 1923.

For Shakespeare's imagery and word-play:

Shakespeare's Imagery and what it tells us, by Caroline F. E. Spurgeon, Oxford University Press, 1935.

The Development of Shakespeare's Imagery, by W. H. Clemen, Methuen, 1951.

Shakespeare's World of Images, by D. A. Stauffer, Oxford University Press, 1952.

Shakespeare's Word-play, by M. M. Mahood, Methuen, 1957.

For Shakespeare, his theatre and his times:

A Companion to Shakespeare Studies, ed. H. Granville Barker and G. B. Harrison, Cambridge University Press, 1934.

Shakespeare's Theatre, by C. Walter Hodges, Oxford University Press, 1964.

For a study of Shakespearian criticism:

Shakespeare's Tragedies. A Selection of Modern Criticism, ed. L. Lerner, Penguin Books, 1963.

Shakespeare and his Critics, by F. E. Halliday, Duckworth, 1958.

For a study of the sources of the play:

Narrative and Dramatic Sources of Shakespeare, Vol. I, by G. Bullough, Routledge & Kegan Paul, 1957.

For a study of *Romeo and Juliet*:

Prefaces to Shakespeare, by H. Granville Barker, Batsford, 1958.

Shakespearian Tragedy, by H. B. Charlton, Cambridge University Press, 1948.

"*Romeo and Juliet*" by John Lawlor, an essay in *Early Shakespeare*, Stratford-upon-Avon Studies 3, Edward Arnold, 1961.

Patterns in Shakespearian Tragedy, by I. Ribner, Methuen, 1960.

On the Design of Shakespearian Tragedy, by H. S. Wilson, Oxford University Press, 1957.

Shakespeare and the Rose of Love, by John Vyvyan, Chatto & Windus, 1960.

BENVOLIO

Alas, that Love,[79] so gentle in his view,[80]
Should be so tyrannous and rough in proof.[81]

ROMEO

Alas, that Love, whose view is muffled still,
Should without eyes see pathways to his will.[82]
(I.i.162 – 165)

DRAMATIS PERSONAE

ESCALUS, *Prince of Verona*
PARIS, *a young Count, the Prince's kinsman*
MONTAGUE ⎱ *heads of two families at enmity with each other*
CAPULET ⎰
AN OLD MAN, *Capulet's kinsman*
ROMEO, *Montague's son*
MERCUTIO, *the Prince's kinsman and Romeo's friend*
BENVOLIO, *Montague's nephew and Romeo's friend*
TYBALT, *Lady Capulet's nephew*
FRIAR LAWRENCE ⎱ *members of the Franciscan Order*
FRIAR JOHN ⎰
BALTHASAR, *Romeo's servant*
SAMPSON ⎱
GREGORY ⎰ *Capulet's servants*
A CLOWN ⎰
PETER, *servant of Juliet's Nurse*
ABRAHAM, *Montague's servant*
An Apothecary
Page to Paris

LADY MONTAGUE, *Montague's wife*
LADY CAPULET, *Capulet's wife*
JULIET, *Capulet's daughter*
NURSE to Juliet

Chorus
Kinsmen of Both Families, Musicians, Guests, City Officers,
    Watchmen, Citizens, Servants and Attendants

————————————

The scenes are laid in the Italian cities of Verona and Mantua.

1 A prologue is an introduction, written or spoken, to something longer which follows. In this play, the prologue is spoken by the Chorus, a single speaker, who gives a very short outline of the story.

2 *dignity* – "honour and social rank".

3 *mutiny* – "quarrel".

4 *civil blood . . . hands unclean* – "the blood of fellow-citizens (*civil blood*) makes the hands of citizens (*civil hands*) unclean".

5 *the fatal loins . . . foes* – "parents who were enemies in this fatal way".

6 *star-crossed* – "opposed by the unfriendly influence of the stars". It was believed by many in Shakespeare's time that the stars and other heavenly bodies influenced the events of a man's life. For example, a man's character and fortunes would depend on whether the star he was born under was a friendly or an unfriendly one.

7 *Whose misadventured piteous overthrows* – "whose unfortunate and pitiful downfalls".

8 *Doth.* In Shakespeare's time writers frequently used the singular form of the verb, as here, where today we would have to use the grammatically correct plural, in this case, *do*. Compare *puts* (I.i.224), *faints* (II.iii.63), *glides* (II.iv.5), *idles* (II.v.19), and *makes* (III.ii.49).

9 *fearful passage* – "terrible course".

10 *death-marked love* – "love destined to be cut short by death". Here, and in line 6 above, and repeatedly throughout the play, Shakespeare stresses that the lives of Romeo and Juliet are ruled by supernatural forces and by natural events which are beyond their control. Although their own mistakes hasten their tragic end, it is their *stars* or fate which cause it.

11 *Which, but . . . could remove* – "which nothing could take away except (*but*) the death of their children".

12 *two hours' traffic . . . stage* – "the action which we are presenting for two hours on the stage". Today the play takes much longer than two hours to perform, since we have pauses while the stage-curtain is closed and the scenery changed, and there is usually a long interval halfway through the play. In Shakespeare's time, however, there was no curtain or scene-changing and the play was performed swiftly without a break.

13 *What here . . . to mend* – "whatever is lacking in our performance we shall work hard to remedy".

ROMEO AND JULIET

Prologue[1]

Enter CHORUS

CHORUS

Two households, both alike in dignity,[2]
  In fair Verona where we lay our scene,
From ancient grudge break to new mutiny,[3]
  Where civil blood makes civil hands unclean.[4]
From forth the fatal loins of these two foes[5]   5
  A pair of star-crossed[6] lovers take their life;
Whose misadventured piteous overthrows[7]
  Doth[8] with their death bury their parents' strife.
The fearful passage[9] of their death-marked love,[10]
  And the continuance of their parents' rage,   10
Which, but their children's end, nought could remove,[11]
  Is now the two hours' traffic of our stage;[12]
The which, if you with patient ears attend,
  What here shall miss, our toil shall strive to mend.[13]

                                                          [*Exit*

(I.i) Sampson and Gregory, servants of the Capulet family, quarrel with two servants of the Montague household. Benvolio, a Montague, tries to separate them, but is attacked by Tybalt, a Capulet. A fight develops which ends when Prince Escalus, the ruler of Verona, enters with his men. Benvolio, alone with his uncle and aunt, Lord and Lady Montague, assures them that he will discover why Romeo, their son, is behaving so moodily. As Romeo approaches, his parents leave, and Romeo reveals to his cousin that Rosaline whom he loves has sworn never to marry. He rejects Benvolio's advice to forget her by turning his interest to other ladies.

1 *bucklers*. Small round shields.

2 *carry coals*. As a saying, to *carry coals* is to "do dirty work which is beneath our dignity" and this is what Sampson means. Gregory pretends to understand the words in their ordinary meaning; this is the reason for his reference to *colliers*, men who carry coal.

3 *and we be in choler, we'll draw* – "if (*and*) we are angry (*in choler*) we will draw our swords, ready to fight".

4 *draw your neck . . . collar*. Gregory mistakes Sampson's word *choler* (anger) as a reference to the *collar*, i.e. the rope put round the neck of a condemned man by the hangman. Note the play on the words *colliers*, *choler* and *collar*, which are all similar in sound.

5 *moved*. Shakespeare plays on various meanings of the verb as follows: (a) "to anger" (lines 5, 7, 9); (b) "to force to action" (lines 5, 6, 7, 9, 10); (c) "to change position" (line 8). The Elizabethan audience greatly enjoyed this kind of word-play. It is often used to cause laughter, as it is here, but can be used for many other dramatic effects as will be seen later in the play.

6 *to stand* – "to hold one's ground, prepared to fight".

7 *take the wall of* – "take the position closest to the wall". In Shakespeare's London rubbish was thrown into the centre of the streets which were narrow and without pavements, so that the walls on each side were the cleanest and safest area. For this reason the strongest walked by the wall, forcing others into the centre.

2

ACT ONE

Scene I. A street in Verona.

Enter SAMPSON *and* GREGORY, *servants of the Capulet household, armed with swords and bucklers.*[1]

SAMPSON

Gregory, on my word, we 'll not carry coals.[2]

GREGORY

No, for then we should be colliers.

SAMPSON

I mean, and we be in choler, we 'll draw.[3]

GREGORY

Ay, while you live, draw your neck out of collar.[4]

SAMPSON

I strike quickly, being moved.[5]   5

GREGORY

But thou art not quickly moved to strike.

SAMPSON

A dog of the house of Montague moves me.

GREGORY

To move is to stir, and to be valiant is to stand:[6] therefore, if thou art moved thou runn'st away.

SAMPSON

A dog of that house shall move me to stand: I will take   10
the wall of[7] any man or maid of Montague's.

GREGORY

That shows thee a weak slave, for the weakest goes to the
wall.[8]

SAMPSON

'Tis true, and therefore women, being the weaker vessels,[9]
are ever thrust to the wall: therefore I will push Monta-   15
gue's men from the wall, and thrust his maids to the wall.

GREGORY

The quarrel is between our masters, and us their men.[10]

SAMPSON

'T is all one. I will show myself a tyrant: when I have
fought with the men, I will be civil with the maids; I will
cut off their heads.   20

GREGORY

The heads of the maids?

SAMPSON

Ay, the heads of the maids, or their maidenheads;[11] take
it in what sense[12] thou wilt.

---

8 *weakest goes to the wall*. In street dis-
   turbances the weakest are pushed
   against the wall.
9 *vessels* – "persons".
10 *The quarrel ... their men* – "Our
   masters, the Capulets, are enemies of
   the Montagues, and we, the Capulets'
   servants, are enemies of the Montagues' servants". The quarrel, he is saying, involves only men, not the *maids*
   mentioned by Sampson.
11 *maidenheads* – "virginity".
12 *sense* – "meaning". In line 22 it means
   "feeling".
13 *hadst* – "had (been)".
14 *poor John* – "salted fish", of a coarse
   and inferior kind.

15 *tool* – "weapon".
16 *back thee* – "support you". Gregory
   takes Sampson to mean "turn my
   back on you and run away".
17 *Fear me not* – "Do not fear that I will
   run away". Gregory understands
   Sampson's words in their ordinary
   sense to mean, "Do not be afraid of
   me". His exclamation, "I fear thee!"
   indicates his scorn at such an idea.
18 *take the law of our sides* – "have the law
   on our side", i.e. by not starting the
   quarrel.
19 *take it as they list* – "consider it an insult, or not notice it, just as they
   please".

4

GREGORY

They must take it in sense that feel it.

SAMPSON

Me they shall feel while I am able to stand; and 't is   25
known I am a pretty piece of flesh.

GREGORY

'T is well thou art not fish; if thou hadst,[13] thou hadst
been poor John.[14] Draw thy tool:[15] here comes two of
the house of Montagues.

Enter ABRAHAM *and another* Servant, *both*
of the Montague household

SAMPSON

My naked weapon is out. Quarrel; I will back thee.[16]   30

GREGORY

How? Turn thy back and run?

SAMPSON

Fear me not.[17]

GREGORY

No, marry; I fear thee!

SAMPSON

Let us take the law of our sides;[18] let them begin.

GREGORY

I will frown as I pass by, and let them take it as they list.[19]   35

SAMPSON

Nay, as they dare. I will bite my thumb at them,[20] which
is disgrace to them if they bear it.

ABRAHAM

Do you bite your thumb at us, sir?

SAMPSON

I do bite my thumb, sir.

ABRAHAM

Do you bite your thumb at us, sir?   40

SAMPSON

[*Aside to* GREGORY] Is the law of our side if I say "Ay"?

GREGORY

[*Aside to* SAMPSON] No.

SAMPSON

[*Replying to* ABRAHAM] No, sir, I do not bite my thumb
at you, sir, but I bite my thumb, sir.

---

20 *bite my thumb at them.* This was an
action which indicated contempt or
defiance.
21 *I am for you* – "I am ready to fight
you".
22 *Well, sir* – . Sampson hesitates to say
"better" because of his unwillingness
to start a quarrel, but he is encouraged
to do so by Gregory who sees Tybalt,
his master's nephew, approaching.
They know that they can count on
the hot-tempered Tybalt to help them
against the Montagues. In their ex-

changes (lines 38–52) the servants
mockingly call each other *sir*, intending to anger each other. The entry of
Benvolio, who balances Tybalt,
means that both sides are evenly
matched, and an open fight unavoid-
able.
23 *washing blow* – "swinging blow".
Gregory has apparently often boasted
about his *washing blow*. Sampson re-
minds him that now is the time for
him to use it.

GREGORY

Do you quarrel, sir?   45

ABRAHAM

Quarrel, sir? No, sir.

SAMPSON

But if you do, sir, I am for you.[21] I serve as good a man as
you.

ABRAHAM

No better?

SAMPSON

Well, sir –[22]   50

Enter BENVOLIO

GREGORY

[*Interrupting* SAMPSON *as he sees* TYBALT *approaching*]
Say "Better"; here comes one of my master's kinsmen.

SAMPSON

[*To* ABRAHAM] Yes, better, sir.

ABRAHAM

You lie.

SAMPSON

Draw, if you be men. Gregory, remember thy washing
blow.[23]   55

[*They fight*] BENVOLIO *draws his sword and tries to separate
them*

7

BENVOLIO

Part, fools!
Put up your swords;[24] you know not what you do.

Enter TYBALT

TYBALT

What, art thou drawn among these heartless hinds?[25]
Turn thee, Benvolio; look upon thy death.

BENVOLIO

I do but keep the peace. Put up thy sword,   60
Or manage it to part these men with me.[26]

TYBALT

What, drawn, and talk of peace? I hate the word
As I hate hell, all Montagues, and thee.
Have at thee,[27] coward!

[*They fight*

---

24 *Put up your swords* – "Replace your swords".

25 *heartless hinds* – (a) "cowardly, spiritless servants (*hinds*)"; (b) "female deer (*hinds*) without a male deer (*hart*) to lead and protect them". Both senses convey Tybalt's contempt for the servants.

26 *manage it ... with me* – "make use of (*manage*) your sword (*it*) with me to separate (*part*) these men".

27 *Have at thee.* An exclamation which warns that the speaker intends to attack.

28 *bills and partisans.* A *bill* is a weapon with a head like an axe set on a wooden handle; a *partisan* is a broad-headed, long-handled spear.

29 *A crutch!* Lady Capulet thinks that a stick to support his body is more suited to her husband's years than a sword to fight with. The fact that he enters in his nightgown (worn in the house after undressing, but not in bed) helps to impress upon us that he is an old man, who ought to be setting a better example.

30 *flourishes ... of me* – "waves (*flourishes*) his sword (*blade*) in scornful defiance (*spite*) of me".

31 *train.* A group of followers serving someone of high rank.

32 *Rebellious subjects ...* The entry of the Prince puts an immediate stop to the fighting; everyone listens to his words and obeys his commands. In Shakespeare's time the ruler was held in great respect because he was regarded as God's representative on earth. The Prince's speech, which is ordered, dignified and full of authority as suits his position, is in contrast to the coarse speech of the servants and the undignified quarrelling of the Capulets and Montagues.

8

Enter an Officer *with three or four armed* Citizens

OFFICER

Clubs, bills and partisans,[28] strike! Beat them down!   65
Down with the Capulets! Down with the Montagues!

Enter CAPULET *in his nightgown, with* LADY CAPULET,
his wife

CAPULET

What noise is this? Give me my long sword, ho!

LADY CAPULET

A crutch,[29] a crutch! Why call you for a sword?

CAPULET

My sword I say! Old Montague is come,
And flourishes his blade in spite of me.[30]   70

Enter MONTAGUE *and* LADY MONTAGUE, *his wife*

MONTAGUE

Thou villain, Capulet. [*To his wife*] Hold me not; let me
go.

LADY MONTAGUE

Thou shalt not stir one foot to seek a foe.

Enter PRINCE ESCALUS *with his train*[31]

PRINCE

Rebellious subjects,[32] enemies to peace,

Profaners of this neighbour-stainèd steel –[33]   75
Will they not hear? What ho! you men, you beasts,
That quench the fire of your pernicious rage
With purple fountains[34] issuing from your veins,
On pain of torture, from those bloody hands
Throw your mistempered weapons[35] to the ground,   80
And hear the sentence of your movèd Prince.
Three civil brawls bred of an airy word[36]
By thee, old Capulet, and Montague,
Have thrice disturbed the quiet of our streets,
And made Verona's ancient citizens   85
Cast by their grave beseeming ornaments[37]
To wield old partisans in hands as old,[38]
Cankered with peace, to part your cankered hate.[39]
If ever you disturb our streets again,

---

33 *Profaners of . . . steel.* By staining their swords with the blood of their neighbours (*neighbourèd stainèd steel*) they have *profaned* them, i.e. used them dishonourably.

34 *purple fountains* – "streams of blood".

35 *On pain of . . . mistempered weapons* – "if you do not drop your wicked swords out of your murderous hands, the punishment will be torture". To temper a weapon is to make the steel of just the right hardness. *Mistempered weapons* are those tempered for an evil use, but the Prince also refers to the ill-temper of those using them.

36 *bred of an airy word* – "started by some unimportant remark".

37 *Cast by . . . ornaments* – "throw on one side (*cast by*) the dignified (*grave*) attire (*ornaments*) suited to them (*beseeming*)."

38 *as old*, i.e. as old as the partisans.

39 *Cankered with . . . hate* – "rusted (*cankered*) through lack of use (owing to peace), to separate you both in your state of diseased (*cankered*) hatred".

40 *pay the forfeit of the peace* – Either (a) "pay for the violation of law and order", or (b) "pay the punishment due for breaking the law".

41 *our farther pleasure* – "what further steps I decide to take". The ruler often referred to himself in the plural as "We", and "our". His *pleasure* is his will or choice.

42 *common* – "public".

43 *new abroach* – "in action again".

44 *close fighting* – "fighting at close quarters, hand to hand".

45 *Who . . . hissed him in scorn.* Benvolio speaks as if the winds were Tybalt's enemies whom he cuts with his sword. He does not hurt them though he cuts them, and the noise which his sword makes as it is waved in the air is compared to the hissing of enemies.

46 *Came* – "there came".

47 *part and part* – "some on one side, some on the other".

48 *parted either part* – "separated both sides".

49 *Right* – "Very".

10

Your lives shall pay the forfeit of the peace.[40]   90
For this time, all the rest depart away.
You, Capulet, shall go along with me,
And Montague, come you this afternoon,
To know our farther pleasure[41] in this case,
To old Freetown, our common[42] judgement-place.   95
Once more, on pain of death, all men depart.

[*Exeunt all except* MONTAGUE, LADY MONTAGUE *and*
BENVOLIO

MONTAGUE

Who set this ancient quarrel new abroach?[43]
Speak, nephew. Were you by when it began?

BENVOLIO

Here were the servants of your adversary
And yours, close fighting[44] ere I did approach.   100
I drew to part them; in the instant came
The fiery Tybalt, with his sword prepared,
Which, as he breathed defiance to my ears,
He swung about his head and cut the winds,
Who, nothing hurt withal, hissed him in scorn.[45]   105
While we were interchanging thrusts and blows,
Came[46] more and more, and fought on part and part,[47]
Till the Prince came, who parted either part.[48]

LADY MONTAGUE

O where is Romeo? Saw you him to-day?
Right[49] glad I am he was not at this fray.   110

BENVOLIO

Madam, an hour before the worshipped sun
Peered forth the golden window of the east,

A troubled mind drive[50] me to walk abroad,[51]
Where, underneath the grove of sycamore
That westward rooteth[52] from this city side,[53]   115
So early walking did I see your son.
Towards him I made,[54] but he was ware of me,[55]
And stole into the covert of the wood.
I, measuring his affections[56] by my own,
Which then most sought where most might not be found,[57]   120
Being one too many by my weary self,[58]
Pursued my humour not pursuing his,[59]
And gladly shunned who[60] gladly fled from me.

MONTAGUE

Many a morning hath he there been seen,
With tears augmenting the fresh morning's dew,   125

---

50 *drive* – "drove". *Drive* is an old form of the past tense.

51 *abroad* – "out of doors".

52 *rooteth* – "has its roots, grows".

53 *this city side* – "this side of the city".

54 *made* – "went".

55 *was ware of me* – "knew I was there".

56 *measuring his affections* – "judging his desires".

57 *most sought where most might not be found.* There is play on the word *most*. Benvolio's desires (*affections*) urged him more than anything else (*most*) to seek out a place where there would not be a crowd (*most*) of people.

58 *Being one . . . self.* Benvolio wanted to be alone so much that even his own company was too much for him.

59 *Pursued . . . pursuing his* – "followed my desire for solitude (*humour*) by not following Romeo (who also had the same desire to be alone)".

60 *shunned who* – "avoided one who".

61 *Adding to clouds . . . deep sighs.* The cold morning air made the breath of Romeo's sighs become visible, like clouds.

62 *all so soon as* – "as soon as".

63 *Aurora's bed.* Aurora was the ancient Greek goddess of dawn. The Elizabethan "four-poster" bed had a roof supported by an upright post at each corner, and curtains which could be drawn all round the bed.

64 *heavy* – "sorrowful". Notice the contrast with *light* in this line.

65 *his own affections' counsellor.* Romeo keeps the secret of his desires to himself.

66 *close* – "reserved".

67 *sounding and discovery* – "the measuring (*sounding*) and exploration (*discovery*) of his hidden depths", i.e. by others. It is as impossible to discover Romeo's hidden thoughts as it is to see the worm hidden in the bud.

68 *bit with* – "bitten by".

69 *envious* – "full of ill-will".

70 *We would . . . as know* – "We are as anxious to cure his sorrow as we are to learn its cause".

71 *So please you* – "If you please".

72 *I'll know . . . much denied* – "I will learn the cause of his sorrow unless he is very firm in his refusal to reveal it."

12

Adding to clouds more clouds with his deep sighs;[61]
But all so soon as[63] the all-cheering sun
Should in the farthest east begin to draw
The shady curtains from Aurora's bed,[63]
Away from light steals home my heavy[64] son,   130
And private in his chamber pens himself,
Shuts up his windows, locks fair daylight out,
And makes himself an artificial night.
Black and portentous must this humour prove,
Unless good counsel may the cause remove.   135

BENVOLIO

My noble uncle, do you know the cause?

MONTAGUE

I neither know it, nor can learn of him.

BENVOLIO

Have you importuned him by any means?

MONTAGUE

Both by myself and many other friends:
But he, his own affections' counsellor,[65]   140
Is to himself – I will not say how true –
But to himself so secret and so close,[66]
So far from sounding and discovery[67]
As is the bud bit with[68] an envious [69] worm
Ere he can spread his sweet leaves to the air,   145
Or dedicate his beauty to the same.
Could we but learn from whence his sorrows grow,
We would as willingly give cure as know.[70]

Enter ROMEO

BENVOLIO

See where he comes. So please you,[71] step aside;
I 'll know his grievance or be much denied.[72]   150

13

MONTAGUE

I would thou wert so happy by thy stay
To hear true shrift.[73] Come, madam, let 's away.

[*Exeunt* MONTAGUE *and* LADY MONTAGUE

BENVOLIO

Good morrow,[74] cousin.

ROMEO

Is the day so young?[75]

BENVOLIO

But new-struck nine.[76]

---

73 *I would* (line *151*) . . . *true shrift* – "I hope you will be so successful (*thou wert so happy*) by staying here as to hear a confession of the truth (*true shrift*) from him".

74 *morrow* – "morning".

75 *Is the day so young?* – "Is it still only morning?". The lovesick Romeo has lost all sense of time.

76 *But new-struck nine* – "It has only just struck nine".

77 *Not having . . . short* – "Not having that (i.e. Rosaline's love) which would make time fly if I had it".

78 *Out of . . . in love* – "Out of favour with the one I love".

79 *Love*. A reference to Cupid, the ancient Roman god of love, who is represented in art as a naked boy whose eyes are covered with a cloth. He carries a bow and arrows which he shoots at those whom he wishes to fall in love.

80 *in his view* – "in appearance".

81 *in proof* – "when tested by experience" (and not just when thought about).

82 *Alas, that Love* (line *164*) . . . *will* – "Alas, that Cupid whose sight is always covered up (*muffled still*), should, though unable to see (*without eyes*), be able to find ways (*see pathways*) to make things happen in the way he desires". The whole of Romeo's speech (lines 164–176) with its list of conflicting opposites reflects his deep unhappiness and confusion of mind, which spring partly from the evil quarrel between the two families. The brawling which he has just heard strengthens his feeling that life is upside down, a *misshapen chaos*. It should be remembered that Rosaline is a Capulet, and would therefore be considered an enemy by his family.

83 *Here's much . . . love*. The *hate* refers to the fight (*fray*) which has just taken place between the Montagues and Capulets; the *love* to Romeo's passion for Rosaline.

84 *of nothing first create* – "created originally from nothing".

85 *well-seeming forms* – "apparently beautiful shapes".

14

ROMEO

Ay me, sad hours seem long.
Was that my father that went hence so fast?   155

BENVOLIO

It was. What sadness lengthens Romeo's hours?

ROMEO

Not having that which, having, makes them short.[77]

BENVOLIO

In love?

ROMEO

Out –

BENVOLIO

Of love?   160

ROMEO

Out of her favour where I am in love.[78]

BENVOLIO

Alas, that Love,[79] so gentle in his view,[80]
Should be so tyrannous and rough in proof.[81]

ROMEO

Alas, that Love, whose view is muffled still,
Should without eyes see pathways to his will.[82]   165
Where shall we dine? O me! What fray was here?
Yet tell me not, for I have heard it all.
Here's much to do with hate, but more with love.[83]
Why then, O brawling love, O loving hate,
O anything of nothing first create,[84]   170
O heavy lightness, serious vanity,
Misshapen chaos of well-seeming forms,[85]

15

Feather of lead, bright smoke, cold fire, sick health,
Still-waking[86] sleep that is not what it is,[87]
This love feel I, that feel no love in this.[88]   175
Dost thou not laugh?

BENVOLIO

No, coz,[89] I rather weep.

ROMEO

Good heart, at what?

BENVOLIO

At thy good heart's oppression.[90]

ROMEO

Why, such is love's transgression.[91]
Griefs of mine own lie heavy in my breast,
Which thou wilt propagate to have it pressed   180
With more of thine.[92] This love that thou hast shown
Doth add more grief to too much of mine own.

---

86 *Still-waking* – "always awake".
87 *sleep that is not what it is*. If sleep is always awake, it is no longer sleep.
88 *in this* – "in return".
89 *coz* – "cousin". The word is also often used for any close relative.
90 *oppression* – "heavy burden".
91 *love's transgression* – "love's way of doing wrong (by going beyond the limits)."
92 *Griefs of mine* (line *179*) . . . *of thine* – "My griefs are heavy in my breast, and you will increase them if you add your griefs (i.e. those caused by sympathy for Romeo's distress) to this weight on my heart".
93 *Being purged* – "when the smoke has cleared away".
94 *A madness most discreet* – "A very wise madness"; another of the many impossible opposites in Romeo's description of love.

95 *A choking . . . sweet* – "a deadly poison and a sweet healing medicine".
96 *some other where* – "somewhere else".
97 *in sadness . . . love?* – "seriously, who is she whom you love?" *Sadly* (line 194) also means "seriously".
98 *groan*. Romeo pretends to misunderstand *sadness* as meaning "sorrow".
99 *A sick man* (line *195*) . . . *so ill*. Romeo objects to Benvolio's use of the words *sadly* and *in sadness* because they remind him of his sorrow; he is so sick that it would be more fitting for him *in sadness* to make his will than to talk of his love.
100 *I aimed so near* – "I knew as much".
101 *mark-man* – "bowman skilled in hitting the object aimed at (*mark*) with his arrows". Romeo here takes up Benvolio's use of the word *aimed* in the previous line.

16

Love is a smoke made with the fume of sighs:
Being purged,[93] a fire sparkling in lovers' eyes;
Being vexed, a sea nourished with loving tears.   185
What is it else? A madness most discreet,[94]
A choking gall, and a preserving sweet.[95]
Farewell, my coz.

BENVOLIO

                        Soft, I will go along;
And if you leave me so, you do me wrong.

ROMEO

Tut, I have lost myself; I am not here.   190
This is not Romeo; he 's some other where.[96]

BENVOLIO

Tell me in sadness, who is that you love?[97]

ROMEO

What, shall I groan[98] and tell thee?

BENVOLIO

                                    Groan? Why no.
But sadly tell me who.

ROMEO

A sick man in sadness makes his will –   195
A word ill urged to one that is so ill.[99]
In sadness, cousin, I do love a woman.

BENVOLIO

I aimed so near[100] when I supposed you loved.

ROMEO

A right good mark-man![101] And she's fair I love.

BENVOLIO

A right fair mark, fair coz, is soonest hit. 200

ROMEO

Well, in that hit you miss.[102] She 'll not be hit
With Cupid's arrow; she hath Dian's wit,[103]
And in strong proof[104] of chastity well-armed,
From Love's weak childish bow she lives uncharmed.[105]
She will not stay the siege of loving terms,[106] 205
Nor bide th' encounter of assailing eyes,[107]
Nor ope her lap to saint-seducing gold.[108]
O, she is rich in beauty; only poor
That when she dies, with beauty dies her store.[109]

---

102 *in that hit you miss* – "in that remark (*hit*) you miss your aim", i.e. "you are wrong".
103 *Dian's wit* – "the wisdom of Diana." Diana was the Roman goddess of hunting, and a symbol of chastity. Love's *bow* is described as *childish* (line 204) because Cupid was a child-god.
104 *proof* – "armour which cannot be pierced".
105 *uncharmed* – "free from the bewitching power of Cupid's arrows".
106 *stay . . . loving terms* – "wait, and allow herself to be attacked (*stay the siege*) by expressions of love".
107 *Nor bide . . . assailing eyes* – "nor wait for (*bide*) the attack (*encounter*) of loving looks (*assailing eyes*)".
108 *ope her lap . . . gold* – "accept a bribe of gold which would lead a saint into sin". *Ope* is an old form of *open*.
109 *only poor (line 208) . . . her store* – "only poor in that when she dies, her fertility, or power to increase (*store*), perishes with her beauty".
110 *chaste* – "unmarried".

111 *sparing* – "careful saving" (of herself, by not marrying).
112 *Cuts beauty . . . posterity* – "prevents all future ages (*posterity*) from inheriting the beauty she would have passed on to her children".
113 *She is too fair (line 214) . . . despair* – "She is being excessively good, wise, and virtuous in seeking to win heaven by making me despair". It was widely believed that heaven was the reward for those who did not marry but lived a chaste life for the love of God.
114 *Examine other beauties* – "look at other beautiful women".
115 *To call hers . . . more* – "to make me think (*call in question*) more about the perfect (*exquisite*) beauty of Rosaline (*hers*)".
116 *puts* for *put*. Compare the note to the opening Prologue, line 8.
117 *passing fair* – "extremely beautiful".
118 *a note*, i.e. a note in the margin of a book, explaining something in the text.

18

BENVOLIO

Then she hath sworn that she will still live chaste?[110]   210

ROMEO

She hath, and in that sparing[111] makes huge waste,
For beauty, starved with her severity,
Cuts beauty off from all posterity.[112]
She is too fair, too wise, wisely too fair,
To merit bliss by making me despair.[113]   215
She hath forsworn to love, and in that vow
Do I live dead, that live to tell it now.

BENVOLIO

Be ruled by me; forget to think of her.

ROMEO

O, teach me how I should forget to think!

BENVOLIO

By giving liberty unto thine eyes: 220
Examine other beauties.[114]

ROMEO

'T is the way
To call hers – exquisite – in question more.[115]
These happy masks that kiss fair ladies' brows,
Being black, puts[116] us in mind they hide the fair.
He that is strucken blind cannot forget   225
The precious treasure of his eyesight lost.
Show me a mistress that is passing fair:[117]
What doth her beauty serve, but as a note[118]

119 *passed* – "exceeded". Masks were commonly worn in public by ladies of fashion at this time. They were also worn by both men and women at balls (masques) as in I.iv. In lines 223–29 Romeo argues that just as ladies' masks suggest the beauties hidden behind them, and just as a blind man remembers beauties he can no longer see, so, when he (Romeo) sees a woman of great beauty he is reminded of the even greater beauty of Rosaline. *Fair* (line

224) means (a) "light in colour" and is contrasted with the black mask, and (b) "beautiful". The blackness of the mask ties up with the darkness of the blind man, and the lack of brightness in the beauty of other women when compared with Rosaline.

120 *pay that doctrine* – "satisfy you in full (*pay*) that my doctrine is right", i.e. that Romeo's cure is to forget Rosaline by turning to *other beauties*.

(I.ii) It is evening of the same day, Sunday. Capulet and Montague have been ordered to keep the peace. Count Paris asks Capulet for the hand of his daughter Juliet in marriage, but Capulet insists that Paris must first gain Juliet's approval. He invites Paris to a feast he is giving that night, and they leave after Capulet has given his servant, the Clown, a list of the guests to invite. When Romeo and Benvolio enter, the Clown, who cannot read, gives Romeo the list to read for him. From it Romeo learns that Rosaline will be at the feast, and he and Benvolio decide to go to it although they have not been invited.

1 *The same*, i.e. the same place as the scene before, a street in Verona. The play would have continued in Shakespeare's day without any break here.

2 *bound* – "obliged by law to keep the peace".

3 *In penalty alike* – "subject to the same penalty" (i.e. if he breaks the peace).

4 *and 'tis not hard* (line 2) . . . *peace.* Capulet's failure to act in the way he knows to be right is a major cause of the tragedy which follows. Despite what he says, he and Montague have already caused *three civil brawls* without reason, and even now they make no attempt to end the quarrel. Although he insists that Juliet cannot marry before two years have passed because she is too young, and that she

must be free to choose her husband, it is not long before he is trying to force her to marry within a few days. Again, his failure to act in the way he knows to be right and wise has tragic results.

5 *honourable reckoning* – (a) "an age worthy of respect", (b) "honourable reputation".

6 *my suit* – "my request" (to marry Juliet).

7 *But saying o'er* – "I only repeat".

8 *change* – "passage".

9 *are happy mothers made* – "have become happy mothers". Capulet's reply (line 13) echoes the proverb. "Soon married, soon marred".

10 *Earth hath swallowèd . . . she.* All his other children have died.

20

Where I may read who passed[119] that passing fair?
Farewell; thou canst not teach me to forget.   230

BENVOLIO

I 'll pay that doctrine,[120] or else die in debt.

[*Exeunt*

Scene II. The same.[1]

Enter CAPULET, PARIS, *and the* CLOWN,
Capulet's *servant*

CAPULET

But Montague is bound[2] as well as I,
In penalty alike[3], and 't is not hard, I think,
For men so old as we to keep the peace.[4]

PARIS

Of honourable reckoning[5] are you both,
And pity 't is you lived at odds so long.   5
But now, my lord, what say you to my suit?[6]

CAPULET

But saying o'er[7] what I have said before:
My child is yet a stranger in the world;
She hath not seen the change[8] of fourteen years;
Let two more summers wither in their pride   10
Ere we may think her ripe to be a bride.

PARIS

Younger than she are happy mothers made.[9]

CAPULET

And too soon marred are those so early made.
Earth hath swallowéd all my hopes but she;[10]

21

She's the hopeful lady of my earth.[11]
But woo her, gentle Paris, get her heart;
My will to her consent is but a part.[12]
And she agreed,[13] within her scope of choice
Lies my consent and fair according[14] voice.
This night I hold an old accustomed[15] feast,   20
Whereto I have invited many a guest,
Such as I love; and you among the store,[16]

---

11 *She's the hopeful . . . earth* – Either (a) "She is the one who can hope for my estate (*my earth*) when I die", or (b) "She is the one lady in the world who inspires me with hope", taking *my earth* to mean "my body", i.e. "me".

12 *My will . . . a part* – "my will is less important than her agreement (which is the main thing)".

13 *And she agreed* – "Once she has agreed".

14 *according* – "agreeing".

15 *old accustomed* – "according to an old custom".

16 *store* – "number".

17 *look* – "expect".

18 *Earth-treading stars* – "ladies of heavenly beauty who walk on earth".

19 *well-apparelled* – "well clothed (in the leaves of springtime)".

20 *female buds* – "young girls about to grow into womanhood". Shakespeare continues the image from nature. The young girls who are soon to become women bring the same joy as young buds which will become beautiful flowers.

21 *Inherit* – "possess".

22 *Which one (line 32) . . . reckoning none* – "your examination (*one more view*) of the many ladies, including my daughter (*mine being one*), may be numbered among all the others (*may stand in number*), though it will not increase the total (*reckoning*) of those looking at them". It was a common saying

that "Among a number, one is reckoned none". Capulet is saying that so many will be looking at the ladies that another one will not make any apparent difference.

23 *on their pleasure stay* – "wait for the pleasure of their company".

24 Shakespeare cleverly combines the Clown's comic function of providing amusement for the audience with the important dramatic function of advancing the action of the play. The Clown uses many words to say very little and gets thoroughly mixed up, but his stupidity and inability to read and write, which cause laughter, are the very reasons which make him ask Romeo to read the list. In this economical and believable way Romeo is given knowledge of the feast which leads to his meeting with Juliet.

25 *yard* – "measuring-rod" (used by tailors to measure cloth).

26 *pencil* – "paintbrush".

27 *writ* – "written".

28 *In good time! The learned*, i.e. those who can read, are coming just when he wants them.

29 *another's anguish* – "the suffering caused by another pain".

30 *Turn giddy . . . turning* – "if your head spins you will be helped (*holp*) by turning in the opposite direction".

31 *cures with another's languish* – "is cured by the suffering (*languish*) caused by another pain".

One more most welcome, makes my number more.
At my poor house look[17] to behold this night
Earth-treading stars[18] that make dark heaven light.   25
Such comfort as do lusty young men feel
When well-apparelled[19] April on the heel
Of limping winter treads, even such delight
Among fresh female buds[20] shall you this night
Inherit[21] at my house; hear all, all see,   30
And like her most whose merit most shall be:
Which one more view of many, mine being one,
May stand in number, though in reckoning none.[22]
Come, go with me. [*To the* CLOWN, *giving him a paper*]
    Go, sirrah, trudge about
Through fair Verona; find those persons out   35
Whose names are written there, and to them say
My house and welcome on their pleasure stay.[23]

                                    [*Exeunt* CAPULET *and* PARIS

                              CLOWN[24]

Find them out whose names are written here? It is written
that the shoemaker should meddle with his yard[25] and the
tailor with his last, the fisher with his pencil[26] and the   40
painter with his nets. But I am sent to find those persons
whose names are here writ,[27] and can never find what
names the writing person hath here writ. I must to the
learned. [*He sees* BENVOLIO *and* ROMEO *approaching*]
In good time![28]   45

                    Enter BENVOLIO *and* ROMEO

                             BENVOLIO

Tut, man, one fire burns out another's burning,
One pain is lessened by another's anguish;[29]
Turn giddy, and be holp by backward turning.[30]
One desperate grief cures with another's languish:[31]

Take thou some new infection to thy eye,   50
And the rank[32] poison of the old will die.

ROMEO

Your[33] plantain[34] leaf is excellent for that.

BENVOLIO

For what, I pray thee?

ROMEO

For your broken shin.[35]

BENVOLIO

Why, Romeo, art thou mad?

ROMEO

Not mad, but bound more than a madman is;   55
Shut up in prison, kept without my food,
Whipped and tormented, and – Good e'en,[36] good fellow.

CLOWN

God gi' good e'en. I pray, sir, can you read?

---

32 *rank* – "foul".
33 *Your* was commonly used in Shakespeare's time to mean, "That you know about".
34 *plantain*, a plant whose leaves were noted for their power to stop bleeding.
35 *broken shin*. Romeo hints that there is more point in discussing the cure for a minor wound like a cut leg than that for a disease like love for which there is no cure.
36 *Good e'en* – "Good evening". The Clown replies, "God give you good evening (*God gi' good e'en*)". Evening was any time after noon.

37 *without book* – "by memory".
38 *rest you merry* – "may God keep you happy"; a conventional farewell phrase. The Clown thinks Romeo cannot read.
39 *County* – "Count".
40 *Up* – Romeo is so impatient to learn where the feast is being held that he cannot wait for the Clown to finish telling him.

24

ROMEO

Ay, mine own fortune in my misery.

CLOWN

Perhaps you have learned it without book.[37] But I pray, 60
can you read anything you see?

ROMEO

Ay, if I know the letters and the language.

CLOWN

Ye say honestly; rest you merry.[38] [*He moves off*]

ROMEO

Stay, fellow; I can read. [*He reads the list*]
"Signor Martino and his wife and daughters; 65
County[39] Anselme and his beauteous sisters;
The lady widow of Vitruvio;
Signor Placentio and his lovely nieces;
Mercutio and his brother Valentine;
Mine uncle Capulet, his wife and daughters, 70
My fair niece Rosaline and Livia;
Signor Valentio and his cousin Tybalt;
Lucio and the lively Helena".
A fair assembly. Whither should they come?

CLOWN

Up – [40] 75

ROMEO

Whither? To supper?

CLOWN

To our house.

25

ROMEO

Whose house?

CLOWN

My master's.

ROMEO

Indeed, I should have asked thee that before.   80

CLOWN

Now I 'll tell you without asking. My master is the great
rich Capulet; and if you be not of the house of Montagues,
I pray come and crush⁴¹ a cup of wine. Rest you merry.

[*Exit* CLOWN

---

41 *crush* – "remove the liquid from", i.e.
"drink".

42 *thou so loves*. This form of the second
person of the verb, without the –t at
the end, was occasionally used in
Shakespeare's time. Compare *thou
loves* (I.v.7) and *thou expects* (III.v.109).

43 *unattainted* – "unprejudiced".

44 *think thy swan a crow* – "think that
Rosaline whom you consider beautiful (*thy swan*) is ugly (*a crow*)". The
white swan was a common symbol for
beauty, the black crow for ugliness.
Note how often blackness and white-
ness, darkness and light are contrasted
in this way throughout the play.

45 *devout religion of mine eye*. Romeo's
belief in the supremacy of Rosaline's
beauty is like a firmly held religious
faith, and is confirmed by the evi-
dence of his eyes.

46 *And these* (line *92*) . . . *liars* – "And
may these (eyes) which, though often
drowned (in tears) could never die, be
burnt because they would be clearly
opponents of the truth (*transparent*

heretics)", i.e. the truth that Rosaline
is the most beautiful of women. There
is play on *transparent* meaning (a)
"apparent", (b) "which can be seen
through". Romeo continues the
religious imagery. A *heretic* is one who
holds a religious belief contrary to the
general belief. In Shakespeare's day
heretics were often burnt to death at
the stake.

47 *saw her . . . being by* – "thought her
beautiful (*fair*) because there was no
other woman beside her" (to compare
her with).

48 *crystal scales*. Romeo's eyes are the
two pans of a balance. Rosaline's
image is reflected and balanced
(*poised*) in each of them. They are
called *crystal* because they reflect like
glass.

49 *Your lady's love* – "your lady-love",
i.e. "the lady you love."

50 *she shall scant . . . best* – "she (Rosaline)
who now seems best shall hardly
(*scant*) appear at all beautiful".

(I.iii) Lady Capulet comes to tell Juliet that Count Paris wishes to marry
her, and instructs her to observe him closely at the feast that night. Juliet
dutifully replies that she will try to like him.

26

BENVOLIO

At this same ancient feast of Capulet's
Sups the fair Rosaline whom thou so loves,[42]   85
With all the admiréd beauties of Verona.
Go thither, and with unattainted[43] eye,
Compare her face with some that I shall show,
And I will make thee think thy swan a crow.[44]

ROMEO

When the devout religion of mine eye[45]   90
Maintains such falsehood, then turn tears to fire;
And these, who, often drowned, could never die,
Transparent heretics, be burnt for liars.[46]
One fairer than my love? The all-seeing sun
Ne'er saw her match since first the world begun.   95

BENVOLIO

Tut, you saw her fair, none else being by,[47]
Herself poised with herself in either eye;
But in that crystal scales[48] let there be weighed
Your lady's love[49] against some other maid
That I will show you shining at this feast,   100
And she shall scant show well that now seems best.[50]

ROMEO

I'll go along, no such sight to be shown,
But to rejoice in splendour of mine own.

                                                      [*Exeunt*

Scene III. A room in Capulet's house.

Enter LADY CAPULET *and* NURSE

LADY CAPULET

Nurse, where's my daughter? Call her forth to me.

NURSE

Now, by my maidenhead at twelve year old, I bade her
come. What, lamb! What, lady-bird! God forbid![1]
Where's this girl? What, Juliet!

Enter JULIET

JULIET

How now?[2] Who calls?   5

NURSE

Your mother.

JULIET

Madam, I am here. What is your will?

---

1 *What, lady-bird! God forbid!* "What!"
 is a call for Juliet to come. Having
 used the word *lady-bird*, which is a
 term of affection, the Nurse remembers that it could also mean "a woman
 of bad reputation", and prays that
 Juliet may never become such a
 woman.
2 *How now?* – "What is the matter?"
3 *matter* – "subject I want to discuss".
4 *give leave* – "leave us alone".
5 *I have remembered me* – "I have remembered (my intention to let the
 Nurse hear our conversation)".
6 *thou's* – "you shall".
7 *of a pretty age* – "at an attractive age".
8 *lay* – "promise to pay if I prove
 wrong".
9 *teen* – "sorrow".
10 *be it spoken* – "let it be said".
11 *Lammas-tide*. Lammas Day, August
 1st, was a harvest festival. Lammas-
 Eve, July 31st, is Juliet's birthday; she
 is thus named after the month of her
 birth.

12 *odd days* – "a few more days". The
 Nurse takes up the word (line 18) in
 its more common meaning, "an uneven number".
13 *Susan*, the Nurse's daughter, now
 dead.
14 *God rest* – "may God give rest to".
15 *of an age* – "the same age".
16 *But, as I said*. The Nurse repeats herself in this way throughout her speech.
 Although she knows she is doing it,
 she does not realise that others find
 such repetition boring to listen to.
17 *the earthquake*. The Nurse refers to a
 particular earthquake which she remembers.
18 *wormwood*, an extremely bitter oil ob-
 tained from a plant.
19 *dug* – "breast".
20 *dove-house wall* – "the wall of the
 house containing the doves".
21 *I do bear a brain* – "I have a splendid
 memory".
22 *it*, i.e. the baby, Juliet.
23 *felt it bitter* – "experienced the bitter
 taste of it".
24 *tetchy* – "ill-tempered".

LADY CAPULET

This is the matter.[3] Nurse, give leave[4] a while;
We must talk in secret. [NURSE *begins to leave*] Nurse,
   come back again;
I have remembered me,[5] thou's[6] hear our counsel.   10
Thou know'st my daughter's of a pretty age.[7]

NURSE

Faith, I can tell her age unto an hour.

LADY CAPULET

She's not fourteen.

NURSE

I 'll lay[8] fourteen of my teeth – and yet, to my teen[9] be it
spoken,[10] I have but four – she's not fourteen. How long   15
is it now to Lammas-tide?[11]

LADY CAPULET

A fortnight and odd days.[12]

NURSE

Even or odd, of all days in the year, come Lammas-Eve at
night shall she be fourteen. Susan[13] and she – God rest[14]
all Christian souls – were of an age.[15] Well, Susan is with   20
God; she was too good for me. But, as I said,[16] on
Lammas-Eve at night shall she be fourteen; that shall she,
marry; I remember it well. 'T is since the earthquake[17]
now eleven years, and she was weaned – I never shall forget it – of all the days of the year, upon that day; for I had   25
then laid wormwood[18] to my dug,[19] sitting in the sun
under the dove-house wall.[20] My lord and you were then
at Mantua – nay, I do bear a brain![21] But, as I said, when
it[22] did taste the wormwood on the nipple of my dug and
felt it bitter,[23] pretty fool, to see it tetchy,[24] and fall out   30

29

with[25] the dug! "Shake", quoth the dove-house[26]. 'Twas
no need, I trow,[27] to bid me trudge. And since that time it
is eleven years, for then she could stand high-lone[28]; nay,
by the rood,[29] she could have run and waddled all about,
for even the day before, she broke her brow,[30] and then   35
my husband – God be with his soul, 'a was a merry man –
took up the child. "Yea,"[31] quoth he, "dost thou fall
upon thy face? Thou wilt fall backward when thou hast
more wit, wilt thou not, Jule?" And, by my holidame,[32]
the pretty wretch left crying, and said "Ay". To see now   40
how a jest shall come about![33] I warrant[34], and[35] I should
live a thousand years, I never should forget it. "Wilt thou
not, Jule?" quoth he; and, pretty fool, it stinted,[36] and
said "Ay".

LADY CAPULET

Enough of this. I pray thee hold thy peace[37].   45

---

25 *fall out with* – "find disagreeable".
26 *"Shake", quoth the dove-house*. The
shaking of the dove-house in the
earthquake warned her to go away.
27 *I trow* – "I am sure".
28 *high-lone* – "quite alone and unsup-
ported".
29 *rood* – "the cross on which Christ was
put to death".
30 *broke her brow* – "cut her head open".
31 *Yea* – "Yes".
32 *by my holidame* – "by my holy mother
(*dame*)," i.e. the Virgin Mary.
33 *how a jest . . . about* – "how something
said as a joke will turn out to be true".
34 *warrant* – "say positively as true".
35 *and* – "if".
36 *stinted* – "stopped" (crying).
37 *hold thy peace* – "be quiet".
38 *leave* – "stop".
39 *it* – "its".
40 *stone* – "reproductive organ".
41 *And stint thou too . . . say I*. Juliet uses
the Nurse's own word, *stint*, to try to

stop her talking. The Nurse has just
told her little joke for the third time.
Note the play on *said "Ay"* (line 52)
and *say I*.
42 *God mark thee to his grace* – "May God
mark you out for His special favour".
43 *And I might (line 55) . . . once* – "If I
could once see you married".
44 *Marry, that "marry"* – "By Mary, that
word "marry" of yours".
45 *How stands . . . married?* – "How do
you feel about the idea of getting
married?"
46 *Were not I thine only nurse . . . from thy
teat* – "If it were not for the fact that I
was the only Nurse you had, I would
say that you had drawn your wisdom
from my breast (*thy teat*)". The Nurse
pretends to be too modest to make the
claim, although she no doubt believes
it.
47 *count* – "reckoning".
48 *much upon these years* – "at just about
the same age".

30

NURSE

Yes, madam; yet I cannot choose but laugh, to think it
should leave[38] crying, and say "Ay"; and yet I warrant it
had upon it[39] brow a bump as big as a young cockerel's
stone[40] – a perilous knock – and it cried bitterly. "Yea,"
quoth my husband, "fall'st upon thy face? Thou wilt fall   50
backward when thou comest to age, wilt thou not, Jule?"
It stinted, and said "Ay".

JULIET

And stint thou too, I pray thee, Nurse, say I.[41]

NURSE

Peace, I have done. God mark thee to his grace,[42] thou
wast the prettiest babe that e'er I nursed. And I might live   55
to see thee married once,[43] I have my wish.

LADY CAPULET

Marry, that "marry"[44] is the very theme
I came to talk of. Tell me, daughter Juliet,
How stands your dispositions to be married?[45]

JULIET

It is an honour that I dream not of.   60

NURSE

An honour! Were not I thine only nurse, I would say thou
hadst sucked wisdom from thy teat.[46]

LADY CAPULET

Well, think of marriage now. Younger than you,
Here in Verona, ladies of esteem,
Are made already mothers. By my count,[47]   65
I was your mother much upon these years[48]

That you are now a maid. Thus then in brief,
The valiant Paris seeks you for his love.

NURSE

A man, young lady! Lady, such a man as all the world . . .
why, he's a man of wax!⁴⁹   70

---

49 *a man of wax* – "a man of perfect
beauty, like a wax image".

50 *Read o'er the volume.* Lady Capulet's
speech (lines 75–86) is an extended
metaphor in which she speaks of
Paris's face as a book (*volume*) with the
various characteristics of the book
corresponding to parts of the face.
The rich poetry and complicated
imagery are intended to persuade
Juliet into accepting Paris as her husband. Lady Capulet's excessive praise
of Paris, and the language in which
she expresses it are in striking contrast
with the simple, repetitive chatter of
the Nurse, but the latter reveals more
true affection for Juliet than Lady
Capulet's polished and clever speech.

51 *writ* – "written".

52 *every married lineament* – "all the har-
moniously united (*married*) parts of his
face (*every lineament*)". *Lineament* can
mean a line on a page or a line of the
face, and so fits cleverly into Lady
Capulet's book metaphor.

53 *one another lends content* – "each part
(*one*) makes the next one (*another*)
satisfying and gives it meaning (*content*)". There is play on *content* meaning (a) "satisfaction", and (b) "the
substance or contents of a book".

54 *And what obscured* (*line 79*) . . . *his eyes.*
Difficulties in the text of a book were
often explained by notes at the side of
the page (*margent*). Lady Capulet
means that if Juliet cannot read what
Paris is thinking from his face, his eyes
will explain everything.

55 *unbound lover.* Paris, not yet bound by
the vows of marriage, is like a book
without a cover, or binding. There is
also possibly a suggestion that his love
is boundless.

56 *The fish lives in the sea.* The meaning
of this puzzling phrase seems to be
that just as the fish cannot live without
the sea which encloses it, so Paris
needs a Juliet. This connects with the
idea of Paris as the inside of a book,
the fair within, and Juliet as the *cover*,
the *fair without*.

57 *'tis much pride* (*line 83*) . . . *hide* – "it is
an occasion for pride (*much pride*)
when a beautiful woman (the *fair
without*, or outside cover) holds a
good-looking man (*the fair within*, or
content) bound in marriage".

58 *That book* (*line 85*) . . . *golden story* –
"Many people (*in many's eyes*) think
that when golden clasps enclose
splendid contents (*golden story*), they
share the glory of the book". *Golden
clasps* are also intended to refer to
Juliet's loving embraces.

59 *like of* – "approve of".

60 *I'll look . . . liking move* – "If looking
at someone leads one to like him, then
I may expect to (*look to*) like Paris".
Juliet is obedient and anxious to do
what her parents wish.

61 *endart* – "bury like a dart, or spear".

62 *gives strength to make it fly* – "gives me
authority to do". *Fly* continues the
image of Juliet's glance as a weapon
thrown through the air at Paris.

32

LADY CAPULET

Verona's summer hath not such a flower.

NURSE

Nay, he's a flower; in faith, a very flower.

LADY CAPULET

What say you? Can you love the gentleman?
This night you shall behold him at our feast.
Read o'er the volume[50] of young Paris' face,   75
And find delight writ[51] there with beauty's pen;
Examine every married lineament,[52]
And see how one another lends content;[53]
And what obscured in this fair volume lies,
Find written in the margent of his eyes.[54]   80
This precious book of love, this unbound lover,[55]
To beautify him, only lacks a cover.
The fish lives in the sea;[56] and 't is much pride
For fair without, the fair within to hide.[57]
That book in many's eyes doth share the glory,   85
That in gold clasps locks in the golden story:[58]
So shall you share all that he doth possess
By having him, making yourself no less.

NURSE

No less? Nay, bigger! Women grow by men.

LADY CAPULET

Speak briefly: can you like of[59] Paris' love?   90

JULIET

I 'll look to like, if looking liking move;[60]
But no more deep will I endart[61] mine eye
Than your consent gives strength to make it fly.[62]

33

Enter CLOWN

CLOWN

Madam, the guests are come, supper served up, you called,
my young lady asked for,⁶³ the Nurse cursed in the   95
pantry,⁶⁴ and everything in extremity.⁶⁵ I must hence to
wait.⁶⁶ I beseech you, follow straight.

---

63 *you called, my young lady asked for.* The
guests are anxious to meet Lady
Capulet and are inquiring for Juliet.

64 *cursed in the pantry,* i.e. because she is
not there to help. The pantry is the
storeroom where such things as cups,
plates and knives are kept in a house.

65 *everything in extremity* – "everything
needs doing at once".

66 *wait* – "serve and attend the guests".

67 *stays* – "waits (for you)".

(I.iv) Romeo and his friends, disguised in masks except for Mercutio,
arrive outside Capulet's house. Romeo says he is too heavy-hearted to dance,
and Mercutio tries unsuccessfully to argue him into a happier mood. Benvolio
points out that they will be too late for the feast if they go on talking, and
this puts an end to the discussion.

1 *Torchbearers* were men who carried
flaming lights to show the way in the
dark.

2 *shall this speech . . . apology?* – "shall
we deliver this speech excusing our
uninvited appearance, or shall we
enter without apology?" *Spoke* –
"spoken".

3 *The date . . . prolixity* – "It is no longer
the fashion to make long apologies".

4 *We'll have no Cupid (line 4) . . . crow-
keeper* – "we will not follow the custom of being led to the feast by someone dressed as Cupid, his eyes covered
(*hoodwinked*) with a scarf, carrying a
toy bow of thin wood (*lath*) painted
to look like a Tartar's, and frighten-
ing the ladies like a boy employed to
keep crows off the cornfields with a
bow and arrows". The Tartars, in-
habitants of central Asia, were famous
bowmen.

5 *Nor no without-book (line 7) . . .
prompter* – "nor an introductory
speech (*prologue*) spoken from memory
(*without-book*) but feebly recited
(*faintly spoke*) following the prompter". The *prompter* was out of sight
near the stage to remind the actors of
their lines when they forgot them.

6 *But let them (line 9) . . . be gone* – "But
let them judge (*measure*) us by what
standard they like, we will perform
the steps (*measure*) of a stately dance
(*measure*) for them and then go".

7 *for this ambling* – "in favour of this
dancing".

8 *Being but heavy . . . light* – "Since I feel
sad I will hold the light", i.e. rather
than dance. Note the play on the contrast between *heavy* and *light*.

LADY CAPULET

We follow thee. Juliet, the County stays.[67]

NURSE

Go, girl; seek happy nights to happy days.

[*Exeunt*

Scene IV. Outside Capulet's house.

Enter torchbearers,[1] followed by ROMEO, MERCUTIO,
BENVOLIO *and five or six other masked men*

ROMEO

What, shall this speech be spoke for our excuse,
Or shall we on without apology?[2]

BENVOLIO

The date is out of such prolixity:[3]
We 'll have no Cupid hoodwinked with a scarf,
Bearing a Tartar's painted bow of lath,   5
Scaring the ladies like a crow-keeper;[4]
Nor no without-book prologue, faintly spoke
After the prompter,[5] for our entrance.
But let them measure us by what they will,
We 'll measure them a measure and be gone.[6]   10

ROMEO

Give me a torch: I am not for this ambling;[7]
Being but heavy, I will bear the light.[8]

MERCUTIO

Nay, gentle Romeo, we must have you dance.

35

ROMEO

Not I, believe me. You have dancing shoes
With nimble soles:[9] I have a soul of lead   15
So stakes me[10] to the ground I cannot move.

MERCUTIO

You are a lover: borrow Cupid's wings,
And soar with them above a common bound.[11]

---

9 *nimble soles* – (a) "shoes suitable for dancing", (b) "active spirits (souls) which make you want to dance". The word *soul* draws attention to the pun on *soles*.

10 *So stakes me* – "(which) fixes me so that".

11 *a common bound* – "the usual limits".

12 *I am too sore (line 19) . . . dull woe* – "I am too painfully pierced with his arrow to fly high (*soar*) with his light feathers; and restrained in this way (*so bound*) I cannot ascend to anything higher than dull grief". The imagery is based on the sport of hawking. Hawks were trained to soar to a height (*pitch*) then fly down on their prey. Note the puns on *sore*, *soar* and *bound*.

13 *And to sink . . . love* – "And if you sank into love you would burden it".

14 *Prick love . . . down* – "If you attack love for attacking you, you will overcome it".

15 *a case to put my visage in* – "a mask for my face".

16 *A visor for a visor!* He means that he is going to put an ugly mask (*visor*) on his ugly face (*visor*).

17 *quote deformities* – "notice ugly details".

18 *beetle brows shall blush* – "overhanging (*beetle*) brows which shall blush". They *blush* (i.e. look red) because they are painted red or pink.

19 *betake him to his legs* – "begin to dance".

20 *wantons light of heart* – "light-hearted merry-makers".

21 *rushes*, tall grass-like leaves which were dried and spread on the floors of houses at this time. It is a waste of time to *tickle* them (by dancing on them) since they are without feeling (*senseless*).

22 *proverbed with (line 37) . . . look on* – "the popular saying (*proverb*) of our grandfathers (that the man who looks on sees most of the game) fits my case".

23 *The game . . . I am dun* – "The entertainment is at its brightest and I am in gloomy spirits". *Dun* – "dark brown in colour". Romeo is playing on the contrast between *fair* and *dun*.

24 *dun's the mouse* – "the mouse is dark brown". This was a proverbial phrase meaning, "Keep quiet and hidden" (like a mouse). It is described as the *constable's own word* possibly because the officials responsible for keeping the peace (constables) kept quiet and hidden when pursuing law-breakers, or possibly because they used it to keep their prisoners quiet when making an arrest.

36

ROMEO

I am too sore empiercéd with his shaft
To soar with his light feathers; and so bound,   20
I cannot bound a pitch above dull woe.[12]
Under love's heavy burden do I sink.

MERCUTIO

And to sink in it should you burden love —[13]
Too great oppression for a tender thing.

ROMEO

Is love a tender thing? It is too rough,   25
Too rude, too boisterous, and it pricks like thorn.

MERCUTIO

If love be rough with you, be rough with love:
Prick love for pricking, and you beat love down.[14]
Give me a case to put my visage in:[15]
A visor for a visor![16] What care I   30
What curious eye doth quote deformities?[17]
Here are the beetle brows shall blush[18] for me.

[*He puts on a mask*

BENVOLIO

Come, knock and enter; and no sooner in,
But every man betake him to his legs.[19]

ROMEO

A torch for me: let wantons light of heart[20]   35
Tickle the senseless rushes[21] with their heels,
For I am proverbed with a grandsire phrase:
I 'll be a candle-holder and look on.[22]
The game was ne'er so fair, and I am dun.[23]

MERCUTIO

Tut, dun's the mouse,[24] the constable's own word;   40

37

If thou art Dun, we 'll draw thee from the mire,[25]
Or, save your reverence,[26] love, wherein thou stickest
Up to the ears. Come, we burn daylight, ho.

ROMEO

Nay, that's not so.

MERCUTIO

I mean, sir, in delay
We waste our lights in vain, like lights by day.[27]   45
Take our good meaning, for our judgement sits
Five times in that, ere once in our fine wits.[28]

ROMEO

And we mean well in going to this masque,
But 't is no wit[29] to go.

---

25 *If thou art Dun . . . mire* – "If you are
Dun (a popular name for a horse at
that time) we will pull you out of the
mud (*mire*)." Horses often got stuck
in the mud since the roads were un-
surfaced, and "Dun in the mire"
became a common expression. Mercutio is suggesting that Romeo is a
"stick-in-the-mud", i.e. he is spoiling
the fun; he is also mocking the state of
being in love by comparing it with
being stuck in the mud.

26 *save your reverence* – "begging your
pardon", a phrase of mock apology.

27 *I mean (line 44) . . . by day.* Mercutio
explains that by the words *we burn
daylight* he meant that letting their
lights burn away and not taking part
in the feast was as much a waste of
time as burning lights in daytime.

28 *Take our good meaning (line 46) . . .
wits* – "Understand (*take*) my words
in their true sense (*good meaning*) since

the correct understanding (*judgement*)
is found five times as often in the
simple meaning as in clever explanations of hidden meanings (*fine wits*)".

29 *no wit* – "not wise".

30 *tonight* – "last night". This meaning of
the word was common in Shakes-
peare's time. Compare II.iii.2.

31 *lie* – "tell lies". Romeo takes up the
word in its other sense, "lie down".

32 *fairies' midwife.* Among the fairies she
is the one who brings to life the
imaginary ideas which men have in
their dreams.

33 *shape* – "size".

34 *Drawn with a team . . . atomi,* i.e. her
waggon is pulled along by a group
(*team*) of tiny creatures (*atomi*).

35 *Athwart* – "across".

36 *spinners'* – "spiders'".

37 *cover,* i.e. the hood covering the
waggon.

MERCUTIO

Why, may one ask?

ROMEO

I dreamt a dream tonight.[30]

MERCUTIO

And so did I.   50

ROMEO

Well, what was yours?

MERCUTIO

That dreamers often lie.[31]

ROMEO

In bed asleep while they do dream things true.

MERCUTIO

O then I see Queen Mab hath been with you.

BENVOLIO

Queen Mab? What's she?

MERCUTIO

She is the fairies' midwife,[32] and she comes   55
In shape[33] no bigger than an agate stone
On the forefinger of an alderman,
Drawn with a team of little atomi[34]
Athwart[35] men's noses as they lie asleep.
Her waggon spokes made of long spinners'[36] legs,   60
The cover[37] of the wings of grasshoppers,
Her traces of the smallest spider-web,

Her collars of the moonshine's watery beams,[38]
Her whip of cricket's bone, the lash of film,[39]
Her waggoner a small grey-coated gnat,   65
Not half so big as a round little worm
Pricked[40] from the lazy finger of a maid.[41]
Her chariot is an empty hazel-nut,
Made by the joiner-squirrel[42] or old grub,[43]
Time out o' mind[44] the fairies' coachmakers.   70
And in this state she gallops night by night
Through lovers' brains, and then they dream of love;
O'er courtiers' knees, that dream on curtsies straight;

---

38 *the moonshine's watery beams* – "the thin shafts of moonlight when it is reflected in water".

39 *film* – "fine thread".

40 *Pricked* – "removed with a needle".

41 *lazy finger of a maid*. Worms were said to breed in lazy fingers.

42 *joiner-squirrel*, so-called because with its sharp teeth it can cut through wood like a carpenter (*joiner*).

43 *grub*, the worm that eats away the inside of nuts.

44 *Time out o' mind* – "for longer than anyone can remember".

45 *Which oft* (line 76) *... tainted are.* She is angry because they attempt to disguise their bad breath with perfumed sweets, and raises watery swellings on their lips.

46 *smelling out a suit* – "discovering someone who will pay him to deliver a request (*suit*) at court to the king".

47 *tithe-pig's tail.* The tithe-pig was every tenth pig born which was paid as a tax to the parson.

48 *benefice* – "paid appointment in the church".

49 *ambuscadoes* – "surprise attacks by hidden men".

50 *Spanish blades* – "Spanish swords". They were valued for their high quality.

51 *healths five fathom deep* – "deep drinking". To drink a health was to wish someone good health and fortune before drinking.

52 *plaits the manes* – "makes the hair knotted and untidy".

53 *bakes the elf-locks* – "knots the hair (*locks*)". The elves were said to be responsible for making the hair untidy.

54 *Which once ... bodes* – "when the knots in the hair are removed (*untangled*) great misfortune is likely to follow".

55 *learns them first to bear* – "first teaches them to bear children".

56 *of good carriage* – "able to bear children well".

57 *True, I talk of dreams.* Mercutio's purpose in his long speech about Queen Mab has been to cheer up Romeo by persuading him that he should dismiss his dream from his mind, since dreams are meaningless. Possibly, also, he wants to convince Romeo that his love for Rosaline is *vain fantasy*, the product of *an idle brain*; the image of the inconstant wind, rejected by the cold north and turning to woo the warm south, soon has a parallel when Romeo turns from Rosaline to Juliet.

O'er lawyers' fingers, who straight dream on fees;
O'er ladies' lips, who straight on kisses dream,   75
Which oft the angry Mab with blisters plagues,
Because their breaths with sweetmeats tainted are.[45]
Sometime she gallops o'er a courtier's nose
And then dreams he of smelling out a suit;[46]
And sometime comes she with a tithe-pig's tail,[47]   80
Tickling a parson's nose as 'a lies asleep,
And then dreams he of another benefice;[48]
Sometime she driveth o'er a soldier's neck,
And then dreams he of cutting foreign throats,
Of breaches, ambuscadoes,[49] Spanish blades,[50]   85
Of healths five fathom deep,[51] and then anon
Drums in his ear, at which he starts and wakes,
And being thus frighted, swears a prayer or two,
And sleeps again. This is that very Mab
That plaits the manes[52] of horses in the night,   90
And bakes the elf-locks[53] in foul sluttish hairs,
Which once untangled, much misfortune bodes;[54]
This is the hag, when maids lie on their backs,
That presses them and learns them first to bear,[55]
Making them women of good carriage;[56]   95
This is she –

ROMEO

                Peace, peace, Mercutio, peace!
Thou talk'st of nothing.

MERCUTIO

                True, I talk of dreams,[57]
Which are the children of an idle brain,
Begot of nothing but vain fantasy,
Which is as thin of substance as the air,   100
And more inconstant than the wind, who woos
Even now the frozen bosom of the north,

And being angered,[58] puffs away from thence,
Turning his face to the dew-dropping south.

BENVOLIO

This wind you talk of blows us from ourselves:[59]   105
Supper is done, and we shall come too late.

ROMEO

I fear, too early, for my mind misgives
Some consequence,[60] yet hanging in the stars,[61]

---

58 *angered.* The wind is angry because the north remains cold despite his wooing.

59 *blows us from ourselves* – "turns us aside from our purpose".

60 *misgives some consequence* – "fills me with fear that some future event".

61 *yet hanging in the stars* – "not yet revealed".

62 *expire the term* (line *110*) . . . *my breast* – "end the period (*term*) of the worthless (*despisèd*) life enclosed within me".

63 *By some . . . untimely death* – "by the evil payment (*vile forfeit*) of a death which comes before it is due (*untimely*)".

64 *He that hath the steerage of* – "God, who steers".

65 *drum* – "drummer".

(I.v) Capulet welcomes the disguised Romeo and his friends to the feast, and dancing begins. Tybalt recognises Romeo and is eager to punish what he considers this insult to his family. Capulet refuses to allow this and Tybalt angrily leaves the room. Romeo, captivated by the beauty of Juliet, talks with her and kisses her. After she has left him he learns to his grief that she is a Capulet. He then leaves, and Juliet, finding out his name, is equally shocked to discover that she has fallen in love with a Montague.

1 *take away* – "remove the dishes (*trenchers*)".

2 *He shift . . . a trencher?* – "You will never find him doing such humble tasks as removing and cleaning dirty dishes".

3 *one or two men's hands.* He means their own.

4 *joint-stools*, stools made of parts joined by a skilful carpenter (as distinct from those of rough workmanship).

5 *court-cupboard* – "movable cupboard in which plate and kitchen ware were displayed".

6 *look to the plate* – "take care of the silverware".

7 *Good thou* – "My good fellow".

8 *marchpane* – "marzipan", a sweet made of powdered nut, sugar and egg.

9 *thou loves* – "you love". See the note to I.ii.85.

Shall bitterly begin his fearful date
With this night's revels, and expire the term   110
Of a despiséd life closed in my breast,[62]
By some vile forfeit of untimely death:[63]
But He[64] that hath the steerage of my course
Direct my sail. On, lusty gentlemen.

BENVOLIO

Strike, drum.[65]   115

[*Exeunt*

Scene V. The hall in Capulet's house.

Enter ROMEO *and the other* Maskers *and stand at one side
of the stage. Enter two* Servants

FIRST SERVANT

Where's Potpan, that he helps not to take away?[1] He shift
a trencher? He scrape a trencher?[2]

SECOND SERVANT

When good manners shall lie all in one or two men's
hands,[3] and they unwashed too, 'tis a foul thing.

FIRST SERVANT

Away with the joint-stools,[4] remove the court-cupboard,[5]   5
look to the plate.[6] Good thou,[7] save me a piece of marchpane,[8] and, as thou loves[9] me, let the porter let in Susan
Grindstone and Nell. [*He calls*] Antony and Potpan!

Enter the Servants, ANTONY *and* POTPAN

ANTONY

Ay, boy, ready.

43

FIRST SERVANT

You are looked for and called for, asked for and sought   10
for, in the great chamber.[10]

POTPAN

We cannot be here, and there too. Cheerly,[11] boys; be
brisk a while, and the longer liver take all.[12]

[*Exeunt* Servants

Enter LORD *and* LADY CAPULET, JULIET, TYBALT,
NURSE, *the* Guests *and* Musicians *at one side of the stage,*
meeting the Maskers *who are at the other side*

CAPULET

Welcome, gentlemen. Ladies that have their toes
Unplagued with corns will walk a bout[13] with you.   15
Ah ha, my mistresses! which of you all
Will now deny to dance? She that makes dainty,[14]
She, I 'll swear, hath corns. Am I come near ye now?[15]
Welcome, gentlemen. I have seen the day
That I have worn a visor, and could tell   20
A whispering tale in a fair lady's ear
Such as would please; 't is gone, 't is gone, 't is gone.

---

10 *great chamber.* This was the main room
of an Elizabethan house.
11 *cheerly* – "cheerfully".
12 *the longer liver take all* – "let the one
who lives longest take everything".
This was a popular saying, to en-
courage cheerfulness which was
thought to lengthen life.
13 *walk a bout* – "join in a round of
dancing".
14 *makes dainty* – "is unwilling".
15 *Am I come near ye now?* – "Have I
touched you on a tender spot (by
guessing the truth)?"
16 *a hall!* – "clear the floor!"

17 *foot it* – "dance".
18 *turn the tables up* – "fold the tables out
of the way".
19 *this unlooked-for sport comes well* – "the
arrival of these unexpected guests is
welcome".
20 *By 'r Lady* – "By Our Lady", i.e. the
Virgin Mary.
21 *nuptial* – "marriage, wedding".
22 *Come Pentecost as quickly as it will* –
"let Whit Sunday (the seventh Sunday after Easter) come as quickly as it
likes", i.e. when Whit Sunday comes.
23 *enrich the hand.* The knight's hand is
richer because it is holding Juliet's.

44

You are welcome, gentlemen. Come, musicians, play!
                              [*Music plays and they dance*
A hall, a hall![16] Give room, and foot it,[17] girls.
[*To the Servants*] More light you knaves, and turn the   25
    tables up,[18]
And quench the fire, the room is grown too hot.
[*To himself*] Ah, sirrah, this unlooked-for sport comes
    well.[19]
[*To his cousin*] Nay sit, nay sit, good cousin Capulet,
For you and I are past our dancing days.
How long is 't now since last yourself and I   30
Were in a mask?

COUSIN

By 'r Lady,[20] thirty years.

CAPULET

What, man? 'T is not so much, 't is not so much:
'T is since the nuptial[21] of Lucentio –
Come Pentecost as quickly as it will –[22]
Some five and twenty years, and then we masked.   35

COUSIN

'T is more, 't is more; his son is elder, sir:
His son is thirty.

CAPULET

                  Will you tell me that?
His son was but a ward two years ago.
[*Observing the dancers*] Good youths i' faith. O youth's a
jolly thing.

ROMEO

[*To a servant*] What lady's that which doth enrich the   40
hand[23] of yonder knight?

45

SERVANT

I know not, sir.

ROMEO

[*To himself*] O she doth teach the torches to burn bright!
It seems she hangs upon the cheek of night
As a rich jewel in an Ethiop's[24] ear;   45
Beauty too rich for use, for earth too dear.[25]
So shows[26] a snowy dove trooping with[27] crows,
As yonder lady o'er her fellows shows.
The measure done,[28] I'll watch her place of stand,[29]
And, touching hers, make blesséd my rude hand.   50
Did my heart love till now? Forswear it, sight,
For I ne'er saw true beauty till this night.

TYBALT

This, by his voice, should[30] be a Montague.
Fetch me my rapier, boy. [*Exit page*] What[31] dares the
    slave
Come hither, covered with an antic face,[32]   55
To fleer and scorn at our solemnity?[33]

---

24 *an Ethiop's* – "belonging to an inhabi-
tant of Ethiopia".
25 *Beauty too rich . . . dear* – "too splendid
to be worn every day, too valuable for
earth".
26 *shows* – "appears".
27 *trooping with* – "following".
28 *The measure done* – "The dance having
finished".
29 *her place of stand* – "the place where
she stands".
30 *should* – "must".
31 *What* – "How".
32 *antic face* – "strange, grinning face".
33 *To fleer . . . solemnity* – "to laugh con-
temptuously (*fleer*) and mock at
(*scorn*) our festivity (*solemnity*)".
34 *Content thee* – "Calm yourself".

35 *portly* – "dignified".
36 *well-governed* – "well-behaved".
37 *do him disparagement* – "do anything to
dishonour him".
38 *fair presence* – "friendly behaviour".
39 *ill-beseeming semblance* – "unfitting
appearance".
40 *It fits* – "It (i.e. Tybalt's unfriendly expression) is fitting".
41 *goodman boy*. *Goodman* was a term
used of men below the rank of
gentleman. Capulet is indicating to
Tybalt that his behaviour is un-
gentlemanly and childish.
42 *Go to!* – "Shame on you"; a common
expression of annoyance or dis-
approval.

Now, by the stock and honour of my kin,
To strike him dead, I hold it not a sin.

CAPULET

Why, how now, kinsman! Wherefore storm you so?

TYBALT

Uncle, this is a Montague, our foe;   60
A villain that is hither come in spite,
To scorn at our solemnity this night.

CAPULET

Young Romeo is it?

TYBALT

                    'T is he, that villain, Romeo.

CAPULET

Content thee,³⁴ gentle coz, let him alone;
'A bears him like a portly³⁵ gentleman: 65
And to say truth, Verona brags of him
To be a virtuous and well-governed³⁶ youth.
I would not, for the wealth of all this town,
Here in my house do him disparagement;³⁷
Therefore be patient, take no note of him.   70
It is my will, the which if thou respect,
Show a fair presence³⁸ and put off these frowns,
An ill-beseeming semblance³⁹ for a feast.

TYBALT

It fits⁴⁰ when such a villain is a guest.
I 'll not endure him.

CAPULET

                    He shall be endured.   75
What, goodman boy?⁴¹ I say he shall. Go to!⁴²
Am I the master here, or you? Go to!

47

You 'll not endure him! God shall mend my soul,
You 'll make a mutiny[43] among my guests!
You will set cock-a-hoop![44] You 'll be the man![45]   80

TYBALT

Why, uncle, 't is a shame.

CAPULET

Go to, go to!
You are a saucy boy. Is 't so indeed?[46]
This trick may chance to scathe[47] you, I know what.[48]
You must contrary[49] me! Marry, 't is time –
[*To the dancers*] Well said, my hearts![50] [*To Tybalt*] You
    are a princox;[51] go   85
Be quiet, or – [*To the Servants*] More light, more light,
    for shame! –

---

43 *make a mutiny* – "start a quarrel".
44 *set cock-a-hoop* – "make mischief and
    cause disorder".
45 *be the man* – "try to rule things like
    the man of the house".
46 *Is 't so indeed?* He refers to Tybalt's
    statement, *'t is a shame*.
47 *scathe* – "injure".
48 *I know what* – "I know what I am
    talking about".
49 *contrary* – "oppose".
50 *hearts* – "dear friends".
51 *princox* – "rude young man".
52 *cheerly* – "cheerfully".
53 *Patience perforce . . . meeting* – "Unwil-
    ling patience meeting with willing
    anger (*wilful choler*)".
54 *different greeting* – "opposed meeting".
55 *this intrusion* (*line 90*) . . . *gall* –
    "Romeo's entrance here (*this intru-
    sion*) which now appears welcome
    (*seeming sweet*) will turn (*convert*) to
    the bitterest hatred".
56 *rough touch*, i.e. of his hand. His kiss is
    the gentle sin which will smooth away
    the *rough* one committed by his hand.

57 *you do wrong* (*line 96*) . . . *in this* – "you
    wrong your hand too much (in saying
    it has sinned) for it shows a proper
    (*mannerly*) devotion in touching mine
    (*in this*)".
58 *saints have hands* (*line 98*) . . . *palmers'
    kiss* – "pilgrims touch the hands of
    saints' statues, and so the proper way
    for pilgrims (*palmers*) to show their
    devotion is hand to hand". Pilgrims
    to Palestine brought back palm leaves
    as a sign that they had visited the
    Christian shrines there, and so were
    called *palmers*.
59 *Grant thou*, i.e. *let lips do what hands do*,
    i.e. kiss.
60 *Saints do not move . . . sake* – "Saints
    (whether invisible in heaven, or in the
    form of statues) do not move physic-
    ally, although they answer prayers".
    Juliet is giving Romeo permission to
    kiss her.

[*To* TYBALT] I 'll make you quiet. – [*To the dancers*]
   What, cheerly,[52] my hearts!
        [*He leaves* TYBALT *and moves among the guests*

TYBALT

[*To himself*] Patience perforce with wilful choler
   meeting,[53]
Makes my flesh tremble in their different greeting.[54]
I will withdraw, but this intrusion shall,   90
Now seeming sweet, convert to bitterest gall.[55]
        [*Exit*

ROMEO

[*Taking* JULIET's *hand*] If I profane with my unworthiest
   hand
This holy shrine, the gentle sin is this:
My lips, two blushing pilgrims, ready stand
To smooth that rough touch[56] with a tender kiss.   95

JULIET

Good pilgrim, you do wrong your hand too much,
Which mannerly devotion shows in this;[57]
For saints have hands that pilgrims' hands do touch,
And palm to palm is holy palmers' kiss.[58]

ROMEO

Have not saints lips, and holy palmers too?   100

JULIET

Ay, pilgrim, lips that they must use in prayer.

ROMEO

O then, dear saint, let lips do what hands do:
They pray, "Grant thou,[59] lest faith turn to despair."

JULIET

Saints do not move, though grant for prayers' sake.[60]

A right good mark-man [101]
(I.i.199)

The shady curtains from Aurora's bed [63]
(I.i.129)

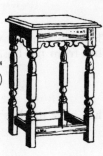

Away with the joint-stools [4]
(I.v.5)

These happy masks that kiss fair ladies' brows,
Being black, puts [116] *us in mind they hide the fair*
(I.i.223 – 224)

a Tartar's painted bow of lath
(I.iv.5)

51

ROMEO

Then move not,[61] while my prayer's effect[62] I take.   105
Thus from my lips, by thine, my sin is purged.

[*He kisses her*

JULIET

Then have my lips the sin that they have took.

ROMEO

Sin from my lips? O trespass sweetly urged![63]
Give me my sin again.

[*He kisses her again*

JULIET

You kiss by the book.[64]

NURSE *comes to* JULIET *from the side of the stage*

---

61 *move not* – "keep still".
62 *my prayer's effect* – "the result of my prayer", i.e. a kiss.
63 *urged* – "argued".
64 *by the book* – "as if you had studied how to do it in a book". Juliet is right: the rather unnatural religious imagery was the conventional language of the lover. Romeo has earlier used it as we have seen (I.ii.90f) to describe his love for Rosaline. The verbal cleverness in which each lover wittily develops and replies to the other's words, however, is not to be taken as a sign of insincerity or lack of true feeling. It is simply a sign that their love is new; as love and understanding grow their exchanges become more direct, informal and passionate in expression.
65 *What* – "Who".
66 *bachelor* – "young gentleman".

67 *the chinks* – "plenty of money". The word comes from the sound which coins make when they are rattled together.
68 *dear account* – (a) "expensive reckoning" (following up the Nurse's word, *chinks*); (b) "an explanation hard to bear".
69 *My life is my foe's debt* – "my life belongs to a Capulet, my enemy". *Debt* continues the money image.
70 *Ay . . . my unrest.* Romeo means that his suffering is even greater since things, now at their best, can only get worse.
71 *foolish banquet* – "a simple (*foolish*) meal of fruit, sweets and wine".
72 *towards* – "about to be served".
73 *honest* – "honourable".

NURSE

Madam, your mother craves a word with you.   110

JULIET *joins her mother at the side of the stage.*

ROMEO

What[65] is her mother?

NURSE

                    Marry, bachelor,[66]
Her mother is the lady of the house,
And a good lady, and a wise and virtuous.
I nursed her daughter that you talked withal.
I tell you, he that can lay hold of her   115
Shall have the chinks.[67]

ROMEO

                    Is she a Capulet?
O dear account![68] My life is my foe's debt.[69]

BENVOLIO

Away, be gone! The sport is at the best.

ROMEO

Ay, so I fear; the more is my unrest.[70]

CAPULET

Nay, gentlemen, prepare not to be gone: 120
We have a trifling foolish banquet[71] towards.[72]
                    [*The maskers whisper their excuses to him*
Is it e'en so? Why, then I thank you all.
I thank you, honest[73] gentlemen; good night.
[*To the servants*] More torches here! Come on, then let's
    to bed.
                    [*Torchbearers show the maskers out*

[*To himself*] Ah, sirrah, by my fay, it waxes late.   125
I 'll to my rest.

            [*Exeunt all except* JULIET *and* NURSE

JULIET

Come hither, Nurse. What is yond gentleman?

NURSE

The son and heir of old Tiberio.

JULIET

What 's he that now is going out of door?

NURSE

Marry, that I think be young Petruchio.   130

JULIET

What 's he[74] that follows there, that would not dance?

NURSE

I know not.

JULIET

Go ask his name [*Exit* NURSE] If he be marriéd,
My grave is like to be my wedding bed.[75]

NURSE

[*Returning*] His name is Romeo, and a Montague,   135
The only son of your great enemy.

---

74 *What 's he.* The answer to this question is the only one Juliet is really
interested in. She is trying to hide her
love for Romeo from the Nurse by
pretending to be interested in the
other guests.

75 *My grave . . . bed.* Juliet means that she
will die unmarried if she cannot marry
Romeo.

76 *Prodigious birth* – "monstrous birth,
likely to end in misfortune".

54

JULIET

[*To herself*] My only love sprung from my only hate!
Too early seen unknown, and known too late!
Prodigious birth[76] of love it is to me,
That I must love a loathéd enemy.   140

NURSE

What 's this, what 's this?

JULIET

A rhyme I learnt even now
Of one I danced withal.
              [JULIET'S *mother calls her from another room*

NURSE

Anon, anon!
Come let's away; the strangers all are gone.
                                        [*Exeunt*

55

(II. Prologue) Romeo's love for Rosaline has been replaced by his new love for Juliet, beside whom Rosaline no longer appears beautiful. Romeo and Juliet, charmed by each other's looks, are in love, but because of the family enmity they have to meet secretly. Their passion overcomes this difficulty, and the joy of their meetings makes the hardship easier to bear.

1 *old Desire* – "Romeo's former desire for Rosaline".
2 *young Affection* – "his new love for Juliet".
3 *gapes* – "opens his mouth hungrily". The usual meaning of *gape* is "to have the mouth open". Shakespeare uses the word metaphorically here to suggest that the mouth is open because of the greedy hunger of *young Affection*.
4 *That fair (line 3) ... not fair* – "the beautiful Rosaline (*that fair*) for whom Romeo groaned and swore he would die, compared with the lovely Juliet is no longer beautiful (*now not fair*) in his eyes".

5 *Alike* – "both", i.e. Romeo and Juliet.
6 *charm* – (a) "magic spell", (b) "attractive beauty".
7 *to his foe-supposed ... complain* – "he must lament in the manner of lovers (*complain*) to his supposed enemy (*foe-supposed*), Juliet".
8 *use to swear* – "are in the habit of swearing".
9 *means* – "opportunity".
10 *Tempering extremities ... sweet* – "softening the hard condition (*extremities*) with the great sweetness (*extreme sweet*) of their meetings".

(II.i) Later that night Romeo climbs over the wall of the Capulets' garden, just before Mercutio and Benvolio arrive looking for him. He does not answer their calls and they give up the search. Juliet appears at her window, and Romeo overhears her talking to herself and revealing her love for him. He speaks to her, telling her of his love for her and promising marriage. She arranges to send a messenger to him the following morning to learn the time and place of the marriage.

1 *go forward*, on his way from the house.
2 *dull earth.* He refers to his own body.

3 *centre* – "heart". Juliet possesses it, and since it was believed that everything tended towards its centre, Romeo moves towards Juliet.

ACT TWO

Prologue

Enter CHORUS

CHORUS

Now old Desire[1] doth in his death-bed lie,
    And young Affection[2] gapes[3] to be his heir;
That fair for which love groaned for and would die,
    With tender Juliet matched, is now not fair.[4]
Now Romeo is beloved and loves again,   5
    Alike[5] bewitchéd by the charm[6] of looks,
But to his foe-supposed he must complain,[7]
    And she steal love's sweet bait from fearful hooks:
Being held a foe, he may not have access
    To breathe such vows as lovers use to swear;[8]   10
And she as much in love, her means[9] much less
    To meet her new-belovéd anywhere;
But passion lends them power, time means, to meet,
    Tempering extremities with extreme sweet.[10]

Scene I. A street beside the wall of Capulet's garden.

Enter ROMEO *walking away from* CAPULET'S *house*

ROMEO

Can I go forward[1] when my heart is here?
Turn back, dull earth,[2] and find thy centre[3] out.
          [*He climbs over the wall into the garden*

Enter MERCUTIO *and* BENVOLIO *in the street.*
ROMEO *listens from inside the garden*

BENVOLIO

Romeo! my cousin Romeo! Romeo!

MERCUTIO

He is wise,
And on my life⁴ hath stolen him to bed.

BENVOLIO

He ran this way and leapt this orchard wall.   5
Call, good Mercutio.

MERCUTIO

Nay, I 'll conjure⁵ too.
Romeo! humours! madman! passion! liver!⁶
Appear thou in the likeness of a sigh;

---

4 *on my life*, an exclamation to assert the truth of what is being said.

5 *conjure* – "call him up", as a magician calls up spirits of the dead.

6 *Romeo! ... liver!* In conjuring up a spirit many names were recited in the hope that one would be correct and make the spirit appear. Mercutio calls out a number of names which he thinks describe Romeo. *Humours* – "moods". The *liver* was thought to be the seat of love.

7 *Cry but ... dove.* Mercutio makes fun of the conventional lover who spent his time sighing and writing love poetry. By *likeness of a sigh* he means "form of a cloud".

8 *gossip Venus.* Mercutio mocks Venus, the Roman goddess of love, by suggesting that she is a talkative person who enjoys idle chatter (*gossip*).

9 *purblind* – "completely blind".

10 *Abraham Cupid.* Mercutio also mocks Cupid by comparing him with the so-called "abraham men", beggars and thieves who, like Cupid, went about half-naked.

11 *trim* – "neatly". A popular song of the time tells how King Cophetua fell in love with Penelophon, a wandering beggar maid.

12 *He,* i.e. Romeo.

13 *ape* – "fool". Mercutio compares Romeo to a performing monkey pretending to be dead.

14 *thy likeness* – "your ghost, in the shape you had when alive".

15 *To raise a spirit* – "If I called up a spirit". He uses several terms used by magicians who made spirits stand inside a magic ring (*circle*), dismissed them (*conjured down*) and made them disappear (*laid*).

16 *That were some spite* – "That would be an annoying matter".

17 *consorted* – "associated".

18 *humorous* – (a) "damp", (b) "moody".

19 *hit the mark* – "achieve its aim". Compare the note to I.i.199.

20 *medlar* a small brown fruit. *Open arse* (line 38) was another name for it.

Speak but one rhyme and I am satisfied;
Cry but "Ay me", pronounce but "love" and "dove";[7]   10
Speak to my gossip Venus[8] one fair word,
One nickname for her purblind[9] son and heir,
Young Abraham Cupid,[10] he that shot so trim[11]
When King Cophetua loved the beggar maid.
He[12] heareth not, he stirreth not, he moveth not;   15
The ape[13] is dead, and I must conjure him.
[*Addressing Romeo*] I conjure thee by Rosaline's bright
    eyes,
By her high forehead and her scarlet lip,
By her fine foot, straight leg and quivering thigh,
And the demesnes that there adjacent lie,   20
That in thy likeness[14] thou appear to us.

BENVOLIO

And if he hear thee, thou wilt anger him.

MERCUTIO

This cannot anger him. 'T would anger him
To raise a spirit[15] in his mistress' circle,
Of some strange nature, letting it there stand   25
Till she had laid it, and conjured it down;
That were some spite.[16] My invocation
Is fair and honest: in his mistress' name
I conjure only but to raise up him.

BENVOLIO

Come; he hath hid himself among these trees   30
To be consorted[17] with the humorous[18] night;
Blind is his love, and best befits the dark.

MERCUTIO

If love be blind, love cannot hit the mark.[19]
Now will he sit under a medlar[20] tree,

And wish his mistress were that kind of fruit   35
As maids call medlars when they laugh alone.
O Romeo, that²¹ she were! O that she were
An open-arse and thou a Poperin²² pear!
Romeo, good night. I 'll to my truckle-bed:²³
This field-bed²⁴ is too cold for me to sleep.   40
Come, shall we go?

BENVOLIO

Go then, for 't is in vain
To seek him here that means not to be found.
[*Exeunt* MERCUTIO *and* BENVOLIO

ROMEO

[*From inside the garden*] He jests at scars that never felt a
     wound.²⁵
[*He sees Juliet*] But soft! What light through yonder
     window breaks?

---

21 *that* – "would that", i.e. "I wish that".
22 *Poperin*, a variety of pear named after the town of Poperinghe in Belgium.
23 *truckle-bed*, a legless bed on wheels.
24 *field-bed* – "sleeping in the open".
25 *He jests . . . wound* – "He (Mercutio) jokes about the wounds of love, having never been in love".
26 *her maid.* The servants of Diana, the virgin goddess of the moon, were unmarried maidens. Juliet is Diana's maid in the sense that she is unmarried.
27 *Her vestal livery . . . green* – "The dress (*livery*) worn by Diana's servants (*vestals*) is sickly green in colour" (like (a) moonlight, and (b) girls suffering from greensickness, or lack of blood). Envious people were said to be "green with envy".
28 *And none but fools do wear it.* The jester, or fool, employed in wealthy house-

holds, usually wore green. Romeo means that anyone who decides never to marry is a fool.
29 *that she knew she were* – "I wish that she knew she is (my love)".
30 *Having some business* – "having to leave on business".
31 *their spheres.* The stars were then thought to be fixed in crystal spheres which turned round the earth.
32 *What if . . . her head?* – "What if her eyes and the two stars changed places?"
33 *shame* – "put to shame".
34 *a wingéd messenger of heaven* – "a flying messenger of the gods".
35 *white-upturnéd* – "looking upwards so that the whites (of the eyes) are showing".
36 *bestrides* – "sits across, as if on a horse".
37 *lazy-pacing* – "slow-moving", like a lazy horse.

60

It is the east, and Juliet is the sun.   45
Arise, fair sun, and kill the envious moon,
Who is already sick and pale with grief
That thou her maid[26] art far more fair than she.
Be not her maid, since she is envious;
Her vestal livery is but sick and green,[27]   50
And none but fools do wear it;[28] cast it off.
It is my lady, O it is my love!
O that she knew she were![29]
She speaks, yet she says nothing. What of that?
Her eye discourses: I will answer it.   55
I am too bold; 't is not to me she speaks.
Two of the fairest stars in all the heaven,
Having some business,[30] do entreat her eyes
To twinkle in their spheres[31] till they return.
What if her eyes were there, they in her head?[32]   60
The brightness of her cheek would shame[33] those stars
As daylight doth a lamp; her eyes in heaven
Would through the airy region stream so bright
That birds would sing and think it were not night.
See how she leans her cheek upon her hand.   65
O that I were a glove upon that hand,
That I might touch that cheek!

JULIET

Ay me.

ROMEO

                                                    She speaks.
O speak again, bright angel, for thou art
As glorious to this night, being o'er my head,
As is a wingéd messenger of heaven[34]   70
Unto the white-upturnéd[35] wondering eyes
Of mortals that fall back to gaze on him
When he bestrides[36] the lazy-pacing[37] clouds,
And sails upon the bosom of the air.

61

JULIET

O Romeo, Romeo! Wherefore art thou Romeo?[38]   75
Deny thy father and refuse thy name:
Or if thou wilt not, be but sworn my love
And I 'll no longer be a Capulet.

ROMEO

[*Aside*] Shall I hear more, or shall I speak at this?

JULIET

'T is but thy name that is my enemy.   80
Thou art thyself, though not a Montague.[39]
What 's "Montague"? It is nor[40] hand, nor foot,
Nor arm, nor face, nor any other part
Belonging to a man. O be some other name!
What 's in a name? That which we call a rose   85
By any other word would smell as sweet.
So Romeo would, were he not Romeo called,
Retain that dear perfection which he owes[41]
Without that title. Romeo, doff[42] thy name,
And for that name,[43] which is no part of thee,   90
Take all myself.

ROMEO

[*To* JULIET]   I take thee at thy word.
Call me but "Love", and I 'll be new baptized;[44]
Henceforth I never will be Romeo.

---

38 *Wherefore art thou Romeo?* – "Why are you Romeo?" Juliet means: "Why have I fallen in love with a Montague?"

39 *Thou art . . . a Montague* – "You would still be the same person even if you were not a Montague".

40 *nor* – "neither".

41 *owes* – "owns".

42 *doff* – "put aside".

43 *for that name* – "in exchange for that name".

44 *new baptized* – "baptized again", i.e. he will take the new name "*Love*" in place of the name he received at baptism, i.e. when, as an infant, he was made a Christian by having water put on his head.

45 *bescreened* – "hidden".

46 *counsel* – "private talk".

47 *thee dislike* – "displeases you".

48 *o'erperch* – "fly over".

62

JULIET

What man art thou, that thus bescreened[45] in night,
So stumblest on my counsel?[46]

ROMEO

               By a name   95
I know not how to tell thee who I am.
My name, dear saint, is hateful to myself
Because it is an enemy to thee.
Had I it written, I would tear the word.

JULIET

My ears have yet not drunk a hundred words   100
Of thy tongue's uttering, yet I know the sound.
Art thou not Romeo, and a Montague?

ROMEO

Neither, fair maid, if either thee dislike.[47]

JULIET

How camest thou hither, tell me, and wherefore?
The orchard walls are high and hard to climb,   105
And the place death, considering who thou art,
If any of my kinsmen find thee here.

ROMEO

With love's light wings did I o'erperch[48] these walls,
For stony limits cannot hold love out;
And what love can do, that dares love attempt: 110
Therefore thy kinsmen are no stop to me.

JULIET

If they do see thee, they will murder thee.

ROMEO

Alack, there lies more peril in thine eye
Than twenty of their swords. Look thou but sweet
And I am proof against their enmity.[49]   115

JULIET

I would not for the world they saw thee here.

ROMEO

I have night's cloak to hide me from their eyes.
And but[50] thou love me, let them find me here;
My life were better ended by their hate
Than death proroguéd,[51] wanting of thy love.[52]   120

JULIET

By whose direction found'st thou out this place?

---

49 *Look thou . . . their enmity* – "If only
you will look with favour on me, then
I cannot be hurt by (*am proof against*)
their hatred".

50 *but* – "unless".

51 *proroguéd* – "postponed".

52 *wanting of thy love* – "(if I should be)
without your love".

53 *adventure for such merchandise* – "risk
anything for such a prize".

54 *bepaint* – "colour".

55 *Fain would I dwell on form* – "I would
gladly behave in the conventional
manner of lovers".

56 *farewell compliment!* – "good-bye to
formal expressions!" (it is too late for
them).

57 *Jove*, or Jupiter, the chief Roman god,
was, among other things, the god of
oaths or solemn promises. He did not
regard the oaths of lovers seriously because he knew that few of them would
be kept.

58 *say thee nay,/ So* – "say no to you, provided that".

59 *else* – "otherwise".

60 *fond* – "foolishly affectionate".

61 *my haviour light* – "my behaviour immodest".

62 *more cunning to be strange* – "greater
skill in pretending to be distant and
reserved".

63 *should* – "would".

64 *ere I was ware* – "before I knew it".

65 *My true-love passion* – "my passionate
declaration of love".

66 *And not impute (line 147) . . . so discoveréd* – "and do not regard this sur-
render (*yielding*) which dark night has
revealed in this way (*so discoveréd*) as
immodest love". Note the play on
light and *dark*.

64

ROMEO

By love, that first did prompt me to inquire;
He lent me counsel, and I lent him eyes.
I am no pilot, yet wert thou as far
As that vast shore washed with the farthest sea,   125
I should adventure for such merchandise.[53]

JULIET

Thou knowest the mask of night is on my face,
Else would a maiden blush bepaint[54] my cheek,
For that which thou hast heard me speak tonight.
Fain would I dwell on form;[55] fain, fain deny   130
What I have spoke: but farewell compliment![56]
<u>Dost thou love me?</u> I know thou wilt say "Ay",
And I will take thy word; yet if thou swear'st
Thou mayst prove false. At lovers' perjuries
They say Jove[57] laughs. O gentle Romeo,   135
If thou dost love, pronounce it faithfully;
Or if thou think I am too quickly won,
I 'll frown, and be perverse, and say thee nay,
So[58] thou wilt woo; but else,[59] not for the world
In truth, fair Montague, I am too fond,[60]   140
And therefore thou mayst think my haviour light.[61]
But trust me, gentleman, I 'll prove more true
Than those that have more cunning to be strange.[62]
I should[63] have been more strange, I must confess,
But that thou overheard'st, ere I was ware,[64]   145
My true-love passion;[65] therefore pardon me,
And not impute this yielding to light love,
Which the dark night hath so discoveréd.[66]

ROMEO

Lady, by yonder blesséd moon I vow,
That tips with silver all these fruit-tree tops –   150

JULIET

O swear not by the moon, th' inconstant moon,
That monthly changes in her circled orb,[67]
Lest that thy love prove likewise variable.

ROMEO

What shall I swear by?

JULIET

                    Do not swear at all;
Or if thou wilt, swear by thy gracious self,   155
Which is the god of my idolatry,
And I 'll believe thee.

ROMEO

                    If my heart's dear love –

JULIET

Well, do not swear. Although I joy[68] in thee,
I have no joy of this contract tonight:
It is too rash, too unadvised, too sudden,   160
Too like the lightning, which doth cease to be
Ere one can say "It lightens." Sweet, good night.
This bud of love, by summer's ripening breath,
May prove a beauteous flower when next we meet.
Good night, good night. As sweet repose[69] and rest   165
Come to thy heart as that within my breast.

---

67 *circled orb* – "circular sphere".
68 *I joy* – "I rejoice".
69 *As sweet repose* – "May as sweet a rest".
70 *I would it were ... again* – "I wish I had it back, to give again".
71 *But to be frank* – "Only to be generous".

72 *And yet ... I have.* As Juliet goes on to explain (lines 176–7), the more she gives her love to him, the more she has.
73 *adieu* – "good-bye".
74 *afeard* – "afraid".
75 *Too flattering-sweet ... substantial* – "too flatteringly pleasant to be real".

ROMEO

O wilt thou leave me so unsatisfied?

JULIET

What satisfaction canst thou have to-night?

ROMEO

Th' exchange of thy love's faithful vow for mine.

JULIET

I gave thee mine before thou didst request it;   170
And yet I would it were to give again.[70]

ROMEO

Would'st thou withdraw it? For what purpose, love?

JULIET

But to be frank[71] and give it thee again:
And yet I wish but for the thing I have.[72]
My bounty is as boundless as the sea,   175
My love as deep; the more I give to thee,
The more I have, for both are infinite.
                              [*The* NURSE *calls*
I hear some noise within. Dear love, adieu.[73]
[*To the* NURSE] Anon, good Nurse! [*To* ROMEO] Sweet
   Montague, be true.
Stay but a little; I will come again.   180
                 [JULIET *leaves the window and goes in*

ROMEO

O blessed, blessed night! I am afeard,[74]
Being in night, all this is but a dream,
Too flattering-sweet to be substantial.[75]
                          [JULIET *returns to the window*

JULIET

Three words, dear Romeo, and good night indeed.
If that thy bent of love[76] be honourable,   185
Thy purpose marriage, send me word to-morrow
By one that I 'll procure to come to thee,
Where and what time thou wilt perform the rite;
And all my fortunes at thy foot I 'll lay,
And follow thee, my lord, throughout the world.   190

NURSE

[*From inside the house*] Madam!

JULIET

[*To the* NURSE] I come, anon. [*To* ROMEO] But if thou
    mean'st not well,
I do beseech thee –

NURSE

[*Calling again from within*] Madam!

JULIET

                By and by,[77] I come –
[*Continuing, to* ROMEO] To cease thy suit,[78] and leave
    me to my grief.
Tomorrow will I send.

---

76 *thy bent of love* – "the intention of your love".

77 *By and by* – "Immediately".

78 *suit* – "wooing".

79 *So thrive my soul* – "As I hope that my soul may thrive –". Romeo was about to assure Juliet of the sincerity of his love, but her haste forces her to interrupt him in the middle of his sentence.

80 *A thousand . . . light* – "(The night is) a thousand times worse (than *good*) without (*to want*) the light you give it".

81 *toward school*, i.e. as schoolboys go towards school.

82 *O for a falconer's* (line *200*) . . . *again*. Juliet wishes she were a falconer (i.e. one who hunts with hawks, or falcons) so that she could recall Romeo, the *tassel-gentle* (the peregrine, the noblest of the falcons).

83 *Bondage is hoarse*. Juliet, bound by the danger of revealing her love, is unable to raise her voice.

84 *tear* – "burst in pieces".

85 *Echo* was a Greek mountain goddess. She fell in love with Narcissus but because he did not return her love, she wasted away to nothing but a voice.

86 *her airy tongue*. Echo's voice is sound thrown back through the air.

ROMEO

So thrive my soul, –[79]   195

JULIET

A thousand times good night!

[JULIET *goes in*

ROMEO

A thousand times the worse, to want thy light![80]
Love goes toward love as schoolboys from their books,
But love from love, toward school[81] with heavy looks.

[ROMEO *is walking away as* JULIET *returns*

JULIET

Hist, Romeo, hist! O for a falconer's voice,   200
To lure this tassel-gentle back again.[82]
Bondage is hoarse,[83] and may not speak aloud,
Else would I tear[84] the cave where Echo[85] lies,
And make her airy tongue[86] more hoarse than mine
With repetition of my "Romeo!"   205

ROMEO

It is my soul that calls upon my name.
How silver-sweet sound lovers' tongues by night,
Like softest music to attending ears.

JULIET

Romeo!

ROMEO

Madam?

JULIET

What o'clock tomorrow
Shall I send to thee?

ROMEO

By the hour of nine.   210

JULIET

I will not fail. 'T is twenty years till then.
I have forgot why I did call thee back.

ROMEO

Let me stand here till thou remember it.

JULIET

I shall forget, to have[87] thee still stand there,
Remembering[88] how I love thy company.   215

ROMEO

And I 'll still stay, to have thee still forget,
Forgetting any other home but this.

---

87 *to have* – "in order to have".
88 *Remembering*. This is related to "I",
    the subject of *shall forget*, as *Forgetting*
    (line 217) is related to the subject of
    'll stay.
89 *a wanton's bird* – "the pet bird kept by
    a playful woman".
90 *silk thread*. This was tied to the bird's
    leg.
91 *loving-jealous of his liberty*, i.e. wanting,
    yet fearing, to give it freedom.

92 *much cherishing* – "over-kindness".
93 *so sweet to rest* – "to rest so sweetly".
94 *my ghostly sire's close cell* – "the private
    room (*close cell*) of my spiritual father
    (*ghostly sire*)". Just as the natural father
    looks after the bodily welfare of his
    children, so the priest looks after the
    welfare of people's souls, and so is re-
    garded as a spiritual father.
95 *dear hap* – "good fortune".

(II.ii) As day breaks, Romeo hurries to Friar Lawrence's cell. He tells him
of his love for Juliet and begs him to marry them later that day. Although
he thinks Romeo rash and wavering, Friar Lawrence agrees to marry them,
hoping that this will end the quarrel between the two families.

1 *Check'ring* – "checkering", i.e. "breaking up the darkness with patches of a
   lighter colour".

2 *fleckled* – (a) "varied with red streaks"
   (like *darkness*); (b) "having the face
   covered with red patches" (like a
   drunkard).

70

JULIET

'T is almost morning. I would have thee gone,
And yet no farther than a wanton's bird,[89]
Who lets it hop a little from her hand,   220
Like a poor prisoner in his twisted gyves,
And with a silk thread[90] plucks it back again,
So loving-jealous of his liberty.[91]

ROMEO

I would I were thy bird.

JULIET

                    Sweet, so would I,
Yet I should kill thee with much cherishing.[92]   225
Good night, good night. Parting is such sweet sorrow,
That I shall say "good night" till it be morrow.

ROMEO

Sleep dwell upon thine eyes, peace in thy breast.
Would I were sleep and peace, so sweet to rest.[93]
                                    [JULIET *goes in*
Hence will I to my ghostly sire's close cell,[94]   230
His help to crave, and my dear hap[95] to tell.

                                    [*Exit*

Scene II. FRIAR LAWRENCE's *cell.*

Enter FRIAR LAWRENCE *with a basket*

FRIAR LAWRENCE

The grey-eyed morn smiles on the frowning night,
Check'ring[1] the eastern clouds with streaks of light;
And fleckled[2] darkness like a drunkard reels

71

From forth day's path and Titan's fiery wheels.[3]
Now, ere the sun advance[4] his burning eye   5
The day to cheer and night's dank dew to dry,
I must upfill this osier cage[5] of ours[6]
With baleful weeds and precious-juicéd flowers.
The earth that 's nature's mother is her tomb:
What is her burying grave, that is her womb,[7]   10
And from her womb children of divers kind
We sucking on her natural bosom find:[8]
Many for many virtues excellent,[9]

---

3 *Titan's fiery wheels*. Titan was the Greek sun-god. The *fiery wheels* are those of his chariot, the sun, which traces its path each day across the sky.

4 *advance* – "raise" (like an eyelid).

5 *upfill this osier cage* – "fill up this willow basket".

6 *of ours*, i.e. belonging to his brotherhood, the Franciscans, named after St. Francis.

7 *The earth* (line *9*) . . . *her womb*. The earth receives dead things back into itself, is fed by them, and produces new life with their help. Friar Lawrence believes firmly in the unity of man with nature, and the fact that all things are part of one another. His knowledge of plants is later displayed when he gives Juliet the sleeping potion, but his speech has the more important dramatic purpose of making the audience see at once that he is a good and wise man whose remarks on the events that follow are a trustworthy guide.

8 *And from* (line *11*) . . . *bosom find* – "and we find various (*divers*) plants (*children*) drawing their life from the earth's surface (*her natural bosom*)".

9 *Many . . . virtues excellent* – "Many (plants) have numerous excellent properties".

10 *None but for some* – "there is none without some excellent quality".

11 *mickle* – "great".

12 *powerful grace* – "beneficial power".

13 *For nought* (line *17*) . . . *abuse* – "There is no living thing so vile that it does not enrich the earth in some way, and nothing so good that it does not produce evil (*abuse*) when forced (*strained*) into some use contrary to its true nature".

14 *And vice . . . dignified* – "and deeds which are the result of evil intentions may sometimes produce good effects".

15 *Poison . . . medicine power* – "poison dwells and healing medicine has power". The same plant has power to heal and to destroy.

16 *For this . . . each part* – "because the smell (*that part*) of this flower (*this*) comforts (*cheers*) the whole body (*each part*)".

17 *stays all . . . the heart* – "stops the heart and all the senses together".

18 *Two such* (line *27*) . . . *plant*. Divine grace and the human passions are always at war in man; if passion wins, spiritual death follows.

19 *Benedicite* – "Bless you".

20 *distempered* – "disturbed in mind".

21 *bid good morrow to* – "leave".

22 *unbruiséd youth . . . brain* – "a young man not yet hurt (by the experiences of life) whose mind (*brain*) is not full of troubles (*unstuffed*)".

None but for some,[10] and yet all different.
O mickle[11] is the powerful grace[12] that lies   15
In plants, herbs, stones, and their true qualities:
For nought so vile that on the earth doth live
But to the earth some special good doth give;
Nor aught so good but, strained from that fair use,
Revolts from true birth, stumbling on abuse.[13]   20
Virtue itself turns vice, being misapplied,
And vice sometime by action dignified.[14]

Enter ROMEO, *unseen by the Friar*

Within the infant rind of this weak flower
Poison hath residence and medicine power:[15]
For this, being smelt, with that part cheers each part;[16]   25
Being tasted, stays all senses with the heart.[17]
Two such opposéd kings encamp them still
In man as well as herbs, grace and rude will;
And where the worser is predominant,
Full soon the canker death eats up that plant.[18]   30

ROMEO

Good morrow, father.

FRIAR LAWRENCE

Benedicite.[19]
What early tongue so sweet saluteth me?
Young son, it argues a distempered[20] head
So soon to bid good morrow to[21] thy bed.
Care keeps his watch in every old man's eye,   35
And where care lodges, sleep will never lie;
But where unbruiséd youth with unstuffed brain[22]
Doth couch his limbs, there golden sleep doth reign.
Therefore thy earliness doth me assure
Thou art uprousèd with some distemperature;   40
Or if not so, then here I hit it right,
Our Romeo hath not been in bed to-night.

73

ROMEO

That last is true: the sweeter rest was mine.

FRIAR LAWRENCE

God pardon sin! Wast thou with Rosaline?

ROMEO

With Rosaline, my ghostly father? No.   45
I have forgot that name, and that name's woe.

FRIAR LAWRENCE

That 's my good son. But where hast thou been then?

ROMEO

I 'll tell thee ere thou ask it me again:
I have been feasting with mine enemy,
Where on a sudden one hath wounded me
That 's by me wounded. Both our remedies   50
Within thy help and holy physic lies.[23]
I bear no hatred, blessed man, for lo,
My intercession likewise steads my foe.[24]

---

23 *Both our remedies (line 51) ... lies* – "The cure for us both lies in your hands (*thy help*), and in the healing power of marriage (*holy physic*)". *Lies* for lie.

24 *My intercession ... foe* – "my pleading (*intercession*) also benefits (*steads*) Juliet (*my foe*)".

25 *homely in thy drift* – "simple in what you say".

26 *Riddling confession ... shrift* – "a confession which is difficult to understand (*riddling*) will find it difficult to obtain forgiveness (*shrift*)".

27 *pass* – "walk along".

28 *Jesu Maria* – "By Jesus and Mary"; an exclamation.

29 *To season love ... taste* – "to preserve and give a flavour to (*season*) a love that is not love at all".

30 *The sun ... clears* – "The sun has not yet dried up the clouds formed by your sighs". Compare I.i.126.

31 *sentence*, a wise saying, expressed in a few words.

32 *Woman may fall ... men* – "Women can be excused for being unfaithful when men are".

74

FRIAR LAWRENCE

Be plain, good son, and homely in thy drift;[25]   55
Riddling confession finds but riddling shrift.[26]

ROMEO

Then plainly know, my heart's dear love is set
On the fair daughter of rich Capulet:
As mine on hers, so hers is set on mine,
And all combined, save what thou must combine   60
By holy marriage. When and where and how
We met, we wooed, and made exchange of vow,
I 'll tell thee as we pass,[27] but this I pray,
That thou consent to marry us to-day.

FRIAR LAWRENCE

Holy Saint Francis, what a change is here!   *disbelief*   65
Is Rosaline that thou didst love so dear
So soon forsaken? Young men's love then lies
Not truly in their hearts, but in their eyes.   *infatuation: eyes deceiving, heart sincere*
Jesu Maria,[28] what a deal of brine   *salty water = tear*
Hath washed thy sallow cheeks for Rosaline!   70
How much salt water thrown away in waste
To season love, that of it doth not taste![29]
The sun not yet thy sighs from heaven clears,[30]
Thy old groans ring yet in mine ancient ears;
Lo, here upon thy cheek the stain doth sit   75
Of an old tear that is not washed off yet.
If e'er thou wast thyself, and these woes thine,   *If these tears are still there, they are all for Rosaline*
Thou and these woes were all for Rosaline.
And art thou changed? Pronounce this sentence[31] then:
Women may fall, when there's no strength in men.[32]   80

ROMEO

Thou chid'st me oft for loving Rosaline.   *scolded*

75

FRIAR LAWRENCE

For doting, not for loving, pupil mine.

ROMEO

And bad'st *tell* me bury love.

FRIAR LAWRENCE

Not in a grave
To lay one in, another out to have.[33]

ROMEO

I pray thee chide me not. Her I love now   85
Doth grace for grace and love for love allow:
The other did not so.

---

33 *Not in a grave* (*line 83*) . . . *have*. He means that he did not advise Romeo to bury one love in order to give birth to another.

34 *Thy love . . . spell*. The sense is, "you recited words by heart (*rote*) without understanding what love was, just as a child who has learned the words by heart pretends to read".

35 *In one respect* – "for one reason".

36 *I stand . . . haste* – "I insist that we hurry".

(II.iii) It is later that same Monday morning. Benvolio tells Mercutio that Tybalt has sent a letter demanding a fight with Romeo. Mercutio is making fun of Tybalt's affected manners when Romeo enters, and Mercutio tries to make him forget his love affair by engaging him in a battle of wits. The Nurse, sent, as arranged, by Juliet, comes looking for Romeo, and Mercutio and Benvolio leave. Romeo instructs the Nurse to get Juliet to come that afternoon to Friar Lawrence's cell, as if to confession, but really in order to be married. He arranges to send the Nurse a rope ladder, to be let down that night from Juliet's window, so that he can enter unseen by the Capulets.

1 *should* – "can".

2 *tonight* – "last night". Compare I.iv.50 and the note to it.

3 *his man*, i.e. Romeo's servant, Balthasar.

4 *his*, i.e. Romeo's.

SCENE III]

FRIAR LAWRENCE

read by heart

O she knew well
Thy love did read by rote that could not spell.[34]
But come, young waverer, come go with me;
In one respect[35] I 'll thy assistant be,   90
For this alliance may so happy prove
To turn your households' rancour to pure love. *to end the quarrel*
x. Capulet & Montague
through Romeo & Juliet's
union

ROMEO

O let us hence. I stand on sudden haste.[36]

FRIAR LAWRENCE

Wisely and slow. They stumble that run fast.

[*Exeunt*

Scene III. A street.

Enter MERCUTIO *and* BENVOLIO

MERCUTIO

Where the devil should[1] this Romeo be? Came he not
home to-night?[2]

BENVOLIO

Not to his father's; I spoke with his man.[3]

MERCUTIO

Why, that same pale hard-hearted wench, that Rosaline,
torments him so, that he will sure run mad.   5

BENVOLIO

Tybalt, the kinsman to old Capulet, hath sent a letter to
his[4] father's house.

77

5 *a challenge* – "an invitation to fight".

6 *answer it* – "accept the invitation to fight". Mercutio (line 10) takes the word *answer* in its usual sense to mean "reply to", so that Benvolio has to explain his meaning (line 11).

7 *he will answer (line 11) . . . dared* – "he will show Tybalt (*the letter's master*) just how brave he is (*how he dares*), having been dared to fight".

8 *stabbed (line 13) . . . black eye*, i.e. killed by a glance from the pale Rosaline's dark eye. It was one of the conventions of the love literature of the time that looks could kill. Compare the image of Juliet's glance as a dart (I.iii.92–3).

9 *run through* – "pierced through".

10 *pin* – "centre". A small metal button (*pin*) marked the centre of the object aimed at by the bowman.

11 *cleft* – "split".

12 *the blind boy's butt-shaft* – "Cupid's arrow". The butt-shaft was an arrow used in the butts, or practice area. Notice the alliteration, i.e. the repetition of the initial letter, in this case the letter "b". It reveals Mercutio's ready wit, and also draws attention to his contemptuous attitude to Cupid and everything to do with love. From the list of ways in which Romeo has been "killed", it is clear that Mercutio sees him as the passive and helpless victim of love.

13 *And is he . . . Tybalt?* – "Is he (in this condition) any match for Tybalt?"

14 *Prince of Cats*. In certain stories of the time, Tybalt was the name of a cat, called the Prince of Cats.

15 *courageous captain of compliments* – "brave master of the laws of polite behaviour". Again, the alliteration underlines Mercutio's mockery, this time of Tybalt. He goes on to display his contempt for the affected Tybalt and his attempts to keep up-to-date and follow the latest foreign fashion.

16 *sing prick-song* – "sing, carefully following the notes (*pricks*) on a sheet of music". Mercutio makes a comparison between fencing and singing. To keep *time* in music is to give each note its correct value, while in fencing it is to move sword and body at the correct time; *distance* in music refers to the pause between two sounds, and in fencing to the space between the two fencers; *proportion* in music and in fencing is regularity of movement.

17 *he rests me (line 20) . . . bosom* – "he pauses for one, two, minim beats, and on the third pierces you in the breast". The *minim* is a short note in music. *Me* has no grammatical function in this sentence. Compare *Follow me* (line 59), and *claps me* (III.i.6).

18 *The very butcher of a silk button*. i.e. he is so skilful that he can pierce any button on the dress of the man he is fighting.

19 *of the very first house . . . cause* – "of the highest rank (*first house*) in his knowledge of the rules of fighting in single combat". The phrase, *the first and second cause*, refers to the causes which make it necessary for one gentleman to challenge another, according to the fashion which Tybalt follows.

20 *passado . . . hai*. These are Italian fencing terms. The *passado* is a forward thrust, the *punto reverso* a back-handed blow, and the *hai* (Italian for "you have it") is the death blow. (Mercutio's attack on foreign manners and phrases voices Shakespeare's own dislike of them.)

MERCUTIO

A challenge,[5] on my life.

BENVOLIO

Romeo will answer it.[6]

MERCUTIO

Any man that can write may answer a letter.   10

BENVOLIO

Nay, he will answer the letter's master, how he dares, being dared.[7]

MERCUTIO

Alas, poor Romeo, he is already dead – stabbed with a white wench's black eye,[8] run through[9] the ear with a love song, the very pin[10] of his heart cleft[11] with the blind bowboy's butt shaft.[12] And is he a man to encounter Tybalt?[13]

BENVOLIO

Why, what is Tybalt?

MERCUTIO

More than Prince of Cats.[14] O, he 's the courageous captain of compliments.[15] He fights as you sing prick-song,[16] – keeps time, distance, and proportion: he rests me his   20 minim rests – one, two, and the third in your bosom.[17] The very butcher of a silk button,[18] a duellist, a duellist, a gentleman of the very first house of the first and second cause.[19] Ah, the immortal passado, the punto reverso, the hai![20]   25

BENVOLIO

The what?

79

21 *The pox of* – "A plague on".

22 *antic* – "strangely-behaved".

23 *affecting fantasticoes*–"foolishly affected men".

24 *new tuners of accent* – "people who affect a new way of talking". Although the plays of English dramatists in Shakespeare's time were often set in foreign countries, the dramatists did not feel it necessary to make their characters talk and behave as foreigners would. This explains why Mercutio, an Italian, is made to attack Italian speech and manners as if he were an Englishman.

25 *tall* – "valiant".

26 *grandsire* – "grandfather".

27 *strange flies* – "foreign nuisances" (because they introduce foreign fashions).

28 *pardon-me's*. This was a favourite phrase of those seeking to be in the fashion (*fashion-mongers*). Mercutio, with his blunt directness, dislikes excessively polite expressions of this kind.

29 *who stand (line 32) . . . old bench* – "who admire (*stand . . . on*) the new fashions so much that they cannot endure the old ones". There is play on the two meanings of *form*, (a) "mode", (b) "seat", and on the *stand*/*sit* contrast.

30 *their bones*. Sitting on the uncushioned seats of *the old bench*, or in the unpadded clothes of the new fashion, hurt their bones.

31 Romeo's entry has been carefully prepared for. His friends have been searching for him, and discussing him, and now he appears. His sharp wit, a quality of his character which we have not seen before, is revealed in the exchanges which follow, and underlines the contrast between Romeo and the humourless Tybalt, whom Mercutio and Benvolio have also been discussing.

32 *Without his roe* – (a) "without Rosaline". The *roe* is the female deer; (b) "dried up, worthless". Here the

roe is the mass of eggs inside a fish. Mercutio's pun on *roe* was suggested by the first syllable of *Romeo* (line 35).

33 *fishified* – "become fish-like and inhuman".

34 *Now is he . . . flowed in* – "He is all ready to write flowing poetry (*numbers*) like Petrarch's". Petrarch was a fourteenth-century Italian poet famous for his love poetry.

35 *Laura . . . a kitchen wench* – "Laura (whom Petrarch loved) was like a kitchen-maid compared with Rosaline (*to his love*)". Mercutio is imagining Romeo's thoughts.

36 *she had . . . be-rhyme her* – "Laura had a better lover to praise her in verse (*be-rhyme her*)". Mercutio is here adding his own opinion.

37 *Dido (line 40) . . . the purpose*. Mercutio imagines Romeo dismissing with contempt lovers famous for their beauty, as inferior to Rosaline. Dido, the Queen of Carthage, lover of Aeneas of Troy, is plain (*a dowdy*); Cleopatra of Egypt, lover of Julius Caesar and Mark Antony, is a *gipsy*; Helen, who was carried off to Troy by Paris, and Hero, a Greek priestess and lover of Leander, are worthless creatures (*hildings*) and immoral women (*harlots*), and Thisbe, the lover of Pyramus, despite her grey eyes, is of no importance (*not to the purpose*).

38 *bonjour* – "good day". The use of this French phrase was one of the new fashions Mercutio is attacking.

39 *French slop* – "loose French trousers".

40 *fairly* – "completely".

41 *the slip*. To give someone *the slip* is to escape from him. A *slip* was also a false coin, which explains *counterfeit* in line 43. See *counterfeit* in the Glossary.

42 *Can you not conceive?* – "Can you not understand (my pun)?"

43 *strain courtesy* – "show less politeness than he should".

80

MERCUTIO

The pox of[21] such antic,[22] lisping, affecting fantasticoes,[23]
these new tuners of accent![24] "By Jesu, a very good blade!
a very tall[25] man! a very good whore!" Why, is not this a
lamentable thing, grandsire,[26] that we should be thus   30
afflicted with these strange flies,[27] these fashion-mongers,
these "pardon-me's"[28] who stand so much on the new
form that they cannot sit at ease on the old bench?[29] O,
their bones, their bones![30]

Enter ROMEO[31]

BENVOLIO

Here comes Romeo, here comes Romeo.   35

MERCUTIO

Without his roe,[32] like a dried herring. O flesh, flesh, how
art thou fishified![33] Now is he for the numbers that
Petrarch flowed in![34] Laura to his lady was a kitchen
wench[35] – marry, she had a better love to be-rhyme her[36]
– Dido a dowdy, Cleopatra a gipsy, Helen and Hero hild-   40
ings and harlots, Thisbe a grey eye or so, but not to the
purpose.[37] Signior Romeo, bonjour![38] There's a French
salutation to your French slop.[39] You gave us the counterfeit fairly[40] last night.

ROMEO

Good morrow to you both. What counterfeit did I give   45
you?

MERCUTIO

The slip, sir, the slip.[41] Can you not conceive?[42]

ROMEO

Pardon, good Mercutio. My business was great, and in
such a case as mine a man may strain courtesy.[43]

MERCUTIO

That 's as much as to say, such a case as yours constrains a   50
man to bow in the hams.[44]

ROMEO

Meaning to curtsy?

MERCUTIO

Thou hast most kindly[45] hit it.

ROMEO

A most courteous exposition.

---

44 *constrains . . . the hams* – "forces a
man's legs to bend (*bow*)". Mercutio
plays on Romeo's phrase *strain courtesy*, turning *courtesy* into *curtsy* (a
bow).
45 *kindly* – (a) "exactly", (b) "graciously".
46 *the very pink* – "the perfection". *Pink*
is also the name of a flower (line 55),
and *to pink* is to cut holes in cloth or
leather as an ornament. When Romeo
says that his *pump* (single-soled shoe)
is *well-favoured*, he means that it has
been *pinked* in this way.
47 *Sure wit!* Mercutio mockingly praises
Romeo's wit as unerring.
48 *that* – "so that".
49 *solely singular* – "absolutely un-
equalled".
50 *single-soled* – "thin and contemptible".
51 *singular for the singleness* – "remarkable
for (a) the fact that it is the only one,
and (b) its silliness". Romeo thus ends
the play on *sole, solely, single* and
singular.

52 *Come between us . . . faints.* Mercutio
makes fun of Romeo's wit, by begging Benvolio to part them, pretending that the battle of wits is too much
for him. *Faints* for *faint*.
53 *switch and spurs* – "(use the horseman's)
whip (*switch*) and spurs (to urge on
your wit)".
54 *cry a match* – "claim the victory".
55 *wild-goose chase*, a sport in which a
horseman had to follow exactly the
course of the one in front, like a wild-
goose. *Wild-goose* and *goose* also
meant "fool".
56 *I am done* – "I am lost". Mercutio is
saying that Romeo, being a greater
goose (fool), is sure to win.
57 *my whole five.* Mercutio is referring to
the five internal wits, namely, com-
mon-sense, memory, fancy, imagination and estimation (or judgement).
58 *Was I . . . the goose?* – "Am I even
with you now, after that joke about
the goose?"
59 *Thou wast never . . . goose* – "You were
never anything but a goose in my
company".

MERCUTIO

Nay, I am the very pink[46] of courtesy.   55

ROMEO

Pink for flower?

MERCUTIO

Right.

ROMEO

Why, then is my pump well-favoured.

MERCUTIO

Sure wit![47] Follow me this jest now till thou hast worn
out thy pump, that[48] when the single sole of it is worn,   60
the jest may remain, after the wearing, solely singular.[49]

ROMEO

O single-soled[50] jest, solely singular for the singleness![51]

MERCUTIO

Come between us, good Benvolio; my wits faints.[52]

ROMEO

Switch and spurs, switch and spurs![53] or I 'll cry a match.[54]

MERCUTIO

Nay, if our wits run the wild-goose chase,[55] I am done,[56]   65
for thou hast more of the wild-goose in one of thy wits
than, I am sure, I have in my whole five.[57] Was I with
you there for the goose?[58]

ROMEO

Thou wast never with me for anything when thou wast
not there for the goose.[59]   70

83

MERCUTIO

I will bite thee by the ear[60] for that jest.

ROMEO

Nay, good goose, bite not.

MERCUTIO

Thy wit is a very bitter sweeting;[61] it is a most sharp sauce.

ROMEO

And is it not well served in to[62] a sweet goose?

MERCUTIO

O here's a wit of cheveril,[63] that stretches from an inch   75
narrow to an ell[64] broad!

ROMEO

I stretch it out for that word "broad", which, added to the
"goose", proves thee far and wide a broad[65] goose.

---

60 *bite thee by the ear*, a sign of affection.
61 *bitter sweeting*, an apple used for making apple sauce.
62 *well served in to* – "fittingly served with". It was the custom to serve a bitter sauce with sweet meat.
63 *cheveril*, the skin of the young goat which can be stretched easily.
64 *an ell*, a measurement of forty-five inches.
65 *broad* – (a) "plain", (b) "big".
66 *now art thou (line 80) . . . as by nature.* Note the play on *art* (are) and *art* (skill), the contrast between *art* (skill) and *nature* (inherited qualities), and the play on *nature* and *natural* (a born fool).
67 *drivelling* – (a) "talking foolishly", (b) "running at the mouth".

68 *natural* – "a born fool".
69 *lolling* – "with the tongue hanging out".
70 *bauble*, the short stick carried by the professional fool, with a small fool's head at the top.
71 *against the hair* – "against the grain", i.e. "against my natural desire to finish it".
72 *large* – "long".
73 *occupy* – "dwell on".
74 *goodly gear! A sail, a sail!* Romeo is amused by the elegant dress (*gear*) of the Nurse, who imitates the appearance and behaviour of a lady of fashion.
75 *a shirt and a smock*, i.e. a man and a woman.

84

friendly parring
" duel of words "
pun on words

MERCUTIO

Why, is not this better now than groaning for love? Now
art thou sociable; now art thou Romeo; now art thou   80
what thou art, by art as well as by nature.[66] For this
drivelling[67] love is like a great natural[68] that runs lolling[69]
up and down to hide his bauble[70] in a hole.

BENVOLIO

Stop there, stop there.

MERCUTIO

Thou desirest me to stop in my tale against the hair.[71]   85

BENVOLIO

Thou wouldst else have made thy tale large.[72]

MERCUTIO

O thou art deceived. I would have made it short, for I was
come to the whole depth of my tale, and meant indeed to
occupy[73] the argument no longer.

Enter NURSE *and her man* PETER

ROMEO

Here's goodly gear! A sail, a sail![74] → refer to the nurse   90
Romeo is cured

MERCUTIO

Two, two! a shirt and a smock.[75]

NURSE

Peter!

PETER

Anon.

85

NURSE

My fan, Peter.

MERCUTIO

Good Peter, to hide her face, for her fan's the fairer face.   95

NURSE

God ye[76] good morrow, gentlemen.

MERCUTIO

God ye good e'en, fair gentlewoman.

NURSE

Is it good e'en?[77]

MERCUTIO

'T is no less, I tell ye, for the bawdy hand of the dial[78] is
now upon the prick[79] of noon.   100

---

76 *God ye*, short for "God give you".
77 *Is it good e'en* – "Is it afternoon (already)?"
78 *dial* – "clock".
79 *prick* – "point".
80 *Out upon . . . are you?* – "Away with you! What kind of a man are you?" With *out* in this sense, as an exclamation of anger, compare III.v.155, 167.
81 *himself*, i.e. Mercutio himself.
82 *By my troth* – "Upon my word". (*Troth* – "truth").
83 *the youngest*, i.e. because he is the only one.
84 *for fault of a worse* – "for lack of a worse". Romeo jokingly uses *worse* instead of *better*, but the Nurse does not notice, and this causes Mercutio to mock her stupidity in the following line.

85 *well took* – "cleverly understood".
86 *confidence*. In trying to imitate the speech of a lady, the Nurse makes several mistakes. *Conference* is the word she intended here.
87 *endite*. Benvolio, noticing her habit of using the wrong word, suggests that she will *endite* ("write") instead of *invite* Romeo.
88 *A bawd* – (a) "an immoral woman", (b) "a hare".
89 *So ho!* This was the cry used by the hunter when he sighted his prey.
90 *found* – "discovered the prey".

86

NURSE

Out upon you! What a man are you?[80]

ROMEO

One, gentlewoman, that God hath made, for himself[81] to mar. *spoil himself*

NURSE

By my troth,[82] it is well said. "For himself to mar," quoth 'a? Gentlemen, can any of you tell me where I may   105 find the young Romeo?

ROMEO

I can tell you, but young Romeo will be older when you have found him than he was when you sought him. I am the youngest[83] of that name, for fault of a worse.[84]

NURSE

You say well.   110

MERCUTIO

Yea, is the worst well? Very well took,[85] i' faith; wisely, wisely.

NURSE

If you be he, sir, I desire some confidence[86] with you.

BENVOLIO

She will endite[87] him to some supper.

MERCUTIO

A bawd,[88] a bawd, a bawd! So ho![89]   115

ROMEO

What, hast thou found?[90]

87

MERCUTIO

No hare, sir, unless a hare, sir, in a lenten pie[91] that is
something stale and hoar ere it be spent.[92]

[He sings]

An old hare hoar,[93]
And an old hare hoar,   120
Is very good meat in Lent:
But a hare that is hoar
Is too much for a score,[94]
When it hoars ere it be spent.

Romeo will you come to your father's? We 'll to dinner   125
thither.

ROMEO

I will follow you.

MERCUTIO

Farewell, ancient lady; farewell, lady, lady, lady.
[Exeunt MERCUTIO *and* BENVOLIO

---

91 *lenten pie*, a pie containing no meat, eaten during Lent.
92 *Something stale . . . spent* – "somewhat stale and mouldy (*hoar*) before it is used up (*spent*)".
93 *hare hoar*. Mercutio plays on the two meanings of *hare*, (a) "the name of an animal like a large rabbit", (b) "a woman of loose morals". He also plays on the word *hoar*, meaning "old" (and *hoars* – "grows old" in line 124) which has the same sound as "whore", an immoral woman.
94 *too much for a score* – "not good enough to deserve payment (*a score*)".
95 *saucy merchant* – "rude fellow".
96 *ropery* – "tricks".

97 *stand to* – "stand by, uphold".
98 *take him down* – "lower his pride".
99 *Jacks* – "low fellows".
100 *none of his flirt-gills* – "not one of those whom he would consider (*his*) women of loose behaviour (*flirt-gills*)".
101 *skains-mates*. The meaning of the word is unknown, but is thought to be the same as that of *flirt-gills*.
102 *use me at his pleasure* – "treat me as he wishes".
103 *afore God* – "before God".
104 *lead her . . . fool's paradise* – "deceive her into a state of false happiness".
105 *deal double* – "deceive".

88

NURSE

I pray you, sir, what saucy merchant[95] was this that was
so full of his ropery?[96]   130

ROMEO

A gentleman, Nurse, that loves to hear himself talk, and
will speak more in a minute than he will stand to[97] in a
month.

NURSE

And 'a stand to anything against me, I'll take him down[98]
and 'a were lustier than he is, and twenty such Jacks;[99]   135
and if I cannot, I'll find those that shall. Scurvy knave! I
am none of his flirt-gills;[100] I am none of his skains-
mates.[101] [To Peter] And thou must stand by, too, and
suffer every knave to use me at his pleasure![102]

PETER

I saw no man use you at his pleasure. If I had, my weapon   140
should quickly have been out. I warrant you, I dare draw
as soon as another man if I see occasion in a good quarrel,
and the law on my side.

NURSE

Now, afore God,[103] I am so vexed that every part about
me quivers. [Referring to MERCUTIO] Scurvy knave!   145
[To ROMEO] Pray you, sir, a word. And, as I told you, my
young lady bid me inquire you out. What she bid me say
I will keep to myself; but first let me tell ye, if ye should
lead her into a fool's paradise,[104] as they say, it were a very
gross kind of behaviour, as they say; for the gentlewoman   150
is young, and therefore, if you should deal double[105] with
her, truly it were an ill thing to be offered to any gentlewoman, and very weak dealing.

89

ROMEO

Nurse, commend me[106] to thy lady and mistress. I protest
unto thee –[107]   155

NURSE

Good heart! and i' faith I will tell her as much. Lord,
Lord, she will be a joyful woman!

ROMEO

What wilt thou tell her, Nurse? Thou dost not mark me.[108]

NURSE

I will tell her, sir, that you do protest, which, as I take it,
is a gentlemanlike offer.   160

ROMEO

Bid her devise some means to come to shrift this afternoon,
And there she shall, at Friar Lawrence's cell,
Be shrived[109] and married. [*He offers her money*] Here is
   for thy pains.

NURSE

No, truly, sir; not a penny.

---

106 *commend me* – "give my greetings".
107 *I protest unto thee* –. The Nurse inter-
    rupts him, thinking that he is declar-
    ing his love for Juliet, whereas in
    fact he was about to deny any inten-
    tion of deceiving Juliet.
108 *mark me* – "listen to what I am say-
    ing".
109 *Be shrived* – "make her confession
    and have her sins forgiven".
110 *a tackled stair* – "a ship's rope ladder".
111 *topgallant*, the platform at the top of
    a ship's mast.

112 *convoy* – "means of conveyance".
113 *quit thy pains* – "reward you for your
    trouble".
114 *putting one away* – "getting rid of any
    third person", i.e. Balthasar, whom
    she fears may not be trustworthy
    (*secret*).
115 *fain lay knife aboard* – "gladly board
    the ship", i.e. capture Juliet.
116 *as lief* – "as soon".

90

ROMEO

Go to, I say you shall.   165

NURSE

[*Taking the money*] This afternoon, sir? Well, she shall
be there.

ROMEO

And stay, good Nurse, behind the abbey wall:
Within this hour my man shall be with thee,
And bring thee cords made like a tackled stair,[110]
Which to the high topgallant[111] of my joy   170
Must be my convoy[112] in the secret night.
Farewell. Be trusty, and I 'll quit thy pains.[113]
Farewell. Commend me to thy mistress.

NURSE

Now God in heaven bless thee! Hark you, sir.

ROMEO

What say'st thou, my dear Nurse?   175

NURSE

Is your man secret? Did you ne'er hear say,
"Two may keep counsel, putting one away"?[114]

ROMEO

I warrant thee my man's as true as steel. → reliable

NURSE

Well, sir. My mistress is the sweetest lady. Lord, Lord!
when 't was a little prating thing – O, there is a nobleman   180
in town, one Paris, that would fain lay knife aboard,[115]
but she, good soul, had as lief[116] see a toad, a very toad,

as see him. I anger her, sometimes, and tell her that Paris is the properer[117] man, but I 'll warrant you, when I say so, she looks as pale as any clout[118] in the versal[119] world.   185
Doth not "rosemary[120] and "Romeo" begin with a letter?[121]

ROMEO

Ay, Nurse, what of that? Both with an R.

NURSE

Ah, mocker, that's the dog-name.[122] R is for the – No;[123]
I know it begins with some other letter; and she hath the   190

---

117 *properer* – "better-looking".
118 *clout* – "piece of cloth".
119 *versal* – "universal"; another of the Nurse's mistakes with words.
120 *rosemary*, a flower worn by a man at his wedding, and also used at funerals.
121 *a letter* – "the same letter".
122 *dog-name*. The letter R was called the dog's letter because it sounds like the noise a dog makes in its throat.
123 *R is for the – No*. The Nurse thinks that since *rosemary* and *Romeo* do not

begin with the sound "ar", they must begin with some other letter than R. She thinks Romeo is mocking her in saying that they both begin with an R.
124 *the prettiest sententious* – "the pleasantest saying". She means *sententia*, which is Latin for "sentence, wise saying". Compare II.ii.79 and the note to it.
125 *Before and apace* – "Go in front of me, and walk quickly".

(II.iv) Juliet is waiting impatiently at home for the Nurse to return with Romeo's message. When at last the Nurse arrives she increases Juliet's impatience and anxiety by pretending that she is breathless and unwell as a result of her journey, and by making pointless and conflicting remarks about Romeo, and holding back the news which Juliet is so anxious to hear. At last she gives her Romeo's message to meet him for the marriage at Friar Lawrence's cell, and Juliet joyfully hurries away.

1 *Perchance* – "Perhaps".
2 *Love's heralds* (line 4) . . . *louring hills* – "The messengers (*heralds*) of love ought to be thoughts, which travel ten times faster than the sun's rays that drive away the shadows from the gloomy-looking (*louring*) hills". *Glides* for *glide*.

3 *Therefore . . . draw Love* – "That is why swift-winged (*nimble-pinioned*) doves pull (*draw*) the chariot of Venus (*Love*)".
4 *highmost* – "highest".

prettiest sententious[124] of it, of you and rosemary, that it
would do you good to hear it.

ROMEO

Commend me to thy lady.

NURSE

Ay, a thousand times. Peter!

PETER

Anon.   195

NURSE

Before, and apace.[125]

[*Exeunt*

Scene IV. The Capulets' garden.

Enter JULIET

JULIET

The clock struck nine when I did send the Nurse;
In half an hour she promised to return.
Perchance[1] she cannot meet him – that's not so.
O, she is lame! Love's heralds should be thoughts,
Which ten times faster glides than the sun's beams   5
Driving back shadows over louring hills.[2]
Therefore do nimble-pinioned doves draw Love,[3]
And therefore hath the wind-swift Cupid wings.
Now is the sun upon the highmost[4] hill
Of this day's journey, and from nine to twelve   10
Is three long hours, yet she is not come.
Had she affections and warm youthful blood,

93

She would be as swift in motion as a ball:
My words would bandy⁵ her to my sweet love,
And his to me.⁶   15
But old folks – many feign as they were dead:⁷
Unwieldy, slow, heavy, and pale as lead.

Enter PETER *followed by* NURSE

O God, she comes! – O honey Nurse, what news?
Hast thou met with him? Send thy man away.

NURSE

Peter, stay at the gate.   20

[*Exit* PETER

JULIET

Now good sweet Nurse – O Lord, why lookest thou sad?
Though news be sad, yet tell them⁸ merrily:
If good, thou shamest the music of sweet news
By playing it to me with so sour a face.

NURSE

I am aweary;⁹ give me leave a while.¹⁰   25
Fie, how my bones ache! What a jaunce have I!¹¹

---

5 *bandy* – "throw" (like a ball).
6 *And his to me* – "And his words would throw her back to me".
7 *But old folks . . . dead* – "As for old people – many of them act as if (*feign*) they were dead".
8 *them. News* could be a singular or a plural noun in Shakespeare's time.
9 *aweary* – "weary".
10 *give me leave a while* – "allow me a moment (to recover my breath)".
11 *What a jaunce have I!* – "What an exhausting trip I have had!"

12 *The excuse (line 33) . . . dost excuse* – "It takes you longer to make your excuse for your delay than it would to tell me your news".
13 *Say either . . . circumstance* – "Tell me whether your news is good or bad, and I will willingly wait for (*stay*) the details (*circumstance*)".
14 *simple* – "foolish".
15 *be not to be talked on* – "are not worth talking about".
16 *flower* – "essence".
17 *Go thy ways* – "Away with you".
18 *a' t' other side* – "at the other side", i.e. the side opposite to her forehead.

JULIET

I would thou hadst my bones, and I thy news.
Nay, come, I pray thee, speak; good, good Nurse, speak.

NURSE

Jesu, what haste! Can you not stay a while?
Do you not see that I am out of breath?   30

JULIET

How art thou out of breath, when thou hast breath
To say to me that thou art out of breath?
The excuse that thou dost make in this delay
Is longer than the tale thou dost excuse.[12]
Is thy news good or bad? Answer to that.   35
Say either, and I 'll stay the circumstance.[13]
Let me be satisfied; is 't good or bad?

NURSE

Well, you have made a simple[14] choice; you know not
how to choose a man. Romeo? No, not he. Though his
face be better than any man's, yet his leg excels all men's;   40
and for a hand and a foot and a body, though they be not
to be talked on,[15] yet they are past compare. He is not the
flower[16] of courtesy, but, I'll warrant him, as gentle as a
lamb. Go thy ways,[17] wench; serve God. What, have
you dined at home?   45

JULIET

No, no. But all this did I know before.
What says he of our marriage? What of that?

NURSE

Lord, how my head aches! What a head have I!
It beats as it would fall in twenty pieces.
My back a' t' other side;[18] ah, my back, my back!   50

Beshrew[19] your heart for sending me about
To catch my death with jauncing up and down.

JULIET

I' faith, I am sorry that thou art not well.
Sweet, sweet, sweet Nurse, tell me, what says my love?

NURSE

Your love says, like an honest[20] gentleman, and a cour- 55
teous, and a kind, and a handsome, and, I warrant, a
virtuous – Where is your mother?

JULIET

Where is my mother? Why, she is within.
Where should she be? How oddly thou repliest:
"Your love says, like an honest gentleman, 60
'Where is your mother?'"

NURSE

O God's Lady[21] dear!
Are you so hot?[22] Marry, come up, I trow.[23]
Is this the poultice for my aching bones?
Henceforth do your messages yourself.

---

19 *Beshrew* – "Curse".
20 *honest* – "honourable".
21 *God's Lady* – "the Virgin Mary".
22 *hot* – "impatient".
23 *Marry, come up, I trow!* The Nurse pretends, through these rather meaningless exclamations, to be annoyed at Juliet's criticism.
24 *coil* – "noise".
25 *wanton* – "uncontrolled".

26 *They'll be . . . any news* – "Your cheeks turn red whenever you hear a piece of news".
27 *climb a bird's nest*, i.e. climb up to Juliet's room.
28 *in your delight* – "for your happiness".
29 *Hie to high fortune* – "I will hurry (*hie*) to my good fortune", i.e. to marry Romeo. Note the play on *hie* and *high*.

(II.v) The lovers are happily re-united at Friar Lawrence's cell, and leave with him for their secret marriage.

1 *So smile* (line *1*) . . . *us not* – "May the heavens approve this marriage, so that the future (*after-hours*) does not punish (*chide*) us with sufferings".

JULIET

Here 's such a coil!²⁴ Come, what says Romeo?   65

NURSE

Have you got leave to go to shrift to-day?

JULIET

I have.

NURSE

Then hie you hence to Friar Lawrence' cell;
There stays a husband to make you a wife.
Now comes the wanton²⁵ blood up in your cheeks: 70
They 'll be in scarlet straight at any news.²⁶
Hie you to church; I must another way,
To fetch a ladder, by the which your love
Must climb a bird's nest²⁷ soon when it is dark.
I am the drudge, and toil in your delight,²⁸ *one who has to do the work*   75
But you shall bear the burden soon at night.
Go. I 'll to dinner; hie you to the cell.

JULIET

Hie to high fortune!²⁹ Honest Nurse, farewell.

                                                          [*Exeunt*

Scene V. Friar Lawrence's cell.

Enter FRIAR LAWRENCE *and* ROMEO

FRIAR LAWRENCE

So smile the heavens upon this holy act
That after-hours with sorrow chide us not.¹

ROMEO

Amen,[2] amen. But come what sorrow can,[3]
It cannot countervail[4] the exchange of joy
That one short minute gives me in her sight.[5]   5
Do thou but close[6] our hands with holy words,[7]
Then love-devouring death do[8] what he dare;
It is enough I may but call her mine.

FRIAR LAWRENCE

These violent delights have violent ends,[9]
And in their triumph die like fire and powder,   10
Which, as they kiss, consume.[10] The sweetest honey
Is loathsome in his[11] own deliciousness,

---

2 *Amen* – "May it be so", the word
which is said at the end of a prayer,
as Romeo says it here to conclude
Friar Lawrence's prayer.
3 *But come what sorrow can* – "But whatever sorrow may come".
4 *countervail* – "balance".
5 *in her sight* – "at the sight of her".
6 *close* – "join".
7 *holy words*, the words of the marriage
ceremony.
8 *do* – "may do".
9 *These violent . . . ends*. The Friar's
warning, like his prayer (lines 1–2),
helps to create the atmosphere of fore-
boding which surrounds all the events
of the play.
10 *die like fire (line 10) . . . consume* – "end
like fire and gunpowder which are
destroyed (*consume*) when they meet".
11 *his* – "its".
12 *in the taste . . . appetite* – "on account
of its taste (*in the taste*) ruins (*confounds*)
the appetite for it".
13 *Too swift . . . slow*, i.e. those who are
too quick to love are as slow to reach
ideal love as those who are too slow
to love.

14 *so light (line 16) . . . flint*. The Friar
means that anyone so light-hearted as
Juliet will never be able to overcome
the difficulties of the road through
life.
15 *bestride the gossamers* – "stride across
the threads of spiders' webs".
16 *idles* – "move lazily". *Idles* for *idle*.
17 *wanton* – "playful".
18 *vanity* – "worldly delight".
19 *ghostly* – "spiritual".
20 *and that (line 25) . . . blazon it* – "and if
your power to describe (*blazon*) it is
greater than mine".
21 *neighbour* – "neighbouring".
22 *rich music's tongue*, i.e. Juliet's musical
voice.
23 *both/Receive in either* – "we both receive from each other".
24 *Conceit (line 30) . . . of ornament* –
"Imagination (*conceit*) which is richer
in substance (*matter*) than in words,
will only boast (*brag*) of its true reality
(*substance*), not of unimportant details
(*ornament*)". Juliet is saying that their
happiness is too great to put into
words.

And in the taste confounds the appetite.[12]
Therefore love moderately; long life doth so:
Too swift arrives as tardy as too slow.[13]   15

Enter JULIET

Here comes the lady. O, so light a foot
Will ne'er wear out the everlasting flint.[14]
A lover may bestride the gossamers[15]
That idles[16] in the wanton[17] summer air,
And yet not fall, so light is vanity.[18]   20

JULIET

Good even to my ghostly[19] confessor.

FRIAR LAWRENCE

Romeo shall thank thee, daughter, for us both.
                              [ROMEO *kisses her*

JULIET

As much to him, else is his thanks too much.
                              [*She returns his kiss*

ROMEO

Ah, Juliet, if the measure of thy joy
Be heaped like mine, and that thy skill be more   25
To blazon it,[20] then sweeten with thy breath
This neighbour[21] air, and let rich music's tongue[22]
Unfold the imagined happiness that both
Receive in either,[23] by this dear encounter.

JULIET

Conceit more rich in matter than in words   30
Brags of his substance, not of ornament.[24]

25 *They are ... worth* – "Those who can calculate their love exactly in words are poor lovers".

26 *sum up sum* – "add up the total".

27 *by your leaves* – "with your permission".

They are but beggars that can count their worth;[25]
But my true love is grown to such excess
I cannot sum up sum[26] of half my wealth.

FRIAR LAWRENCE

Come, come with me, and we will make short work;   35
For, by your leaves,[27] you shall not stay alone
Till Holy Church incorporate two in one.

[Exeunt

(III.i) Mercutio and Benvolio are talking in the street when Tybalt enters looking for Romeo, and a quarrel develops between Tybalt and Mercutio. At this moment Romeo enters and is insulted by Tybalt, but having just been secretly married to Juliet, he is unwilling to quarrel with any member of her family, and so declines to fight Tybalt. Mercutio, who is ignorant of any relationship between Romeo and Juliet, and is annoyed by what seems to him Romeo's cowardice, fights Tybalt himself. Romeo tries to separate them, and keep the peace, but Tybalt wounds Mercutio with a cowardly blow under Romeo's arm, and runs away. Benvolio helps Mercutio to a neighbouring house, but soon returns to report that Mercutio is dead. Romeo is so angered by this slaying of the friend who had fought on his behalf, that when Tybalt reappears, he fights and kills him. He escapes just before the Prince and the city authorities arrive on the scene. Benvolio tells them all that has happened. The Prince banishes Romeo from the city and declares that he will be put to death if he returns. He also imposes a heavy fine upon the two families whose enmity has been the cause of the bloodshed.

1 *the Capels are abroad* – "the Capulets are roaming out of doors".
2 *scape* – "escape".
3 *claps me* – "puts down hard". *Me* has no grammatical function here.
4 *the operation . . . cup* – "as his second drink begins to work on him". (making him drunk).
5 *draws him on the drawer* – "draws his sword against the barman".
6 *as hot a Jack* – "as violent a fellow".
7 *moody to be moved* – "annoyed at being angry".

The act starts light-heartedly but the mood indicates fighting

ACT THREE

Scene I. A street.

Enter MERCUTIO, *his* Page, BENVOLIO *and Servants*

personal servant

BENVOLIO

I pray thee, good Mercutio, let 's retire: *go*
The day is hot, the Capels are abroad,[1]
And if we meet we shall not scape[2] a brawl, *fight*
For now, these hot days, is the mad blood stirring. → *summer, heat makes him more angry → fight*

MERCUTIO

Thou art like one of these fellows that, when he enters the   5
confines of a tavern, claps me[3] his sword upon the table
and says, "God send me no need of thee"; and by the
operation of the second cup,[4] draws him on the drawer,[5]
when indeed there is no need.

BENVOLIO

Am I like such a fellow?   10

MERCUTIO

Come, come; thou art as hot a Jack[6] in thy mood as any
in Italy, and as soon moved to be moody, and as soon
moody to be moved.[7]

BENVOLIO

And what to?

MERCUTIO

Nay, and there were two such, we should have none   15
shortly, for one would kill the other. Thou? Why, thou
wilt quarrel with a man that hath a hair more or a hair
less in his beard than thou hast. Thou wilt quarrel with a

man for cracking nuts, having no other reason but because
thou hast hazel eyes.[8] What eye but such an eye would   20
spy out such a quarrel? Thy head is as full of quarrels as
an egg is full of meat, and yet thy head hath been beaten
as addle as an egg[9] for quarrelling. Thou hast quarrelled
with a man for coughing in the street because he hath
wakened thy dog that hath lain asleep in the sun. Didst   25
thou not fall out with a tailor for wearing his new doublet[10] before Easter? With another for tying his new shoes
with old ribbon? And yet thou wilt tutor me from
quarrelling![11]

BENVOLIO

And I were so apt to quarrel as thou art, any man should   30
buy the fee-simple of my life for an hour and a quarter.[12]

---

8 *hazel eyes.* Mercutio jokingly paints a
picture of the solid and peace-loving
Benvolio as a highly quarrelsome
man who will fight at the least opportunity. He will fight, says Mercutio,
with a man cracking hazel nuts because they have the same name as the
colour of his eyes.

9 *as addle as an egg* – "as rotten as a bad
egg".

10 *doublet*, a sleeveless garment which
fitted close to the body. It was the
custom to wear new clothes for the
first time on Easter Sunday, though,
of course, it would be foolish to
quarrel with someone for appearing
in new clothes at other times of the
year.

11 *tutor me from quarrelling* – "teach me
not to quarrel".

12 *buy the fee-simple . . . quarter. Fee-
simple* is complete legal possession.
Benvolio says that whoever bought
his life would possess it only a very
short time, if he were as quarrelsome
as Mercutio.

13 *O, simple!* "What a feeble joke!"

14 *And but* – "Only".

15 *apt enough (line 39) . . . occasion* –
"ready enough to do that if (*and*) you
give me any cause".

16 *take some . . . giving* – "find a reason
without my giving you one".

17 *consortest* – "associate".

18 *Consort.* Mercutio, trying to anger
Tybalt, purposely misunderstands
him, taking *consort* in its other meaning, "combine in musical harmony",
and pretending that Tybalt has insulted him by calling him a hired
musician (*minstrel*).

19 *And* – "If".

20 *discords* – (a) "notes played out of
tune", (b) "quarrels".

21 *fiddlestick*, a stick used in playing a
violin, but here Mercutio means his
sword.

22 *Zounds*, an exclamation, short for "By
Christ's wounds" (on the cross).

MERCUTIO

The fee-simple? O, simple!¹³

Enter TYBALT *and his followers*

BENVOLIO

By my head, here comes the Capulets!

MERCUTIO

By my heel, I care not.

TYBALT

[*To his followers*] Follow me close, for I will speak to them.   35
[*To* MERCUTIO *and* BENVOLIO] Gentlemen, good e'en;
  a word with one of you.

MERCUTIO

And but¹⁴ one word with one of us? Couple it with something: make it a word and a blow.

TYBALT

You shall find me apt enough to that, sir, and you will
give me occasion.¹⁵   40

MERCUTIO

Could you not take some occasion without giving?¹⁶

TYBALT

Mercutio, thou consortest¹⁷ with Romeo –

MERCUTIO

Consort?¹⁸ What, dost thou make us minstrels? And¹⁹
thou make minstrels of us, look to hear nothing but dis-
cords.²⁰ Here's my fiddlestick;²¹ here's that shall make   45
you dance. Zounds,²² consort!

BENVOLIO

We talk here in the public haunt of men.
Either withdraw unto some private place,
Or reason coldly²³ of your grievances,
Or else depart.²⁴ Here, all eyes gaze on us.   50

MERCUTIO

Men's eyes were made to look, and let them gaze.
I will not budge for no man's pleasure, I.

Enter ROMEO

TYBALT

[*To* MERCUTIO] Well, peace be with you, sir; here comes
my man.²⁵

MERCUTIO

But I 'll be hanged, sir, if he wear your livery.²⁶
Marry, go before to field, he 'll be your follower: 55
Your worship in that sense may call him "man".²⁷

---

23 *reason coldly* – "debate calmly".

24 *depart* – "separate".

25 *my man* – "the man I am looking for".

26 *your livery* – "the dress worn by your servants".

27 *Marry* (*line 55*) . . . *call him "man"*. Mercutio again pretends to misunderstand Tybalt, taking *man* to mean "servant". The meaning is, "If you lead the way to the field (i.e. to the battlefield, for a fight) Romeo will follow you. Only in that sense is he your follower (*man*)".

28 *Doth much* (*line 60*) . . . *greeting* – "does much to remove (*excuse*) the anger which it would be right for me to feel (*appertaining rage*) at such a greeting as yours". Romeo is unaware of having insulted (*injured*) Tybalt by his presence at the feast.

29 *devise* – "imagine".

30 *tender* – "care for".

31 *"Alla stoccata" . . . away.* "Alla stoccata" is Italian, meaning "in the manner of the thrust". The sense of the line is, "Tybalt, with his Italian fencing fashions, has won the contest."

32 *rat-catcher*, i.e. "cat".

33 *will you walk?* – "will you step aside with me?" i.e. to fight.

34 *nine lives.* The cat is said to have nine lives because it escapes dangers many (eight) times before its death.

35 *make bold withal* – "treat roughly".

36 *as you shall use me hereafter* – "according to whether or not you behave well to me in the future".

37 *dry-beat* – "beat without drawing blood".

106

TYBALT

Romeo, the love I bear thee can afford
No better term than this: thou art a villain. *evil person*

ROMEO

Tybalt, the reason that I have to love thee [*not fighting*]
Doth much excuse the appertaining rage   60
To such a greeting.[28] Villain am I none;
Therefore, farewell; I see thou know'st me not.

TYBALT

Boy, this shall not excuse the injuries
That thou hast done me; therefore turn and draw.

ROMEO

I do protest I never injured thee, *I did not insult you*   65
But love thee better than thou can'st devise[29]
Till thou shalt know the reason of my love.
And so, good Capulet, which name I tender[30]
As dearly as mine own, be satisfied.

MERCUTIO *sees Romeo as traitor*

O calm, dishonourable, vile submission!   70
"Alla stoccata" carries it away.[31]
[*He draws his sword*] Tybalt, you rat-catcher,[32] will you
  walk?[33]

TYBALT

What would'st thou have with me?

MERCUTIO

Good King of Cats, nothing but one of your nine lives[34]
that I mean to make bold withal,[35] and, as you shall use   75
me hereafter,[36] dry-beat[37] the rest of the eight. Will you

107

pluck your sword out of his pilcher by the ears?³⁸ Make
haste, lest mine be about your ears³⁹ ere it be out.

TYBALT

[*Drawing his sword*] I am for you.

ROMEO

Gentle Mercutio, put thy rapier up.   80

MERCUTIO

[*To* TYBALT] Come, sir, your passado.⁴⁰

[MERCUTIO *and* TYBALT *fight*

ROMEO

Draw, Benvolio; beat down their weapons.
Gentlemen, for shame, forbear this outrage!
Tybalt! Mercutio! the Prince expressly hath
Forbid this bandying⁴¹ in Verona streets.   85
Hold, Tybalt! good Mercutio!

ROMEO *comes between them.* TYBALT *wounds* MERCUTIO
from behind ROMEO, *then runs away, followed by his men*

---

38 *pluck your sword . . . ears* – "pull your
sword out of its case (*pilcher*) without
ceremony (*by the ears*)".
39 *lest mine . . . your ears* – "lest I beat you
about the ears with mine".
40 *your passado* – "(Let us see) your
Italian fencing strokes (*passado*)".
Mercutio is contemptuous of them.
41 *bandying* – "exchange of blows".
42 *sped* – "gone", i.e. killed.
43 *hath nothing* – "is not wounded".
44 *'t will serve* – "it will be sufficient", i.e.
to cause his death.

45 *grave* – (a) "serious" (for once), (b) "in
the grave".
46 *peppered . . . this world* – "given the
finishing blow as far as this world is
concerned".
47 *fights by . . . arithmetic* – "fights by the
rules of the (fencing) textbook".
48 *worms' meat* – "food for worms", i.e. a
dead man.
49 *I have it* – "I have my death wound".
50 *soundly* – "thoroughly".

MERCUTIO

I am hurt.
A plague o' both your houses! I am sped.[42]
Is he gone, and hath nothing?[43]

BENVOLIO

What, art thou hurt?

MERCUTIO

Ay, ay, a scratch, a scratch; marry, 't is enough.
Where is my page? Go, villain, fetch a surgeon. *doctor*   90
[*Exit Page*

ROMEO

Courage, man; the hurt cannot be much.

MERCUTIO

No, 't is not so deep as a well, nor so wide as a church
door, but 't is enough, 't will serve.[44] Ask for me to-
morrow and you shall find me a grave[45] man. I am
peppered, I warrant, for this world.[46] A plague o' both   95
your houses! Zounds! a dog, a rat, a mouse, a cat, to
scratch a man to death! A braggart, a rogue, a villain that
fights by the book of arithmetic![47] Why the devil came
you between us? I was hurt under your arm.

ROMEO

I thought all for the best.   100

MERCUTIO

Help me into some house, Benvolio,
Or I shall faint. A plague o' both your houses!
They have made worms' meat[48] of me. I have it,[49]
And soundly[50] too. Your houses!
[BENVOLIO *helps him out*
109

talking about Mercutio

ROMEO

This gentleman, the Prince's near ally,[51]   105
My very[52] friend, hath got this mortal hurt
In my behalf, my reputation stained
With Tybalt's slander – Tybalt that an hour
Hath been my cousin. O sweet Juliet,
Thy beauty hath made me effeminate,   110
And in my temper[53] softened valour's steel.

[BENVOLIO *returns*

BENVOLIO

O Romeo, Romeo, brave Mercutio is dead.
That gallant spirit hath aspired the clouds,
Which too untimely here did scorn the earth.[54]

ROMEO

This day's black fate on more days doth depend;[55]   115
This but begins the woe others must end.

[TYBALT *returns*

BENVOLIO

Here comes the furious Tybalt back again.

ROMEO

Alive, in triumph! and Mercutio slain!
Away to heaven, respective lenity,[56]

He is not going to be merciful to Tybalt anymore

---

51 *ally* – "relative".
52 *very* – "true".
53 *temper* – (a) "character", (b) "quality (of metal)".
54 *That gallant (line 113) . . . earth* – "That brave spirit who, too early in his life, disdained to stay on earth, has ascended (*aspired*) to the clouds".
55 *on more days doth depend* – "hangs (*doth depend*) threateningly over the days to come". Romeo's words point forward to the tragedy to come.

56 *respective lenity* – "mercy (*lenity*) which has respected Tybalt's relationship with Juliet".
57 *conduct* – "guide".
58 *This*, i.e. his sword.
59 *up* – "in arms".
60 *doom thee death* – "pass sentence of death on you".
61 *fortune's fool* – "the sport, or plaything, of fortune".

And fire-eyed fury be my conduct[57] now!   120
Now, Tybalt, take the "villain" back again
That late thou gavest me, for Mercutio's soul
Is but a little way above our heads,
Staying for thine to keep him company.
Either thou or I, or both, must go with him.   125

TYBALT

Thou, wretched boy, that did consort him here,
Shalt with him hence.

ROMEO

[Drawing his sword] This[58] shall determine that.
                    [They fight, and ROMEO kills TYBALT

BENVOLIO

Romeo, away, be gone!
The citizens are up,[59] and Tybalt slain.
Stand not amazed: the Prince will doom thee death[60]   130
If thou art taken. Hence, be gone, away!

ROMEO

O, I am fortune's fool.[61]

BENVOLIO

                    Why dost thou stay?
                              [Exit ROMEO

Enter an Officer and Citizens

OFFICER

Which way ran he that killed Mercutio?
Tybalt, that murderer, which way ran he?

BENVOLIO

There lies that Tybalt.

OFFICER

Up, sir, go with me: 135
I charge thee in the Prince's name, obey.

Enter PRINCE ESCALUS, MONTAGUE, CAPULET,
their wives and servants

PRINCE

Where are the vile beginners of this fray?

BENVOLIO

O noble Prince, I can discover[62] all
The unlucky manage[63] of this fatal brawl.
There lies the man, slain by young Romeo, 140
That slew thy kinsman, brave Mercutio.

LADY CAPULET

Tybalt, my cousin! O my brother's child!
O Prince! O cousin! husband! O the blood is spilled

---

62 *discover* – "reveal".
63 *manage* – "course".
64 *spoke him fair* – "spoke politely to him".
65 *bethink how nice . . . was* – "think how unimportant the quarrel was".
66 *take truce with* – "make peace with".
67 *unruly spleen* – "uncontrolled anger".
68 *but that he tilts* – "but on the contrary, he thrusts".
69 *all as hot* – "equally angry".
70 *It*, i.e. the blow. They fought with rapiers in their right hands, and daggers in their left.
71 *Retorts it* – "returns it".
72 *rushes*, i.e. "he rushes".
73 *envious* – "full of hatred".
74 *stout* – "brave".
75 *by and by* – "very soon".

76 *newly entertained revenge* – "only at that moment conceived the idea of revenge".
77 *the Montague*, i.e. Romeo.
78 *he speaks not true*. Benvolio's account is incorrect; it suggests that Tybalt attacked Mercutio, though in fact Mercutio started the fight. Lady Capulet, however, is guessing when she accuses him of falsehood since she was not present at the fight, and her own account of it is even more incorrect. Both give false accounts out of *affection* for their kinsmen. We see how enmity breeds untruth, makes bad motives appear good, and hinders the operation of justice, since it is difficult for the Prince to discover the truth.

112

SCENE I]

Of my dear kinsman. Prince, as thou art true,
For blood of ours, shed blood of Montague.   145
O cousin, cousin!

PRINCE

Benvolio, who began this bloody fray?

BENVOLIO

Tybalt, here slain, whom Romeo's hand did slay.
Romeo, that spoke him fair,[64] bid him bethink
How nice the quarrel was,[65] and urged withal   150
Your high displeasure. All this, utteréd
With gentle breath, calm look, knees humbly bowed,
Could not take truce with[66] the unruly spleen[67]
Of Tybalt, deaf to peace, but that he tilts[68]
With piercing steel at bold Mercutio's breast,   155
Who, all as hot,[69] turns deadly point to point,
And, with a martial scorn, with one hand beats
Cold death aside, and with the other sends
It[70] back to Tybalt, whose dexterity
Retorts it.[71] Romeo – he cries aloud,   160
"Hold, friends! friends part!" and, swifter than his
    tongue,
His agile arm beats down their fatal points,
And 'twixt them rushes;[72] underneath whose arm
An envious[73] thrust from Tybalt hit the life
Of stout[74] Mercutio, and then Tybalt fled,   165
But by and by[75] comes back to Romeo,
Who had but newly entertained revenge,[76]
And to 't they go like lightning, for, ere I
Could draw to part them, was stout Tybalt slain,
And as he fell, did Romeo turn and fly.   170
This is the truth, or let Benvolio die.

LADY CAPULET

He is a kinsman to the Montague:[77]
Affection makes him false; he speaks not true.[78]

113

Some twenty of them fought in this black strife, And all those twenty could but kill one life. *the life of Tybalt* 175 I beg for justice, which thou, Prince, must give: Romeo slew Tybalt; Romeo must not live.

PRINCE

Romeo slew him; he slew Mercutio.
Who now the price of his dear blood[79] doth owe?

79 *his dear blood.* He is referring to Mercutio, his blood-relation.
80 *His fault (line 181) . . . Tybalt –* "His offence has only done what the law would have had to do, that is, ended Tybalt's life".
81 *I have . . . proceedings –* "I am directly concerned in (*have an interest in*) the actions produced by your hatred (*your hate's proceedings*)".

82 *amerce –* "fine".
83 *loss of mine –* "my loss".
84 *purchase out abuses –* "buy off the punishment due to wrong-doing".
85 *Mercy . . . that kill –* "Mercy that pardons murderers only encourages murder (*but murders*)".

(III.ii) Juliet begs night to come quickly so that Romeo may join her unseen. The Nurse enters, lamenting the death of Tybalt, but without naming him, so that at first Juliet thinks it is Romeo who has been killed. When she learns that Romeo has killed Tybalt she angrily blames him, torn by conflicting feelings of loyalty to her husband and to her family. As she grows calmer she realises that Romeo must have had good reason for his action, and that her first loyalty is to him. She is grieved at the thought that she will never see him again, but the Nurse promises to find him and bring him to her for a last farewell. *Nurse is quite instrumental here*

1 *fiery-footed steed (line 1) . . . lodging.* The horses (*steeds*) are those which drew the chariot of Phoebus, the Greek sun-god, from the east, to his resting place (*lodging*) in the west.
2 *Phaeton,* the son of Phoebus, who attempted to drive his father's chariot, and was killed by Jupiter when he drove too near the earth.
3 *close,* i.e. giving secrecy.

4 *That runaway's . . . wink.* "Phoebus, who runs through the day (*that runaway*), may go to sleep".
5 *Lovers (line 8) . . . own beauties.* The sense is, "The beauties that lovers see in each other are sufficient light for them".
6 *if love (line 9) . . . with night.* If the lovers are blind it does not matter, since they are then most like night.
7 *civil –* "polite".

114

As soon as they get marry, the tragedy begins

MONTAGUE

Not Romeo, Prince; he was Mercutio's friend.   180
His fault concludes but what the law should end –
The life of Tybalt.[80]

Royal plural

PRINCE

                And for that offence *Romeo killing Tybalt*
Immediately we do exile him hence. *banish*
I have an interest in your hate's proceedings:[81]
My blood for your rude brawls doth lie a-bleeding.   185
But I'll amerce [82] you with so strong a fine
That you shall all repent the loss of mine.[83]
I will be deaf to pleading and excuses;   *Not from Lady*
Nor tears, nor prayers shall purchase out abuses.[84] *Capulet nor*
                                                        Benvolio
Therefore use none. Let Romeo hence in haste,   190
Else when he is found, that hour is his last.
Bear hence this body, and attend our will.
Mercy but murders, pardoning those that kill.[85]

[*Exeunt.*

Scene II. Juliet's room.

Enter JULIET

JULIET

Gallop apace, you fiery-footed steeds, *→ horse*
Towards Phoebus' lodging![1] Such a waggoner
As Phaeton[2] would whip you to the west, *make the day end*
And bring in cloudy night immediately. *quickly*
Spread thy close[3] curtain, love-performing night; *→ be together, alone* 5
That runaway's eyes may wink,[4] and Romeo
Leap to these arms untalked of and unseen. *→ night*
Lovers can see to do their amorous rites
By their own beauties;[5] or, if love be blind
It best agrees with night.[6] Come, civil[7] night,   10

115

Thou sober-suited matron all in black,
And learn[8] me how to lose a winning match,[9]
Played for a pair of stainless maidenhoods.
Hood my unmanned blood, bating in my cheeks,
With thy black mantle,[10] till strange love, grown bold,   15
Think true love acted simple modesty.[11]
Come, night; come, Romeo; come, thou day in night,[12]
For thou wilt lie upon the wings of night,
Whiter than new[13] snow upon a raven's back.
Come, gentle night; come, loving, black-browed night,   20
Give me my Romeo; and when I shall die,
Take him and cut him out in little stars,
And he will make the face of heaven so fine
That all the world will be in love with night
And pay no worship to the garish sun.   25
O, I have bought the mansion of a love,
But not possessed it; and though I am sold,
Not yet enjoyed.[14] So tedious is this day
As is the night before some festival
To an impatient child that hath new robes   30
And may not wear them. O here comes my Nurse,

---

8 learn – "teach".
9 to lose a winning match. In surrendering to Romeo, Juliet wins by gaining a husband.
10 Hood (line 14) . . . black mantle. The imagery is taken from hawking. Juliet compares herself to a hawk which is unused to men (unmanned). Just as the hawk is nervous and flutters its wings, and has a hood put over its head to calm it, so Juliet's heart flutters, and the blood comes and goes (bating) in her cheeks, so that she asks night to cover her with its cloak (black mantle). Unmanned also means "without a husband".
11 strange love (line 15) . . . modesty. Juliet's love, which is now shy (strange) will grow bold when night comes,

and her actions will then seem purely modest (simple modesty).
12 thou day in night. Romeo makes the night seem as bright as day. In Come, gentle night, Juliet plays on knight and night.
13 new – "freshly fallen".
14 O, I have (line 26) . . . enjoyed. Juliet suddenly changes the metaphor. At first she is the buyer, then the object bought. This sudden change suggests her impatience.
15 well-a-day – "alas".
16 undone – "ruined".
17 death-darting . . . cockatrice. The cockatrice is an imaginary creature like a serpent, able to kill people by looking at them.

116

Enter NURSE *with the rope ladder* — *her gesture of distress*

And she brings news; and every tongue that speaks
But Romeo's name, speaks heavenly eloquence.
Now, Nurse, what news? What hast thou there?
   The cords→ *rope ladder*
That Romeo bid thee fetch?

NURSE

Ay, ay, the cords.   35

JULIET

Ay me, what news? Why dost thou wring thy hands?

NURSE

Ah, well-a-day![15] He 's dead, he 's dead, he 's dead!
We are undone,[16] lady, we are undone.
Alack the day, he 's gone, he 's killed, he 's dead!

JULIET

Can heaven be so envious?

NURSE

                    Romeo can,   40
Though heaven cannot. O Romeo, Romeo!
Whoever would have thought it? Romeo!

JULIET

What devil art thou dost torment me thus?
This torture should be roared in dismal hell.
Hath Romeo slain himself? Say thou but "Ay",   45
And that bare vowel "I" shall poison more
Than the death-darting eye of cockatrice.[17]

117

I am not I,[18] if there be such an "I",
Or those eyes shut[19] that makes thee answer "Ay".
If he be slain, say "Ay", or if not, "No".   50
Brief sounds determine my weal[20] or woe.

NURSE

I saw the wound, I saw it with mine eyes –
God save the mark![21] – here on his manly breast;
A piteous corse,[22] a bloody, piteous corse;
Pale, pale as ashes, all bedaubed[23] in blood,   55
All in gore blood;[24] I swounded[25] at the sight.

JULIET

O break, my heart! poor bankrupt, break[26] at once![27]
To prison, eyes; ne'er look on liberty!
Vile earth, to earth resign,[28] end motion here,
And thou and Romeo press one heavy bier! – *funeral casket* 60

---

18 *I am not I* – "I am not myself". Note the play, in lines 45–50, on *ay* (yes), *I* (the vowel sound), *I* (the pronoun), and *eye*.

19 *Or those eyes shut* – "or if those eyes (i.e. Romeo's) are shut".

20 *weal* – "welfare".

21 *God save the mark!* This phrase of apology was used when something unpleasant was being said.

22 *corse* – "dead body".

23 *bedaubed* – "painted over".

24 *gore blood*, i.e. blood which has become solid.

25 *swounded* – "fainted".

26 *bankrupt, break*. A *bankrupt* is one who is unable to pay his debts. To *break* means "become bankrupt", and also "be overcome by great sorrow".

27 *at once* – "at one stroke".

28 *Vile earth . . . resign* – "Vile body, submit yourself to the earth". Juliet is addressing herself.

29 *What storm . . . so contrary* – "What kind of storm is this which blow so strongly against me?". Juliet uses this word *storm* because of the great damage done in the deaths of Romeo and Tybalt.

30 *trumpet . . . doom*. In this reference to the trumpet which will sound on the day of general judgement, Juliet is asking for the world to end.

31 *keep* – (a) "guard", (b) "inhabit".

32 *wolvish-ravening lamb*. He appears to be a lamb, but is really a hungry wolf.

33 *divinest show* – "most heavenly appearance".

34 *Just opposite . . . seem'st* – "the exact opposite of what you truly seem".

35 *bower* – "enclose".

118

NURSE

O Tybalt, Tybalt, the best friend I had!
O courteous Tybalt, honest gentleman,
That ever I should live to see thee dead!

JULIET

What storm is this that blows so contrary?[29]
Is Romeo slaughtered, and is Tybalt dead?   65
My dearest cousin, and my dearer lord?
Then, dreadful trumpet, sound the general doom,[30]
For who is living if those two are gone?

NURSE

Tybalt is gone and Romeo banishèd;
Romeo that killed him, he is banishèd.   70

JULIET

O God! did Romeo's hand shed Tybalt's blood?

NURSE

It did, it did! alas the day, it did!

JULIET

O serpent heart, hid with a flowering face!
Did ever dragon keep[31] so fair a cave?
Beautiful tyrant, fiend angelical,   75
Dove-feathered raven, wolvish-ravening[32] lamb,
Despisèd substance of divinest show,[33]
Just opposite to what thou justly seem'st,[34]
A damnèd saint, an honourable villain!
O nature, what hadst thou to do in hell   80
When thou didst bower[35] the spirit of a fiend
In mortal paradise of such sweet flesh?
Was ever book containing such vile matter
So fairly bound? O that deceit should dwell
In such a gorgeous palace!

119

Nurse:
not constant, scattered
She is now criticising
Romeo but later
she bring Juliet
to Romeo

NURSE — *older + experienced*

There 's no trust,   85
No faith, no honesty in men; all perjured,
All forsworn, all naught,[36] all dissemblers.   *not a very good*
Ah, where 's my man?[37] Give me some aqua-vitae.[38] *counsellor*
These griefs, these woes, these sorrows make me old. *Juliet*
Shame come to Romeo!

JULIET

              Blistered be thy tongue   *He is not that*
For such a wish! He was not born to shame. *kind of person,*
Upon his brow shame is ashamed to sit,   *it's not natural*
For 't is a throne where honour may be crowned *for him to do*
Sole monarch of the universal earth.   *such thing*
O what a beast was I to chide at him! *think evil?*   95

                    NURSE — *shocked*
         support
Will you speak well of him that killed your cousin?

---

36 *naught* – "wicked".

37 *my man*, i.e. Peter, her servant.

38 *aqua-vitae*, Latin for "water of life".
She means "strong liquor".

39 *smooth* – (a) "flatter, or speak well of",
(b) "make smooth", as opposed to
mangled, "made rough, or spoilt"
(line 99).

40 *your native spring*, i.e. her eyes.

41 *Your tributary (line 103) . . . joy*. Since
tears are a tribute which should be
paid to woe, she says, in shedding them when
Romeo is alive, since this is a reason
for joy. *Tributary*, like *spring*, also
suggests the flowing stream of her
tears, and thus the depth of her grief.

42 *forget it fain* – "gladly forget it".

43 *That "banishéd" (line 113) . . . Tybalts*.
To have Romeo banished is as griev-
ous to her as the death of ten thousand
Tybalts would be.

44 *if sour woe delights in fellowship* – "if
one sorrow likes to have others to
keep it company".

45 *needly* – "of necessity".

46 *Why followed (line 118) . . . moved?*
Juliet means that if she has to suffer
more than one sorrow, she would
have preferred the death of her father,
or mother, or both, since this would
have caused (*moved*) only an ordinary
(*modern*) grief, not the terrible grief of
Romeo's banishment.

47 *But with (line 121) . . . banishéd!* – "But
to follow the news of Tybalt's death
with the words 'Romeo is banishéd'!"
Rearward – "rearguard, a guard of
men at the rear".

48 *that word's death* – "the death which
that word brings".

49 *sound* – (a) "express in words", (b)
"measure the depth of".

120

Change in Romeo & Juliet
R — not impulsive, X want to fight, but caught in it
J — mature at her age

SCENE II]

JULIET — *loyally defensive with Romeo*

Shall I speak ill of him that is my husband? *She answers question with question.*
Ah, poor my lord, what tongue shall smooth[39] thy name,
When I, thy three-hours' wife, have mangled it?
But wherefore, villain, didst thou kill my cousin? *They both 100*
That villain cousin would have killed my husband. *villain.*
Back, foolish tears, back to your native spring;[40]
Your tributary drops belong to woe,
Which you, mistaking, offer up to joy.[41]
My husband lives, that Tybalt would have slain,   105
And Tybalt's dead that would have slain my husband.
All this is comfort. Wherefore weep I then?
Some word there was, worser than Tybalt's death,
That murdered me. I would forget it fain,[42]
But O, it presses to my memory   110
Like damnèd guilty deeds to sinners' minds:
"Tybalt is dead, and Romeo banishèd."
That "banishèd", that one word "banishèd",
Hath slain ten thousand Tybalts.[43] Tybalt's death
Was woe enough if it had ended there;   115
Or, if sour woe delights in fellowship[44]
And needly[45] will be ranked with other griefs,
Why followed not, when she said, "Tybalt's dead",
"Thy father", or "thy mother", nay, or both,
Which modern lamentation might have moved?[46]   120
But with a rearward following Tybalt's death,
"Romeo is banishèd"![47] To speak that word
Is father, mother, Tybalt, Romeo, Juliet,
All slain, all dead. "Romeo is banishèd".
There is no end, no limit, measure, bound,   125
In that word's death;[48] no words can that woe sound.[49]
Where is my father and my mother, Nurse?

NURSE

Weeping and wailing over Tybalt's corse.
Will you go to them? I will bring you thither.

121

JULIET

Wash they his wounds with tears? Mine shall be spent   130
When theirs are dry, for Romeo's banishment.[50]
Take up those cords. Poor ropes, you are beguiled,[51]
Both you and I, for Romeo is exiled.
He made you for a highway to my bed,
But I, a maid, die maiden-widowéd.[52]   135
Come, cords; come Nurse; I 'll to my wedding bed,
And death, not Romeo, take my maidenhead.

NURSE

Hie to your chamber. I 'll find Romeo
To comfort you; I wot[53] well where he is.

---

50 *Mine shall* (line *130*) ... *banishment* –
"My tears for Romeo's banishment
will continue to pour out when theirs
for Tybalt have ceased".

51 *beguiled* – "cheated" (because they will
not be used by Romeo, as planned).

52 *die maiden-widowéd* – "die a widow,
though never really a wife".

53 *wot* – "know".

(III.iii) <u>Friar Lawrence returns to his cell, where Romeo is hiding after the
killing of Tybalt, with the news that the Prince has banished him. Romeo
argues that banishment from Juliet is worse than death.</u> His despair increases
when the Nurse arrives and tells him of Juliet's misery; he attempts to kill
himself, but is prevented from doing so by the Nurse, who seizes the knife.
The Friar calms him by pointing out that their situation is far from hopeless.
He advises Romeo to go to Juliet, but to leave early in the morning for
<u>Mantua where he must stay until pardon is obtained from the Prince.</u> The
Nurse is sent to prepare Juliet for Romeo's arrival, and the Friar tells Romeo
he will send messages to him in Mantua through Romeo's servant, Balthasar.
Romeo then leaves to join Juliet.

1 *fearful* – "full of fear".
2 *Affliction ... to calamity* – "Misery has
fallen in love with your good qualities and you are wedded to distress".
3 *craves acquaintance ... hand* – "desires
to be introduced to me".

4 *tidings* – "news".
5 *What less ... doom?* – "How much
less than the death sentence is the
Prince's sentence?"
6 *vanished from* – "escaped".

Hark ye, your Romeo will be here at night: 140
I 'll to him; he is hid at Lawrence' cell.

JULIET

O find him! Give this ring to my true knight,
And bid him come to take his last farewell.

[Exeunt

Scene III. Friar Lawrence's cell.

Enter FRIAR LAWRENCE

FRIAR LAWRENCE

Romeo, come forth; come forth, thou fearful[1] man.
Affliction is enamoured of thy parts,
And thou art wedded to calamity.[2]

[ROMEO comes forward from the inner room

ROMEO

Father, what news? What is the Prince's doom?
What sorrow craves acquaintance at my hand[3]   5
That I yet know not?

FRIAR LAWRENCE

Too familiar

Is my dear son with such sour company:
I bring thee tidings[4] of the Prince's doom.

ROMEO

What less than doomsday is the Prince's doom?[5]

FRIAR LAWRENCE

A gentler judgement vanished from[6] his lips: 10
Not body's death, but body's banishment.

123

ROMEO *didn't think banishment is the lesser punishment*

Ha, banishment? Be merciful, say "death", *To him, death is*
For exile hath more terror in his look, *better – he is not*
Much more, than death; do not say "banishment". *concerned with his life if he just lives for Juliet*

FRIAR LAWRENCE

Hence from Verona art thou banishéd. 15
Be patient, for the world is broad and wide.

ROMEO

There is no world without[7] Verona walls,
But purgatory, torture, hell itself. *outside Verona*
Hence "banishéd" is banished from the world,
And world's exile[8] is death. Then "banishéd" *from this world* 20
Is death mis-termed. Calling death "banishéd", *∴ Verona is his world*
Thou cut'st my head off with a golden axe,[9]
And smilest upon the stroke that murders me.

FRIAR LAWRENCE

O deadly sin! O rude unthankfulness!
Thy fault our law calls death,[10] but the kind Prince, 25

---

7 *without* – "outside".
8 *world's exile* – "exile from the world".
9 *a golden axe*. Romeo means that although "banishment" sounds *golden* or pleasant, compared with "death", it will kill him just the same.
10 *Thy fault . . . death* – "Our law pronounces the death sentence on your fault", i.e. the slaying of Tybalt.
11 *rushed aside* – "swept aside".
12 *dear* – "loving", or possibly "great, unusual".
13 *Live* for *Lives*.
14 *validity* – "value".
15 *state* – "rank".
16 *courtship* – (a) "the state fitting for a court or its members", (b) "power to woo".

17 *Who* –"which", i.e. Juliet's lips.
18 *Still blush . . . sin* – "are always red as if with shame because they think the kiss which each lip gives the other (when they are closed) is sinful".
19 *sharp-ground* – "rubbed on a hard stone (ground) until sharp".
20 *mean of death . . . mean* – "means of death, however base (*mean*)".
21 *Howling attends it* – "the wailing (of condemned souls) goes with it".
22 *divine* – "priest".
23 *A sin-absolver* – "one who forgives sins".
24 *fond* – "foolish".

124

SCENE III]

Taking thy part, hath rushed aside[11] the law,
And turned that black word "death" to "banishment".
This is dear[12] mercy, and thou seest it not.

The Prince feels sympathy for you but Romeo is not grateful.

He sees banishment not a merciful act but a continuing torture.

ROMEO

'T is torture and not mercy. Heaven is here
Where Juliet lives, and every cat and dog   30
And little mouse, every unworthy thing,
Live[13] here in heaven and may look on her,
But Romeo may not. More validity,[14]
More honourable state,[15] more courtship,[16] lives
In carrion flies than Romeo: they may seize   35
On the white wonder of dear Juliet's hand,
And steal immortal blessing from her lips,
Who[17] even in pure and vestal modesty
Still blush, as thinking their own kisses sin,[18]
But Romeo may not; he is banishéd.   40
Flies may do this, but I from this must fly;
They are free men, but I am banishéd.
And say'st thou yet that exile is not death?
Hadst thou no poison mixed, no sharp-ground[19] knife,
No sudden mean of death, though ne'er so mean,[20]   45
But "banishéd" to kill me? "Banishéd"!
O Friar, the damnéd use that word in hell;
Howling attends it.[21] How hast thou the heart,
Being a divine,[22] a ghostly confessor,
A sin-absolver,[23] and my friend professed,   50
To mangle me with that word "banishéd"?

How can you say that banishment is not death?

FRIAR LAWRENCE

Thou fond[24] madman, hear me a little speak.

ROMEO

O thou wilt speak again of banishment.

125

FRIAR LAWRENCE

I 'll give thee armour to keep off that word:
Adversity's sweet milk,[25] philosophy, *→Day of life, thinking*   55
To comfort thee though thou art banishéd.

ROMEO

Yet "banishéd"?[26] Hang up philosophy![27]
Unless philosophy can make a Juliet,
Displant a town,[28] reverse a Prince's doom,
It helps not, it prevails not,[29] talk no more.   60

FRIAR LAWRENCE

O, then I see that madmen have no ears.

ROMEO

How should they, when that wise men have no eyes?[30]

FRIAR LAWRENCE

Let me dispute with thee of thy estate.[31]

---

25 *Adversity's sweet milk* – "the comforting food which supports one through *misfortune*".
26 *Yet "banishéd"?* – "Are you still using that word "banishéd"?
27 *Hang up philosophy* – "Hang philosophy (like the *armour* which you say it is) on the wall". Romeo considers philosophy to be ornamental, not useful.
28 *Displant a town* – "pull up a town (i.e. Verona) by the roots, and plant it somewhere else (i.e. in Mantua)".
29 *prevails not* – "is of no benefit".
30 *How should ... no eyes?* – "Why should madmen (like me) listen when wise men (like you) cannot see (how hopeless the situation is)?"

31 *dispute with ... estate* – "discuss (*dispute*) your situation (*estate*) with you".
32 *that* – "that which".
33 *Taking ... unmade grave.* Stretched on the ground, Romeo is measuring how much room will be needed for his grave.
34 *infold* – "wrap itself round me".
35 *taken* – "captured".
36 *my study.* This would be the inner stage (see Introduction p. xiii), in which Romeo was hiding at the beginning of the scene.
37 *simpleness* – "stupidity". The Friar is annoyed by Romeo's refusal to get up and hide.

126

ROMEO

Thou canst not speak of that[32] thou dost not feel.
Wert thou as young as I, Juliet thy love,   65
An hour but married, Tybalt murderéd,
Doting like me, and like me banishéd,
Then mightst thou speak, then mightst thou tear thy
  hair,
And fall upon the ground as I do now,
Taking the measure of an unmade grave.[33]   70

> [ROMEO *flings himself on the floor. There is knocking*
> *at the door*

FRIAR LAWRENCE

Arise; one knocks. Good Romeo, hide thyself.

ROMEO

Not I, unless the breath of heartsick groans
Mist-like infold[34] me from the search of eyes.

> [*More knocking*

FRIAR LAWRENCE

Hark, how they knock! – Who's there? – Romeo, arise;
Thou wilt be taken.[35] – [*He calls*] Stay a while! –
  [*To* ROMEO] Stand up!
Run to my study.[36] – [*He calls*] By and by! –   75
  [*To* ROMEO] God's will,
What simpleness[37] is this? – [*He calls*] I come, I come!

> [*Louder knocking*

Who knocks so hard? Whence come you? What's your
  will?

NURSE

[*From outside*] Let me come in, and you shall know my
  errand.
I come from Lady Juliet.

127

FRIAR LAWRENCE

[*Opening the door*] Welcome then.   80

NURSE

[*Entering*] O holy Friar, O tell me, holy Friar,
Where 's my lady's lord? Where 's Romeo?

FRIAR LAWRENCE

There on the ground, with his own tears made drunk.

NURSE

O he is even in my mistress' case,[38]
Just in her case. O woeful sympathy![39]   85
Piteous predicament! Even so lies she,
Blubbering and weeping, weeping and blubbering.
[*To* ROMEO] Stand up, stand up! Stand, and you be[40] a
    man!
For Juliet's sake; for her sake rise and stand.
Why should you fall into so deep an O?[41]   90

ROMEO

[*Rising*] Nurse!

---

38 *even in . . . case* – "in the same state
    (*case*) as my mistress".
39 *sympathy* – "similarity of feeling".
40 *and you be* – "if you are".
41 *an O* – "a lament". The word prob-
    ably comes from the shape made by
    the mouth of the person lamenting
    aloud.
42 *an old murderer* – "one who has often
    murdered".
43 *blood removed . . . her own*. Tybalt's
    blood is almost the same as Juliet's
    since they are both Capulets.

44 *my concealed lady* – "my secret wife".
45 *cancelled* – "blotted out" (by Romeo's
    exile).
46 *level* – "line of fire".
47 *this anatomy* – "my body".
48 *Unseemly woman (line 111) . . . both* –
    "Since you are apparently a man (*a
    seeming man*) it is not proper (*un-
    seemly*) that you should behave like a
    woman; in appearing to be both (*in
    seeming both*) you are like some mons-
    trous animal (*ill-beseeming beast*)".

NURSE

Ah sir! Ah sir! Death 's the end of all.

ROMEO

Spak'st thou of Juliet? How is it with her?
Doth she not think me an old murderer,[42]
Now I have stained the childhood of our joy
With blood removed but little from her own?[43]   95
Where is she? and how doth she? and what says
My concealed lady[44] to our cancelled[45] love?

NURSE

O she says nothing, sir, but weeps and weeps,
And now falls on her bed, and then starts up,
And Tybalt calls, and then on Romeo cries,   100
And then down falls again.

ROMEO

                As if that name,
Shot from the deadly level[46] of a gun,
Did murder her as that name's curséd hand
Murdered her kinsman. O tell me, Friar, tell me,
In what vile part of this anatomy[47]   105
Doth my name lodge? Tell me, that I may sack
The hateful mansion.

                [*He draws his dagger to kill himself, but
                the Nurse snatches it from him*

FRIAR LAWRENCE

                Hold thy desperate hand!
Art thou a man? Thy form cries out thou art:
Thy tears are womanish, thy wild acts denote
The unreasonable fury of a beast.   110
Unseemly woman in a seeming man,
And ill-beseeming beast in seeming both![48]

129

in the great chamber[10]
(I.v.11)

O for a falconer's voice,
To lure this tassel-gentle back again[82]
(II.i.200 – 201)

cords made like a tackled stair,[110]
Which to the high topgallant[111]
(II.iii.169 – 170)

130

What, dost thou make us minstrels?
(III.i.43)

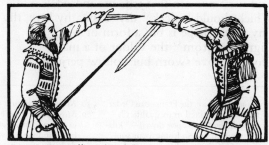

a villain that fights by the book of arithmetic [47]
(III.i.97 – 98)

till the watch be set [68]
(III.iii.147)

Thou hast amazed me. By my holy order,[49]
I thought thy disposition better tempered.[50]
Hast thou slain Tybalt? Wilt thou slay thyself?   115
And slay thy lady, that in thy life lives,
By doing damnéd hate upon thyself?[51]
Why rail'st thou on thy birth, the heaven, and earth,
Since birth, and heaven, and earth, all three, do meet
In thee at once,[52] which thou at once would'st lose?[53]   120
Fie, fie! Thou sham'st thy shape, thy love, thy wit,
Which like a usurer abound'st in all,
And usest none in that true use indeed[54]
Which should bedeck[55] thy shape, thy love, thy wit.
Thy noble shape is but a form of wax,[56]   125
Digressing from[57] the valour of a man;
Thy dear love sworn but hollow perjury,[58]

---

49 *my holy order*, i.e. the Franciscan Order.
50 *tempered* – "mixed in its qualities".
51 *doing damnéd hate upon thyself* – "killing yourself and so losing your soul". Taking one's own life, a mortal sin, results in damnation.
52 *birth and heaven* (*line 119*) . . . *at once*, i.e. man is both body and soul at the same time.
53 *at once wouldst lose*. By killing himself Romeo would lose all hope of heaven in one blow.
54 *Which like* (*line 122*) . . . *use indeed*. A usurer has plenty of everything (*abound'st in all*), but uses nothing as it should be used. *Which* – "who". To *use* was to lend money at interest.
55 *bedeck* – "adorn".
56 *a form of wax* – "a wax figure" (lacking human qualities).
57 *Digressing from* – "(because you) turn aside from".
58 *Thy dear love . . . perjury* – "the devoted love which you have sworn (for Juliet) is simply an empty lie (*hollow perjury*)".

59 *Killing* – "because you kill".
60 *Misshapen . . . in both* – "misdirected in the guidance (*conduct*) it gives your body and your love (*them both*)".
61 *flask*, the container for a soldier's gunpowder.
62 *dismembered . . . own defence* – "blown to pieces (*dismembered*) by the things which should have protected you (*thine own defence*)".
63 *thou wast but lately dead* – "just now you wished to be dead".
64 *light upon* – "come down upon".
65 *fortune*, i.e. good fortune.
66 *decreed* – "decided".
67 *look* – "see to it that".
68 *the watch be set* – "the watchmen are placed in their positions". The *watch* was the police-force of Shakespeare's time.
69 *blaze* – "make public".
70 *apt unto* – "ready for".

Killing[59] that love which thou hast vowed to cherish;
Thy wit, that ornament to shape and love,
Misshapen in the conduct of them both,[60]   130
Like powder in a skilless soldier's flask,[61]
Is set afire by thine own ignorance,
And thou dismembered with thine own defence.[62]
What? Rouse thee, man! Thy Juliet is alive,
For whose dear sake thou wast but lately dead;[63]   135
There art thou happy. Tybalt would kill thee,
But thou slew'st Tybalt; there art thou happy.
The law that threatened death becomes thy friend,
And turns it to exile; there art thou happy too.
A pack of blessings light upon[64] thy back;   140
Happiness courts thee in her best array,
But like a misbehaved and sullen wench
Thou frown'st upon thy fortune[65] and thy love.
Take heed, take heed, for such die miserable.
Go, get thee to thy love, as was decreed;[66]   145
Ascend her chamber; hence, and comfort her,
But look[67] thou stay not till the watch be set,[68]
For then thou can'st not pass to Mantua,
Where thou shalt live till we can find a time
To blaze[69] your marriage, reconcile your friends,   150
Beg pardon of the Prince, and call thee back
With twenty hundred thousand times more joy
Than thou went'st forth in lamentation.
Go before, Nurse. Commend me to thy lady,
And bid her hasten all the house to bed,   155
Which heavy sorrow makes them apt unto.[70]
Romeo is coming.

NURSE

O Lord, I could have stayed here all the night
To hear good counsel. O what learning is!
My lord, I 'll tell my lady you will come.   160

133

ROMEO

Do so, and bid my sweet prepare to chide.

NURSE

Here, sir, a ring she bid me give you, sir.
Hie you, make haste, for it grows very late.

ROMEO

How well my comfort is revived by this.

FRIAR LAWRENCE

Go hence; good night.

[*Exit* NURSE

              r state:[71]   165

Either be gone bef
Or by the break o
Sojourn in Mantua. I 'll find out your man,[72]
And he shall signify from time to time
Every good hap[73] to you that chances here.   170
Give me thy hand. 'T is late; farewell, good night.

---

71 *here stands all your state* – "your whole
    fortune depends on this".
72 *your man,* i.e. Romeo's servant Bal-
    thasar.
73 *good hap* – "piece of good fortune".
74 *But that* – "Were it not that".

75 *a joy past joy* – "a joy greater than joy
    itself".
76 *It were . . . with thee* – "it would be a
    grief to part from you so hastily
    (brief)".

(III.iv) Capulet, without consulting Juliet, assures Paris that Juliet will
agree to marry him. He fixes Thursday as the wedding day.

1 *fallen out* – "happened".
2 *move* – "make any suggestion to" (i.e.
    of marriage to Paris).
3 *promise* – "assure".
4 *a-bed* – "in bed".

5 *These times . . . woo.* Note the play on
    times and *time, woe* and *woo*.
6 *mewed up to her heaviness* – "shut up in
    her grief". *Mew* – "shut a bird in a
    cage".
7 *a desperate tender* – "a bold offer".

ROMEO

But that[74] a joy past joy[75] calls out on me,
It were a grief so brief to part with thee.[76]
Farewell.

[*Exeunt*

Scene IV. Capulet's house.

Enter CAPULET, LADY CAPULET, *and* PARIS

CAPULET

Things have fallen out,[1] sir, so unluckily
That we have had no time to move[2] our daughter.
Look you, she loved her kinsman Tybalt dearly,
And so did I. Well, we were born to die.
'T is very late; she 'll not come down tonight.   5
I promise[3] you, but for your company,
I would have been a-bed[4] an hour ago.

PARIS

These times of woe afford no time to woo.[5]
Madam, good night; commend me to your daughter.

LADY CAPULET

I will, and know her mind early to-morrow;   10
To-night she's mewed up to her heaviness.[6]

CAPULET *calls back* PARIS *who is leaving*

CAPULET

Sir Paris! I will make a desperate tender[7]
Of my child's love. I think she will be ruled
In all respects by me: nay, more, I doubt it not.

135

Wife, go you to her ere you go to bed;　　　　　　　　15
Acquaint her here of my son Paris'⁸ love,
And bid her, mark you me, on Wednesday next –
But soft, what day is this?

PARIS

Monday, my lord.

CAPULET

Monday, ah ha; well, Wednesday is too soon;
O' Thursday let it be. O' Thursday, tell her,　　　　　20
She shall be married to this noble earl.
Will you be ready? Do you like this haste?

---

8 *my son Paris.* Capulet is so confident
that Juliet will obey him, that he refers to Paris as if Paris were already his
son-in-law (i.e. Juliet's husband).
When Juliet refuses, he lacks the
humility to admit that he was wrong
to make this *desperate tender*. His pride
leads to Juliet's death.

9 *keep no great ado* – "we will not make
it a big affair".

10 *late* – "recently".

11 *held him carelessly* – "did not greatly
care for him".

12 *would* – "wish".

13 *against* – "in time for".

14 *Afore me,* a shortened form of the exclamation, "God before me".

15 *so very late (line 34) . . . early.* It is so
near midnight that it will soon be
early morning.

(III.v) Juliet tries to persuade Romeo that morning has not yet arrived,
but when she realises how dangerous it is for him to stay, she insists that he
should leave. When they learn from the Nurse that Lady Capulet is coming,
Romeo descends the ladder and bids farewell to Juliet. Lady Capulet, who
imagines that Juliet is grieving for Tybalt, thinks she will be made happy by
the news of Paris's proposal of marriage, but this only increases Juliet's suffering, and she rejects the offer. In his fury at her refusal Juliet's father threatens
to drive her from the house unless she marries Paris that Thursday. After he
has left, Juliet appeals to her mother for help, but in vain. She then seeks
comfort from her Nurse who urges her to marry Paris. Juliet is shocked to
discover that she can no longer trust the Nurse. She is now cut off from
everyone except Friar Lawrence, whose advice she determines to seek.

1 *Fearful* – "full of fear".

2 *envious streaks.* The lines of light
appear in the early morning sky because they are jealous of the lovers
and wish to part them.

We'll keep no great ado;[9] a friend or two;
For hark you, Tybalt being slain so late,[10]
It may be thought we held him carelessly,[11]   25
Being our kinsman, if we revel much.
Therefore we 'll have some half a dozen friends,
And there an end. [*To* PARIS] But what say you to
    Thursday?

PARIS

My lord, I would[12] that Thursday were to-morrow.

CAPULET

Well, get you gone; o' Thursday be it then.   30
[*To his wife*] Go you to Juliet ere you go to bed;
Prepare her, wife, against[13] this wedding day.
Farewell, my lord. [*To his Servant*] Light to my
    chamber, ho!
Afore me,[14] 't is so very late that we
May call it early[15] by and by. Good night.   35

[*Exeunt*

Scene V. Juliet's bedroom.

ROMEO *and* JULIET *stand at the window*

JULIET

Wilt thou be gone? It is not yet near day.
It was the nightingale, and not the lark,
That pierced the fearful[1] hollow of thine ear.
Nightly she sings on yond pomegranate tree.
Believe me, love, it was the nightingale.   5

ROMEO

It was the lark, the herald of the morn, *announcer*
No nightingale. Look, love, what envious streaks[2]

137

Do lace[3] the severing clouds[4] in yonder east.
Night's candles[5] are burnt out, and jocund day
Stands tiptoe on the misty mountain tops.   10
I must be gone and live, or stay and die.

JULIET

Yond light is not daylight; I know it, I.
It is some meteor that the sun exhales[6]
To be to thee this night a torchbearer
And light thee on thy way to Mantua. *when he was banished* 15
Therefore stay yet; thou need'st not to be gone.

ROMEO

Let me be ta'en,[7] let me be put to death:
I am content, so[8] thou wilt have it so.
I 'll say yon grey is not the morning's eye,
'T is but the pale reflex of Cynthia's brow;[9]   20

---

3 *lace* – "show in lines, like a network, on".

4 *severing clouds* – (a) "clouds which are breaking up", (b) "clouds which part (*sever*) the lovers".

5 *Night's candles*, i.e. the stars.

6 *some meteor . . . exhales*. It was believed that shooting stars (*meteors*) were caused by the sun drawing up (*exhaling*) gases from the earth and setting fire to them with its heat.

7 *ta'en* – "taken", i.e. "captured".

8 *so* – "if".

9 *reflex of Cynthia's brow* – "the reflection of the moon". Cynthia was the moon-goddess.

10 *vaulty* – "arched".

11 *care* – "desire".

12 *sharps* – "high, shrill notes".

13 *division* – "separation", i.e. of long notes into short parts. Juliet plays on this meaning and on the ordinary meaning of "separation".

14 *This doth not so* – "this (lark) does not do so".

15 *the lark . . . changed eyes*. The toad has fine eyes, despite its general ugliness, and the lark ugly ones, despite its general beauty, so it was said that they had changed eyes. If they had changed voices then the harsh noise of the lark would be more suitable as a warning for the lovers to part than its present song.

16 *Since arm . . . affray* – "since the lark's voice frightens us away (*doth us affray*) from each other (*arm from arm*)".

17 *hunt 's-up to the day*. "The hunt is up" was the name of a song used to awaken the huntsmen in the early morning.

18 *look about* – "be watchful".

19 *life*, i.e. Romeo.

138

Nor that is not the lark whose notes do beat
The vaulty[10] heaven so high above our heads.
I have more care[11] to stay than will to go.
Come, death, and welcome! Juliet wills it so.
How is 't my soul? Let's talk; it is not day.   25

JULIET

It is, it is! Hie hence, be gone, away!
It is the lark that sings so out of tune,
Straining harsh discords and unpleasing sharps.[12]
Some say the lark makes sweet division:[13]
This doth not so,[14] for she divideth us.   30
Some say the lark and loathéd toad changed eyes;[15]
O now I would they had changed voices too,
Since arm from arm that voice doth us affray,[16]
Hunting thee hence with hunt 's-up to the day.[17]
O now be gone; more light and light it grows.   35

ROMEO

More light and light, more dark and dark our woes.

Enter NURSE *in a hurry*

NURSE

Madam!

JULIET

Nurse?

NURSE

Your lady mother is coming to your chamber.
The day is broke; be wary, look about.[18]   40

[*Exit* NURSE

JULIET

Then, window, let day in, and let life[19] out.

139

ROMEO

Farewell, farewell. One kiss and I 'll descend.

[*He descends the ladder*

JULIET

Art thou gone so, love, lord, ay husband, friend?[20]
I must hear from thee every day in the hour,
For in a minute there are many days.   45
O, by this count I shall be much in years[21]
Ere I again behold my Romeo.

ROMEO

[*From the garden below*] Farewell. I will omit no
   opportunity
That may convey my greetings, love, to thee.

JULIET

O, think'st thou we shall ever meet again?   50

ROMEO

I doubt it not; and all these woes shall serve
For sweet discourses in our time to come.

JULIET

O God, I have an ill-divining soul![22]
Methinks I see thee, now thou art so low,
As one dead in the bottom of a tomb;   55
Either my eyesight fails, or thou look'st pale.

---

20 *friend* – "lover".
21 *much in years* – "very old".
22 *an ill-divining soul* – "a soul which sees evil ahead".
23 *Dry sorrow ... blood.* It was believed that sorrow caused the blood to return to the heart, so causing paleness.

24 *what dost* (*line 60*) . . . *faith.* Juliet asks the changeable goddess Fortune what she can have to do with one who is so faithful and unchanging as Romeo.
25 *down so late* – "lying down in bed at such a late hour".
26 *procures* – "brings".
27 *how now* – "what is the matter".

140

Line 53: Juliet divines the future forboding evil for them
– It is an accurate omen

ROMEO

And trust me, love, in my eye so do you.
Dry sorrow drinks our blood.[23] Adieu, adieu.

[*Exit* ROMEO

takes him away from Juliet

JULIET

O Fortune, Fortune, all men call thee fickle; — *unreliable*
If thou art fickle, what dost thou with him   60
That is renowned for faith?[24] Be fickle, Fortune,
For then I hope thou wilt not keep him long,
But send him back.

LADY CAPULET

[*Outside* JULIET'S *door*] Ho, daughter, are you up?

JULIET

Who is 't that calls? It is my lady mother.
Is she not down so late,[25] or up so early?   65
What unaccustomed cause procures[26] her hither?

Enter LADY CAPULET

In this scene 1st they talk of R & how he should be punished. 2nd Lady C proposes the marriage.

LADY CAPULET

Why, how now,[27] Juliet?

JULIET

Throughout the conversation the audience is aware of the double meaning of J's words. But Lady C. is not aware.

Madam, I am not well.

LADY CAPULET

Evermore weeping for your cousin's death?
What, wilt thou wash him from his grave with tears?
And if thou could'st, thou could'st not make him live;   70

141

Therefore have done:[28] some grief shows much of love,
But much of grief shows still some want of wit.[29]

JULIET

Yet let me weep for such a feeling loss.[30]

LADY CAPULET

So shall you feel the loss, but not the friend
Which you weep for.[31]

JULIET

Feeling so the loss,   75
I cannot choose but ever weep[32] the friend.

LADY CAPULET

Well, girl, thou weep'st not so much for his death
As that the villain lives which slaughtered him.

---

28 *have done* – "stop (crying)".
29 *some grief* (*line 71*) . . . *of wit* – "mode-
   rate grief shows great love, but great
   grief shows a lack of wisdom (*wit*)".
30 *such a feeling loss* – "a loss which I feel
   so much". Juliet is thinking of Romeo,
   and not, as her mother believes, of
   Tybalt. There is dramatic irony
   throughout their conversation; the
   audience is aware of the double meaning of Juliet's words while Lady
   Capulet is not.
31 *So shall you* (*line 74*) . . . *weep for* – "By
   doing that you will feel your loss (of
   Tybalt) but never feel Tybalt himself", i.e. bring him back to life by
   your grief. *Which* – "whom".
32 *weep* – "weep for".
33 *be* – "are".
34 *no man . . . my heart* – "no man grieves
   my heart as he does", i.e. by his absence. She intends her mother to
   understand her words to mean that
   she grieves for Tybalt, not for any
   man like Romeo.

35 *traitor* – "traitorous".
36 *from* – "away from".
37 *Would none but I might venge* – "I wish
   that none but I might have the power
   to take revenge for (*might venge*)".
38 *runagate* – "wandering, worthless fellow".
39 *Shall* – "who shall".
40 *unaccustomed dram* – "strange drink".
41 *so for a kinsman vexed* – "so troubled at
   the death of a kinsman". Juliet says
   that she will not be satisfied until she
   sees Romeo, but she intends her
   mother to think that she wants to see
   him in order to poison him. It is possible that she scarcely pauses after *him*
   (line 93) in order to mislead her
   mother further.
42 *temper* – (a) "mix", (b) "weaken".
   Juliet intends her mother to understand the word in sense (a).

JULIET

What villain, madam?

LADY CAPULET

That same villain, Romeo.

JULIET

[*Aside*] Villain and he be[33] many miles asunder. –   80
[*To her mother*] God pardon him; I do, with all my heart;
And yet no man like he doth grieve my heart.[34]

LADY CAPULET

That is because the traitor[35] murderer lives.

JULIET

Ay, madam, from[36] the reach of these my hands.
Would none but I might venge[37] my cousin's death!   85

LADY CAPULET

We will have vengeance for it, fear thou not.
Then weep no more. I'll send to one in Mantua,
Where that same banished runagate[38] doth live,
Shall[39] give him such an unaccustomed dram[40]
That he shall soon keep Tybalt company;   90
And then I hope thou wilt be satisfied.

JULIET

Indeed, I never shall be satisfied
With Romeo till I behold him; dead
Is my poor heart, so for a kinsman vexed.[41]
Madam, if you could find out but a man   95
To bear a poison, I would temper[42] it
That Romeo should upon receipt thereof

143

Soon sleep in quiet.[43] O how my heart abhors
To hear him named and cannot come to him
To wreak the love I bore my cousin   *I cannot wait to* 100
Upon his body that hath slaughtered him.[44]   *see him to give him*
                                                                        my love

LADY CAPULET

Find thou the means, and I 'll find such a man.
But now I 'll tell thee joyful tidings, girl.

JULIET

And joy comes well in such a needy time.[45]
What are they, beseech[46] your ladyship?   105

LADY CAPULET

Well, well, thou hast a careful[47] father, child;
One who, to put thee from thy heaviness,
Hath sorted out[48] a sudden day of joy
That thou expects not, nor I looked not for.[49]

JULIET

irony

Madam, in happy time![50] What day is that?   110

---

43 *sleep in quiet.* Juliet means "sleep peacefully" after she has made the poison harmless. Her mother thinks she means "die".

44 *his body . . . him* – "the body of the one who killed him".

45 *a needy time* – (a) "a time when it is needed", (b) "a time of need", i.e. without joy.

46 *beseech* – "(may I) ask".

47 *careful* – "full of care, anxious", i.e. for Juliet's welfare.

48 *sorted out* – "chosen".

49 *nor I looked not for* – "(and which) I did not expect".

50 *in happy time!* An exclamation of pleasure at good news. Ironically, the *joyful tidings* could hardly be worse.

51 *the sunset of my brother's son* – "the death of Tybalt". Note the pun on *sun* and *son*. Tybalt was the son of Capulet's brother-in-law.

52 *It rains downright* – "it pours hard"; a reference to Juliet's tears.

53 *How now, a conduit, girl?* He compares Juliet to one of the statues in human form, popular at that time, from which water flowed. *How now* – "What is the matter?"

54 *Who* – "which".

55 *overset* – "overturn".

144

LADY CAPULET

Marry, my child, early next Thursday morn,
The gallant, young, and noble gentleman,
The County Paris, at Saint Peter's Church,
Shall happily make thee there a joyful bride.

JULIET — *She has to tell the truth*

Now, by Saint Peter's Church, and Peter too,   115
He shall not make me there a joyful bride.
I wonder at this haste, that I must wed
Ere he that should be my husband comes to woo.
I pray you tell my lord and father, madam,
I will not marry yet; and when I do, I swear   120
It shall be Romeo, whom you know I hate,
Rather than Paris. These are news indeed!

LADY CAPULET

Here comes your father; tell him so yourself,
And see how he will take it at your hands.

Enter CAPULET *and* NURSE

CAPULET — *in a happy mood*

When the sun sets, the earth doth drizzle dew;   125
But for the sunset of my brother's son[51]
It rains downright.[52]
How now, a conduit,[53] girl? What, still in tears?
Evermore showering? In one little body
Thou counterfeits a bark, a sea, a wind;   130
For still thy eyes, which I may call the sea,
Do ebb and flow with tears; the bark thy body is,
Sailing in this salt flood; the winds thy sighs,
Who[54] raging with thy tears, and they with them,
Without a sudden calm will overset[55]   135
Thy tempest-tossèd body. How now, wife?
Have you delivered to her our decree?

145

LADY CAPULET

Ay, sir, but she will none,[56] she gives you thanks.
I would the fool were married to her grave![57]

CAPULET

Soft, take me with you,[58] take me with you, wife.   140
How will she none? Doth she not give us thanks?
Is she not proud? Doth she not count her blest,
Unworthy as she is, that we have wrought
So worthy a gentleman to be her bride?[59]

JULIET

Not proud you have, but thankful that you have.   145
Proud can I never be of what I hate,
But thankful even for hate that is meant love.[60]

CAPULET

How, how! how, how, chop-logic![61] What is this?
"Proud", and "I thank you", and "I thank you not",

---

56 *she will none* – "she will not agree".

57 *I would the fool . . . grave* – "I wish she were married to her grave", i.e. were dead.

58 *take me with you* – "explain to me what you mean", i.e. by saying she will have none of it (*will none*).

59 *Doth she not* (line *142*) . . . *her bride* – "Doesn't she, who is so unworthy, consider herself fortunate (*count her blest*) that we have persuaded (*wrought*) such a noble (*worthy*) gentleman to be her bride?" *Bride* could be used, in Shakespeare's time, of either the husband or the wife at a wedding. Pride in the wealth and social position of Paris is certainly part of Capulet's reason for trying to hasten the marriage.

60 *even for hate . . . love* – "even for something hateful to me when it is intended as a sign of love".

61 *chop-logic.* i.e. one who exchanges (*chops*) arguments (*logic*); thus, one who engages in wordy arguments.

62 *mistress minion you* – "you ill-mannered girl".

63 *Thank me no thankings* – "I do not want any of your thanks".

64 *fettle* – "prepare".

65 *hurdle,* the wooden frame on which condemned prisoners were dragged to their death.

66 *green-sickness carrion* – "pale, dead-looking creature". Compare the note to II.i.50. *Carrion* is dead flesh.

67 *tallow-face* – "pale face". Juliet's grief has made her pale. See Glossary for *tallow.*

68 *My fingers itch.* He is tempted to strike her.

69 *hilding* – "worthless creature". Compare the note to II.iii.40.

70 *Smatter* – "Chatter".

And yet "Not proud", mistress minion you?[62]   150
Thank me no thankings,[63] nor proud me no prouds,
But fettle[64] your fine joints 'gainst Thursday next,
To go with Paris to Saint Peter's Church,
Or I will drag thee on a hurdle[65] thither.
Out, you green-sickness carrion![66] out, you baggage!   155
You tallow-face.[67]

LADY CAPULET

[*To her husband*] Fie, fie! what, are you mad?

JULIET

Good father, I beseech you on my knees,
Hear me with patience but to speak a word.

CAPULET

Hang thee, young baggage! disobedient wretch!
I tell thee what: get thee to church o' Thursday,   160
Or never after look me in the face.
Speak not, reply not, do not answer me.
My fingers itch.[68] Wife, we scarce thought us blest
That God had lent us but this only child,
But now I see this one is one too much,   165
And that we have a curse in having her.
Out on her, hilding![69]

NURSE

           God in heaven bless her!
You are to blame, my lord, to rate her so.

CAPULET

And why, my Lady Wisdom? Hold your tongue,
Good Prudence. Smatter[70] with your gossips, go.   170

NURSE

I speak no treason.

CAPULET

O God gi' good e'en!⁷¹

NURSE

May not one speak?

CAPULET

Peace, you mumbling fool!
Utter your gravity⁷² o'er a gossip's bowl,
For here we need it not.

LADY CAPULET

You are too hot.⁷³

CAPULET

God's bread!⁷⁴ it makes me mad.   175
Day, night, hour, tide, time, work, play,
Alone, in company, still my care hath been
To have her matched; and having now provided
A gentleman of noble parentage,
Of fair demesnes, youthful and nobly trained,   180

---

71 *God gi' good e'en!* He is telling her to go.
72 *gravity* – "weighty words".
73 *hot* – "angry".
74 *God's bread!* i.e. the sacred bread used during the Mass.
75 *Proportioned ... wish a man* – "his body as well-proportioned as one could wish a man's to be".
76 *a whining mammet* – "a crying doll".
77 *in her fortune's tender* – "on this offer of her fortune".

78 *pardon you* – "give you permission to go".
79 *Graze* – "feed".
80 *house* – "live".
81 *I do not use* – "it is not my habit".
82 *lay hand on heart* – "think deeply about it".
83 *advise* – "reflect".
84 *And* – "If".
85 *Nor what is mine ... good*, i.e. Juliet will never inherit anything from him.

148

Stuffed, as they say, with honourable parts,
Proportioned as one 's thought would wish a man,[75]
And then to have a wretched puling fool,
A whining mammet,[76] in her fortune's tender,[77]
To answer "I 'll not wed, I cannot love,   185
I am too young, I pray you pardon me"!
But and you will not wed I 'll pardon you:[78]
Graze[79] where you will, you shall not house[80] with me.
Look to 't, think on 't; I do not use[81] to jest.
Thursday is near; lay hand on heart,[82] advise.[83]   190
And[84] you be mine, I 'll give you to my friend:
And you be not, hang, beg, starve, die in the streets,
For, by my soul, I 'll ne'er acknowledge thee,
Nor what is mine shall never do thee good:[85]
Trust to 't, bethink you; I 'll not be forsworn.   195

[Exit CAPULET

See p. 54, 140, 122, 124, 151

JULIET

Is there no pity sitting in the clouds
That sees into the bottom of my grief? → rhetoric question
O sweet my mother, cast me not away!   — showing deep
Delay this marriage for a month, a week;   sense of
Or, if you do not, make the bridal bed   sadness and
In that dim monument where Tybalt lies.   hopeless 200

Her Capulet has left

LADY CAPULET

Talk not to me, for I 'll not speak a word.
Do as thou wilt, for I have done with thee.

[Exit LADY CAPULET

JULIET

O God! O Nurse, how shall this be prevented?
My husband is on earth, my faith in heaven;   205
How shall that faith return again to earth,
Unless that husband send it me from heaven

149

By leaving earth?[86] Comfort me, counsel me.
Alack, alack, that heaven should practise stratagems[87]
Upon so soft a subject as myself!   210
What say'st thou? Hast thou not a word of joy?
Some comfort, Nurse.

NURSE — *very practical*

Faith, here it is: Romeo
Is banishéd; and all the world to nothing[88]   *The harsh*
That he dares ne'er come back to challenge[89] you;   *reality of this situation*
Or if he do, it needs must be[90] by stealth.   215
Then since the case so stands as now it doth,
I think it best you married with the County.
O, he's a lovely gentleman!
Romeo's a dishclout to him.[91] An eagle, madam,
Hath not so green,[92] so quick, so fair an eye   220
As Paris hath. Beshrew[93] my very heart,
I think you are happy in this second match,
For it excels your first; or if it did not,
Your first is dead, or 't were as good he were,
As living here, and you no use of him.[94]   225

---

86 *My husband (line 205) . . . leaving
    earth?* The sense of the passage is,
    "Since my husband is alive, and my
    marriage vow (*faith*) is registered in
    heaven, how can I make the same vow
    to anyone else unless Romeo dies and
    thus releases me from my vow?"
87 *practise stratagems* – "play cruel tricks".
88 *all the world to nothing* – "(I will give
    you) all the world in exchange for
    nothing at all (if I am wrong)". The
    Nurse is certain she is right.
89 *challenge* – "claim".
90 *needs must be* – "is bound to be".
91 *a dishclout to him* – "a dishcloth com-
    pared with him". The word *dishclout*
    was often used to make contemptuous
    comparisons.

92 *green*. Green eyes were thought to be
    beautiful.
93 *Beshrew* – "Curse".
94 *As living . . . of him* – "as have him
    living here on earth and have no use
    of him".
95 *Amen!* Juliet agrees to curse (*beshrew*)
    the Nurse's heart and soul. See the
    note to II.v.3.
96 *Ancient damnation!* – "You old devil!"
97 *to wish me thus forsworn* – "to wish me
    to break my marriage vow in this
    way".
98 *Thou and my . . . twain* – "from now
    on (*henceforth*) you will be a stranger
    to my secrets (*bosom*)".

150

JULIET

Speak'st thou from thy heart?

NURSE

And from my soul too; else beshrew them both.

JULIET

Amen!⁹⁵

NURSE

What?

JULIET

Well, thou hast comforted me marvellous much.   230
Go in and tell my lady I am gone,
Having displeased my father, to Lawrence' cell
To make confession and to be absolved.

NURSE

Marry, I will; and this is wisely done.

[*Exit* NURSE

JULIET

Ancient damnation!⁹⁶ O most wicked fiend!   →refers to nurse 235
Is it more sin to wish me thus forsworn,⁹⁷   She is like a devil
Or to dispraise my lord with that same tongue she is urging
Which she hath praised him with above compare me to break
                                                the vow
So many thousand times? Go, counsellor,
Thou and my bosom henceforth shall be twain.⁹⁸   240
I 'll to the Friar, to know his remedy.
If all else fail, myself have power to die.

[*Exit* JULIET

151

*Like Romeo, Juliet seeks a solution from
Friar & like Romeo she believes that death
maybe the only solution.*

(IV.i) Paris has come to Friar Lawrence's cell to arrange for his marriage to Juliet. Juliet enters, and Paris, believing that she has come for confession, leaves them. Juliet tells the Friar that unless he can help her she will kill herself. He gives her a drug which will produce all the appearances of death for forty-two hours. If she takes this drug on Wednesday night she will be found as if dead on Thursday morning, the day fixed for her marriage to Paris, and will be laid in the family tomb of the Capulets. The Friar explains that he will help her to escape to Mantua.

1 *I am nothing ... haste* – "There is nothing slow about me which will lessen (*slack*) his speed (*haste*)". Paris refers to Capulet as his *father*, just as Capulet had called him *son* (III.iv.16), both of them taking Juliet's approval for granted.

2 *the lady's mind*, i.e. whether Juliet approves or not.

3 *Uneven is the course* – "This course of action is not straightforward".

4 *For Venus ... tears* – "since love does not flourish in a house of sorrow".

5 *counts* – "reckons".

6 *give her sorrow so much sway* – "allow her sorrow to rule her so much".

7 *Which, too much (line 13) ... society* – "her tears, to which she is too much inclined (*minded*) when alone, may be removed (*put from her*) if she has company (*society*)".

8 *I would ... be slowed* – "I wish I did not know why it must be delayed".

Timewise the scene is positioned mid-way in the drama. It occurs on Tuesday, two days since Juliet met Romeo, & 2 days before J's father promised her to Paris. J is placed ½ R & Paris, ½ life & death. We've known J for 2 days — the ball on Sunday, her wedding on Monday & in 2 days she will be 'dead' on Wednesday, she will be discovered. On Thursday, J will commit suicide. The subject of death permeates the 2nd half of this scene.

152

ACT FOUR

Scene I. Friar Lawrence's cell.

Enter FRIAR LAWRENCE *and* PARIS

FRIAR LAWRENCE

On Thursday, sir? The time is very short.

PARIS

My father Capulet will have it so,
And I am nothing slow to slack his haste.[1]

FRIAR LAWRENCE

You say you do not know the lady's mind?[2]
Uneven is the course;[3] I like it not.   5

PARIS

Immoderately she weeps for Tybalt's death,
And therefore have I little talked of love,
For Venus smiles not in a house of tears.[4]
Now, sir, her father counts[5] it dangerous
That she do give her sorrow so much sway,[6]   10
And in his wisdom hastes our marriage,
To stop the inundation of her tears,
Which, too much minded by herself alone,
May be put from her by society.[7]
Now do you know the reason of this haste.   15

FRIAR LAWRENCE

[*Aside*] I would I knew not why it should be slowed. –[8]
Look, sir, here comes the lady toward my cell.

Enter JULIET

153

PARIS

Happily met, my lady and my wife!

JULIET

That may be, sir, when I may be a wife.

PARIS

That "may be" must be, love, on Thursday next.   20

JULIET

What must be shall be.⁹

FRIAR LAWRENCE

That 's a certain text.¹⁰

PARIS

Come you to make confession to this father?

JULIET

To answer that, I should confess to you.

PARIS

Do not deny to him that you love me.

---

9 *What must be shall be.* Juliet means that
   what is destined to happen will happen. She is not agreeing with Paris
   that she must be his wife.
10 *a certain text* – "a true saying".
11 *price* – "value".
12 *is much abused with tears* – "has been
   badly ill-treated by your tears".

13 *The tears (line 30)* . . . *spite* – "my face
   had so little beauty before their injury
   (*spite*) that the tears have gained only a
   small victory by destroying it".
14 *to my face* – (a) "about my face",
   (b) "openly".
15 *It may be so . . . own* – "Maybe I have
   slandered it since it is not mine".
   Juliet means that it is Romeo's, and
   also that it is so changed by her grief
   that it is not her usual face.

JULIET

I will confess to you that I love him.   25

PARIS

So will ye, I am sure, that you love me.

JULIET

If I do so, it will be of more price,[11]
Being spoke behind your back, than to your face.

PARIS

Poor soul, thy face is much abused with tears.[12]

JULIET

The tears have got small victory by that,   30
For it was bad enough before their spite.[13]

PARIS

Thou wrong'st it more than tears with that report.

JULIET

That is no slander, sir, which is a truth,
And what I spake, I spake it to my face.[14]

PARIS

Thy face is mine, and thou hast slandered it.   35

JULIET

It may be so, for it is not mine own. —[15]
Are you at leisure, holy Father, now,
Or shall I come to you at evening Mass?

155

FRIAR LAWRENCE

My leisure serves me, pensive[16] daughter, now.
My lord, we must entreat the time alone.[17]   40

PARIS

God shield[18] I should disturb devotion.
Juliet, on Thursday early will I rouse ye;
Till then, adieu, and keep this holy kiss.

[He kisses her and leaves

JULIET — *her feeling of helpless*

O shut the door, and when thou hast done so,
Come weep with me, past hope, past care, past help.   45

FRIAR LAWRENCE

O Juliet, I already know thy grief;
It strains me past the compass of my wits.[19]
I hear thou must, and nothing may prorogue[20] it,
On Thursday next be married to this County.

---

16 *pensive* – "sorrowful".

17 *entreat the time alone* – "ask you to leave us alone now".

18 *God shield* – "God forbid".

19 *It strains . . . wits* – "it strains my mind (*wits*) beyond its limits (*compass*)".

20 *prorogue* – "postpone".

21 *presently* – "immediately". See also line 95.

22 *the label to another deed* – "the wax seal (*label*) fixed to another written agreement (*deed*)". This *label* made it binding in law. Juliet refuses to enter into any other contract than her marriage contract with Romeo.

23 *this shall slay them both* – "this (knife) shall destroy both my hand and my heart".

24 *out of thy long-experienced time* – "from your long years of experience".

25 *'Twixt my extremes* (line 62) . . . *umpire* – "this bloody knife shall be the judge (*umpire*) of the struggles between my sufferings (*extremes*) and me".

26 *commission* – "authority".

27 *art* – "skill".

28 *Could . . . honour bring* – "could not bring to an honourable conclusion (*issue*)".

29 *As that . . . would prevent.* His plan will be as dangerous to carry out as the situation which they are trying to prevent is dangerous.

30 *That cop'st . . . from it* – "you who struggle (*That cop'st*) with death himself to escape from this shame (*it*)", i.e. of marrying Paris.

Friar Lawrence acknowledge the uses of herbs can be fatal or life-saving & he uses his knowledge to help Juliet as he truely believes sancitity of marriage & that that it is the only way to make Capulets & Montagues unite.

JULIET — *show her absolute determination*

Tell me not, Friar, that thou hearest of this,   50
Unless thou tell me how I may prevent it.
If in thy wisdom thou can'st give no help,
Do thou but call my resolution wise,
And with this knife I 'll help it presently.[21]
God joined my heart and Romeo's, thou our hands;   55
And ere this hand, by thee to Romeo's sealed,
Shall be the label to another deed,[22]
Or my true heart with treacherous revolt
Turn to another, this shall slay them both.[23]
Therefore, out of thy long-experienced time,[24]   60
Give me some present counsel; or, behold,
'Twixt my extremes and me, this bloody knife
Shall play the umpire,[25] arbitrating that
Which the commission[26] of thy years and art[27]
Could to no issue of true honour bring.[28]   65
Be not so long to speak; I long to die
If what thou speak'st speak not of remedy.

FRIAR LAWRENCE

Hold, daughter: I do spy a kind of hope,
Which craves as desperate an execution
As that is desperate which we would prevent.[29]   70
If, rather than to marry County Paris,
Thou hast the strength of will to slay thyself,
Then is it likely thou wilt undertake
A thing like death to chide away this shame,
That cop'st with death himself to scape from it;[30]   75
And, if thou darest, I 'll give thee remedy.

JULIET

O bid me leap, rather than marry Paris,
From off the battlements of any tower,

157

Or walk in thievish ways,[31] or bid me lurk
Where serpents are; chain me with roaring bears,   80
Or hide me nightly[32] in a charnel house,[33]
O'ercovered quite with dead men's rattling bones,
With reeky shanks[34] and yellow chapless[35] skulls;
Or bid me go into a new-made grave,
And hide me with a dead man in his shroud –   85
Things that, to hear them told, have made me tremble –
And I will do it without fear or doubt,
To live an unstained wife to my sweet love.

FRIAR LAWRENCE *give her a solid plan, explo*
everything to her, s
Hold, then. Go home, be merry, give consent   *she won't be astra*
To marry Paris. Wednesday is to-morrow: 90
To-morrow night look[36] that thou lie alone;
Let not the Nurse lie with thee in thy chamber.
Take thou this vial, being then in bed,
And this distilléd liquor drink thou off,
When presently through all thy veins shall run   95
A cold and drowsy humour,[37] for no pulse
Shall keep his native progress, but surcease;[38]
No warmth, no breath, shall testify thou livest;

---

31 *thievish ways* – "roads where there are thieves".
32 *nightly* – "at night".
33 *charnel house*, a building where bones and dead bodies are laid.
34 *reeky shanks* – "evil-smelling limbs".
35 *chapless* – "without the lower jaw (*chap*)".
36 *look* – "see to it".
37 *A cold and drowsy humour* – "a fluid (*humour*) which will make you feel cold and drowsy".
38 *no pulse (line 96)* . . . *surcease* – "no pulse will keep its (*his*) natural movement (*native progress*) but it will stop completely (*surcease*)".

39 *wanny* – "pale".
40 *eyes' windows* – "eyelids". The *windows* here (as in I.i.132) are wooden coverings or shutters, not glass windows.
41 *supple government* – "power of movement".
42 *against thou shalt awake* – "in preparation for the time when you will wake up".
43 *drift* – "intention".
44 *inconstant toy* – "idle notion (*toy*) which makes you change your mind".
45 *prosperous* – "successful".
46 *shall help afford* – "will give help".

158

The roses in thy lips and cheeks shall fade
To wanny[39] ashes, thy eyes' windows[40] fall   100
Like death when he shuts up the day of life.
Each part, deprived of supple government,[41]
Shall, stiff and stark and cold, appear like death,
And in this borrowed likeness of shrunk death
Thou shalt continue two and forty hours,   105
And then awake as from a pleasant sleep.
Now, when the bridegroom in the morning comes
To rouse thee from thy bed, there art thou dead.
Then, as the manner of our country is,
In thy best robes, uncovered on the bier,   110
Thou shalt be borne to that same ancient vault
Where all the kindred of the Capulets lie.
In the meantime, against thou shalt awake,[42]
Shall Romeo by my letters know our drift,[43]
And hither shall he come; and he and I   115
Will watch thy waking, and that very night
Shall Romeo bear thee hence to Mantua.
And this shall free thee from this present shame,
If no inconstant toy[44] nor womanish fear
Abate thy valour in the acting it.   120

JULIET

Give me, give me! O tell not me of fear!

FRIAR LAWRENCE

Hold; get you gone. Be strong and prosperous[45]
In this resolve. I 'll send a friar with speed
To Mantua, with my letters to thy lord.

JULIET

Love give me strength! and strength shall help afford.[46]   125
Farewell, dear Father.

                                        [*Exeunt*

Scene II. Capulet's house.

Enter CAPULET, LADY CAPULET, NURSE *and Servants*

CAPULET

[*Giving a paper to a Servant*] So many guests invite as
   here are writ.

[*Exit Servant*

[*To another Servant*] Sirrah, go hire me twenty cunning[1]
   cooks.

SERVANT

You shall have none ill,[2] sir, for I 'll try if they can lick
their fingers.

CAPULET

How can'st thou try them so?   5

SERVANT

Marry, sir, 't is an ill cook that cannot lick his own
fingers.[3] Therefore he that cannot lick his own fingers
goes not with me.

CAPULET

Go, be gone.

[*Exit Servant*

We shall be much unfurnished[4] for this time.   10
What, is my daughter gone to Friar Lawrence?

(IV.ii) Juliet enters while her father is making preparations for the wedding,
and says that she is sorry for her disobedience and begs his pardon. He decides
to have the wedding the following day, Wednesday, instead of Thursday,
and leaves to tell Paris of his change of plan.

1 *cunning* – "skilful".
2 *ill* – "unskilled".
3 *'t is an ill cook . . . fingers,* i.e. if a cook
   cannot taste his own cooking it must
   be very bad.
4 *unfurnished* – "unprovided".
5 *forsooth* – "in truth, certainly".

6 *harlotry it is* – "foolish girl she is".
7 *shrift* – "confession".
8 *headstrong* – "stubborn one".
9 *knot*, i.e. the marriage.
10 *to-morrow morning*, i.e. Wednesday,
   not Thursday as planned.
11 *becoméd* – "fitting".

NURSE

Ay, forsooth.[5]

CAPULET

Well, he may chance to do some good on her.
A peevish, self-willed harlotry it is.[6]

Enter JULIET

NURSE

See where she comes from shrift[7] with merry look.   15

CAPULET

How now, my headstrong?[8] Where have you been
gadding? *running around*

JULIET

Where I have learnt me to repent the sin
Of disobedient opposition
To you and your behests, and am enjoined
By holy Lawrence to fall prostrate here *fall on your knees* 20
To beg your pardon. [*She kneels*] Pardon, I beseech you.
Henceforward I am ever ruled by you.

CAPULET *—he is very impulsive*

Send for the County; go, tell him of this.
I 'll have this knot[9] knit up to-morrow morning.[10]

JULIET

I met the youthful lord at Lawrence' cell,   25
And gave him what becoméd[11] love I might,
Not stepping o'er the bounds of modesty.

CAPULET

Why, I am glad on 't; this is well. Stand up.
This is as 't should be. Let me see the County: *He wants to go
+ tell Paris*

161

Ay, marry, go, I say, and fetch him hither.
Now, afore God, this reverend holy Friar –
All our whole city is much bound to him.[12]

JULIET

Nurse, will you go with me into my closet
To help me sort[13] such needful ornaments
As you think fit to furnish me to-morrow?   35

LADY CAPULET

No, not till Thursday; there is time enough.

CAPULET

Go, Nurse, go with her. We 'll to church to-morrow.
[*Exeunt* JULIET *and* NURSE

LADY CAPULET

We shall be short in our provision:[14]
'T is now near night.

---

12 *is much bound to him* – "owes him a great debt (of gratitude)".
13 *sort* – "choose".
14 *short in our provision*. Lady Capulet opposes the change to Wednesday because they will not have enough time to prepare everything necessary.

15 *deck up her* – "adorn her".
16 *all forth* – "all gone out".
17 *against* – "ready for".
18 *reclaimed* – "brought back to the right course of action".

(IV.iii) Having pretended to choose her clothes for the wedding to Paris the next day, Juliet dismisses the Nurse and says good-bye to her mother. Alone, she begins to be afraid, and turns over in her mind all the terrors and difficulties of Friar Lawrence's plan. She has a vision of Tybalt's ghost which seems to be threatening Romeo in the tomb. Anxious to join Romeo and protect him, she swallows the drink.

1 *orisons* – "prayers".
2 *cross* – "perverse, stubborn".

3 *behoveful* – "fitting".

CAPULET *impulsive + bossy*

Tush, I will stir about,
And all things shall be well, I warrant thee, wife.   40
Go thou to Juliet: help to deck up her.[15]
I 'll not to bed to-night. Let me alone;
I 'll play the housewife for this once. [*He calls the Servants*]
   What ho!
They are all forth.[16] Well, I will walk myself
To County Paris, to prepare up him   45
Against[17] to-morrow. My heart is wondrous light
Since this same wayward girl is so reclaimed.[18]
            [*Exeunt* CAPULET *and* LADY CAPULET

Scene III. Juliet's bedroom.

Enter JULIET *and* NURSE

JULIET

Ay, those *clothes* attires are best; but, gentle Nurse,
I pray thee leave me to myself to-night,
For I have need of many orisons[1]
To move the heavens to smile upon my state,
Which well thou knowest is cross[2] and full of sin.   5

Enter LADY CAPULET

LADY CAPULET

What, are you busy, ho? Need you my help?

JULIET

No, madam; we have culled such necessaries
As are behoveful[3] for our state to-morrow:
So please you, let me now be left alone,

163

And let the Nurse this night sit up with you,   10
For I am sure you have your hands full all
In this so sudden business.

LADY CAPULET

Good night.
Get thee to bed and rest, for thou hast need.

[*Exeunt* LADY CAPULET *and* NURSE

JULIET – *her doubt , 'if' – uncertainty*

Farewell. – God knows when we shall meet again.
I have a faint cold fear[4] thrills[5] through my veins,   15
That almost freezes up the heat of life.
I 'll call them back again to comfort me.
[*She calls*] Nurse! – What should she do here?
My dismal[6] scene I needs must act alone.
Come, vial. *Friar's container*   20
What if this mixture do not work at all?
Shall I be married then to-morrow morning?
No, no. This shall forbid it. [*She lays down her knife*]
   Lie thou there.

---

4 *a faint cold fear* – "a fear which causes
   faintness and coldness".
5 *thrills* – "(which) trembles".
6 *dismal* – "horrible".
7 *still been tried* – "always been proved".
8 *healthsome* – "healthy".
9 *like* – "likely". Compare *like* in line 45.
10 *conceit of death and night* – "thoughts
    aroused by death and night".
11 *green in earth* – "just recently buried".
12 *mandrakes.* The mandrake plant, with
    its forked root, was thought to look
    like a man. It was believed that it
    shrieked when pulled from the
    ground, and that anyone hearing it
    would either die or go mad.

13 *That* – "so that".
14 *walk*, i.e. about the tomb.
15 *rage* – "madness".
16 *spit* – "pierce".
17 *Stay.* Juliet imagines she sees Tybalt
    about to attack Romeo, and begs him
    to stop.
18 *She falls on her bed.* The bed would be
    on the inner stage and Juliet would be
    hidden from the audience by the cur-
    tains which surrounded the bed. This
    made it easier for the audience to
    imagine the next scene, which fol-
    lowed straight on from this one, as
    taking place in Capulet's hall.

er fear: ① wake up before
Romeo come for her
② suffocate to death
③ see Tybalt's rotting body
④ killed by her ancestors

Her doubt: ① doubt Friar Lawrence
(temporary doubt)

SCENE III]

What if it be a poison which the Friar
Subtly hath ministered to have me dead,   25
Lest in this marriage he should be dishonoured
Because he married me before to Romeo?
I fear it is; and yet methinks it should not,
For he hath still been tried[7] a holy man.
How if, when I am laid into the tomb,   30
I wake before the time that Romeo
Come to redeem me? There 's a fearful point!
Shall I not then be stifled in the vault,
To whose foul mouth no healthsome[8] air breathes in,
And there die strangled ere my Romeo comes?   35
Or, if I live, is it not very like[9]
The horrible conceit of death and night,[10]
Together with the terror of the place –
As in a vault, an ancient receptacle,
Where, for this many hundred years, the bones   40
Of all my buried ancestors are packed;
Where bloody Tybalt yet but green in earth,[11]
Lies festering in his shroud; where, as they say,
At some hours in the night spirits resort –
Alack, alack! is it not like that I,   45
So early waking, what with loathsome smells
And shrieks like mandrakes[12] torn out of the earth,
That[13] living mortals, hearing them run mad –
O, if I walk,[14] shall I not be distraught,
Environed with all these hideous fears,   50
And madly play with my forefathers' joints,
And pluck the mangled Tybalt from his shroud,
And in this rage,[15] with some great kinsman's bone,
As with a club, dash out my desperate brains?
O look! methinks I see my cousin's ghost,   55
Seeking out Romeo that did spit[16] his body
Upon a rapier's point. Stay,[17] Tybalt, stay!
Romeo, I come! this do I drink to thee.

[*She falls on her bed*[18]

165

Scene IV. The hall in Capulet's house.

Enter LADY CAPULET *and* NURSE *who carries herbs*

LADY CAPULET

Hold, take these keys and fetch more spices, Nurse.

NURSE

They call for dates and quinces in the pastry.[1]

Enter CAPULET

CAPULET

Come, stir, stir, stir! The second cock hath crowed,
The curfew bell hath rung, 't is three o'clock.
Look to the baked meats, good Angelica;[2]   5
Spare not for cost.

NURSE

Go, ye cot-quean,[3] go.
Get you to bed. Faith, you 'll be sick to-morrow
For this night's watching.[4]

(IV.iv) Busy preparations for the wedding feast have been going on all night at the Capulets' house. It is now early morning, as Paris is heard approaching, and Capulet orders the Nurse to waken Juliet.

1 *the pastry*, the room where the pastry, or *baked meats* (line 5), was made.
2 *Angelica.* Capulet is probably addressing the Nurse, though possibly his wife.
3 *cot-quean*, a name given to a man who interfered in the housewife's affairs. The word means "cottage-wife".
4 *watching* – "staying awake".
5 *been a mouse-hunt* – "been pursuing women".
6 *watch* – "prevent".
7 *a jealous hood* – "a jealous woman".

8 *spits.* These are the thin metal bars on which meat is turned round and roasted over a fire.
9 *I have a head . . . logs* – "I am clever at finding logs".
10 *Mass*, a shortened form of "By the Mass" (the chief religious ceremony in the Catholic Church).
11 *whoreson* – "fellow".
12 *Thou shalt be loggerhead* – "We will call you wooden-head", i.e. a stupid fellow.

166

CAPULET

No, not a whit. What! I have watched ere now
All night for lesser cause and ne'er been sick.   10

LADY CAPULET

Ay, you have been a mouse-hunt[5] in your time,
But I will watch[6] you from such watching now.
                    [*Exeunt* LADY CAPULET *and* NURSE

CAPULET

A jealous hood,[7] a jealous hood!

Enter Servants with spits,[8] *logs, and baskets*

                    Now, fellow, what is there?

SERVANT

Things for the cook, sir, but I know not what.

CAPULET

Make haste, make haste, sirrah. Fetch drier logs.   15
Call Peter; he will show thee where they are.

SERVANT

I have a head, sir, that will find out logs.[9]
And never trouble Peter for the matter.

CAPULET

Mass,[10] and well said; a merry whoreson,[11] ha!
Thou shalt be loggerhead.[12] – Good faith, 't is day!   20
The County will be here with music straight,
For so he said he would. [*Music sounds*] I hear him near.
Nurse! Wife! What ho! What, Nurse, I say!

167

Enter NURSE

Go waken Juliet; go, and trim her up.
I 'll go and chat with Paris. Hie, make haste, 25
Make haste! The bridegroom he is come already.
Make haste, I say.

[*Exeunt all except* NURSE[13]

Scene V. Juliet's bedroom.

NURSE

[*Calling outside the bed-curtains*] Mistress! what, mistress!
Fast,[1] I warrant her, she.
Why, lamb! why, lady! Fie, you slug-a-bed![2]

---

13 The next scene continues without interruption. As the others leave the stage, the Nurse moves to the back and stands outside the curtain of the inner stage which conceals the bed on which Juliet is lying.

(IV.v) The Nurse tries in vain to wake Juliet, and at last discovers that she is, as she supposes, dead. Her cries attract Lady Capulet, and soon Capulet and Paris arrive and join in the lamentation. Friar Lawrence calms them, and tells them to prepare Juliet's body for burial.

1 *Fast* – "Fast asleep".
2 *slug-a-bed*, a lazy person who stays late in bed.
3 *You take your pennyworths* – "See that you get your money's worth (of sleep)". *Pennyworths* is pronounced "penn'orths".
4 *set up his rest* – "staked everything", i.e. made up his mind. The phrase was used in gambling. (See *gamble* in the Glossary.)

5 *take* – "find".
6 *Will it not be?* – "Will you not wake up?"
7 *What dressed . . . again?* – "Have you dressed, and got ready, and then lain down again?"
8 *aqua-vitae*. See III.ii.88 and the note to it.

168

Why, love, I say! madam! sweetheart! why, bride!
What, not a word? You take your pennyworths[3] now;
Sleep for a week; for the next night, I warrant,⁣   5
The County Paris hath set up his rest[4]
That you shall rest but little. God forgive me!
Marry, and amen! How sound is she asleep!
I needs must wake her. Madam, madam, madam!
Ay, let the County take[5] you in your bed;   10
He 'll fright you up, i' faith. Will it not be?[6]
                 [*She opens the bed-curtains*
What, dressed, and in your clothes, and down again?[7]
I must needs wake you. Lady, lady, lady!
Alas, alas! Help, help! My lady's dead!
O well-a-day that ever I was born!   15
Some aqua-vitae,[8] ho! My lord! my lady!

Enter LADY CAPULET

LADY CAPULET

What noise is here?

NURSE

O lamentable day!

LADY CAPULET

What is the matter?

NURSE

Look, look! O heavy day!

LADY CAPULET

O me, O me! My child, my only life,
Revive, look up, or I will die with thee!   20
Help, help! Call help!

Enter CAPULET

CAPULET

For shame, bring Juliet forth; her lord is come.

NURSE

She 's dead, deceased; she 's dead, alack the day!

LADY CAPULET

Alack the day, she 's dead, she 's dead, she's dead!

CAPULET

Ha, let me see her. Out,[9] alas! she's cold;   25
Her blood is settled,[10] and her joints are stiff.
Life and these lips have long been separated.
metaphor ⌈Death lies on her like an untimely frost[11]⌉ *Too young to die*
Upon the sweetest flower of all the field.

NURSE

O lamentable day!

LADY CAPULET

O woeful time!   30

CAPULET

Death, that hath ta'en her hence to make me wail,
Ties up my tongue and will not let me speak.

---

9 *Out*, an exclamation of grief.
10 *settled* – "stopped flowing".
11 *untimely frost* – "frost which comes at the wrong time", i.e. late.
12 *Ready to go*, i.e. to the burial ceremony.
13 *living* – "that which provides a living", e.g. property, or money.
14 *thought long* – "been impatient".
15 *In lasting . . . pilgrimage* – "in the unending toil (*labour*) of his journey".
16 *But one poor one* – "Only one unfortunate child".
17 *solace in* – "delight in".
18 *catched* – "snatched".

170

Enter FRIAR LAWRENCE *and* PARIS

FRIAR LAWRENCE

Come, is the bride ready to go to church?

CAPULET

Ready to go,[12] but never to return.
O son, the night before thy wedding day   35
Hath Death lain with thy wife. There she lies,
Flower as she was, deflouréd by him.
Death is my son-in-law, Death is my heir;
My daughter he hath wedded. I will die
And leave him all. Life, living,[13] all is Death's.   40

PARIS

Have I thought long[14] to see this morning's face,
And doth it give me such a sight as this?

LADY CAPULET

Accursed, unhappy, wretched, hateful day!
Most miserable hour that e'er Time saw
In lasting labour of his pilgrimage.[15]   45
But one poor one,[16] one poor and loving child;
But one thing to rejoice and solace in,[17]
And cruel Death hath catched[18] it from my sight.

NURSE

O woe! O woeful, woeful, woeful day!
Most lamentable day, most woeful day   50
That ever, ever I did yet behold!
O day, O day, O day, O hateful day!
Never was seen so black a day as this.
O woeful day, O woeful day!

PARIS

Beguiled, divorcéd, wrongéd, spited, slain!¹⁹   55
Most detestable Death, by thee beguiled;
By cruel, cruel thee quite overthrown!
O love! O life! Not life, but love in death!²⁰

CAPULET

Despised, distressed, hated, martyred, killed!
Uncomfortable²¹ Time, why cam'st thou now   60
To murder, murder our solemnity?²²
O child, O child! my soul, and not my child!
Dead art thou. Alack, my child is dead,
And with my child my joys are buriéd.

FRIAR LAWRENCE

Peace, ho, for shame! Confusion's cure lives not   65
In these confusions.²³ Heaven and yourself

---

19 *Beguiled . . . slain!* Paris is referring to himself in this line, as Capulet is in line 59. *Spited* – "injured".

20 *Not life . . . death* – "You are no longer my life, but still my love, though dead (*love in death*)".

21 *Uncomfortable* – "Distressing".

22 *solemnity* – "marriage festivity".

23 *Confusion's . . . confusions* – "The remedy for disaster (*confusion*) is not noisy lamentation (*confusion*)".

24 *Your part*, i.e. the body.

25 *his part*, i.e. the soul.

26 *'t was your heaven . . . advanced* – "your highest aim was that she should be raised up", i.e. by marriage to Paris, who is of a higher social rank.

27 *in this love (line 75) . . . is well* – "you show a misplaced love for your child in loving her in such a way that you go mad with grief, considering that all is well with her" (i.e. she is in heaven).

28 *rosemary*, an evergreen shrub, and so a symbol of lasting remembrance, was used at funerals and weddings.

29 *fond* – (a) "foolish", (b) "affectionate".

30 *nature* – "natural affection".

31 *nature's tears . . . merriment* – "our natural tears of sorrow make reason laugh", i.e. it is unreasonable to weep for one who has gone to a better place.

32 *All things (line 84) . . . funeral* – "Change the purpose (*office*) of everything that we designed for the marriage festivity (*ordainéd festival*), and use it for the funeral".

33 *cheer* – "food".

34 *solemn hymns* – "hymns suited to the occasion", i.e. joyful ones.

35 *ill* – "evil" (done by them, the Capulets).

172

Had part in this fair maid: now Heaven hath all,
And all the better is it for the maid.
Your part[24] in her you could not keep from Death,
But Heaven keeps his part[25] in eternal life.   70
The most you sought was her promotion,
For 't was your heaven she should be advanced;[26]
And weep ye now, seeing she is advanced
Above the clouds, as high as heaven itself?
O, in this love you love your child so ill   75
That you run mad, seeing that she is well.[27]
She 's not well married that lives married long,
But she 's best married that dies married young.
Dry up your tears, and stick your rosemary[28]
On this fair corse, and as the custom is,   80
In all her best array bear her to church,
For though fond[29] nature[30] bids us all lament,
Yet nature's tears are reason's merriment.[31]

CAPULET

All things that we ordainéd festival
Turn from their office to black funeral:[32]   85
Our instruments to melancholy bells,
Our wedding cheer[33] to a sad burial feast,
Our solemn hymns[34] to sullen dirges change,
Our bridal flowers serve for a buried corse,
And all things change them to the contrary.   90

FRIAR LAWRENCE

Sir, go you in; and, madam, go with him;
And go, Sir Paris. Everyone prepare
To follow this fair corse unto her grave.
The heavens do lour upon you for some ill:[35]
Move them no more by crossing their high will.   95
    [*They place rosemary on* JULIET'S *body and close the
                bed-curtains. Exeunt all except* NURSE

the label to another deed [22]
(IV.i.57)

mandrake
(IV.iii.47)

a cook
(IV.ii.2)

174

I do remember an apothecary[13]
(V.i.37)

As violently as hasty powder fired[26]
Doth hurry from the fatal cannon's womb
(V.i.64 – 65)

Enter Musicians

FIRST MUSICIAN

Faith, we may put up[36] our pipes and be gone.

NURSE

irony Honest good fellows, ah, put up, put up,
For well you know this is a pitiful case.[37]

FIRST MUSICIAN

Ay, by my troth, the case may be amended.[38]

[*Exit* NURSE

Enter PETER

PETER

Musicians, O musicians, "Heart's ease", "Heart's ease"![39]   100
O, and[40] you will have me live, play "Heart's ease".

FIRST MUSICIAN

Why "Heart's ease"?

---

36 *put up* – "pack away in their cases".

37 *a pitiful case* – "a sad state of affairs".

38 *the case . . . amended* – "the case does need repair". He is talking about his instrument case, taking the Nurse's *case* in the wrong sense.

39 *"Heart's ease"* was a popular song of the time.

40 *and* – "If".

41 *"Mў heart is full"*. These were the first words of another popular song.

42 *merry dump*. A *dump* is a sad tune. A *merry dump* is thus an impossibility.

43 *give it you soundly* – (a) "pay you out thoroughly", (b) "pay you out musically".

44 *gleek*. To "give someone the gleek" was to mock him.

45 *give you the minstrel* – "call you a minstrel". *Minstrel* was a term of contempt.

46 *give you the serving-creature* – "call you a slave".

47 *carry* – "endure".

48 *crotchets* – (a) "musical notes", (b) "strange ideas".

49 *I 'll re . . . fa you. Re* and *fa* are the second and fourth notes in the musical scale.

50 *note*. Peter plays on the two meanings, "musical note", "take note of".

PETER

O musicians, because my heart itself plays "My heart is
  full" [41]
O play me some merry dump[42] to comfort me.

FIRST MUSICIAN

Not a dump, we. 'T is no time to play now.   105

PETER

You will not then?

FIRST MUSICIAN

No.

PETER

I will then give it you soundly.[43]

FIRST MUSICIAN

What will you give us?

PETER

No money, on my faith, but the gleek.[44] I will give you   110
the minstrel.[45]

FIRST MUSICIAN

Then will I give you the serving-creature.[46]

PETER

Then will I lay the serving-creature's dagger on your
  pate.*head*
I will carry[47] no crotchets.[48] I 'll re you, I 'll fa you.[49]
Do you note me?[50]   115

177

FIRST MUSICIAN

And you re us and fa us, you note us.[51]

SECOND MUSICIAN

Pray you, put up your dagger, and put out[52] your wit.

PETER

Then have at you with my wit![53] I will dry-beat[54] you
with an iron wit,[55] and put up my iron dagger. Answer
me like men: 120

>   When griping grief the heart doth wound,
>   And doleful dumps the mind oppress,
>   Then music with her silver sound –

Why "silver sound"? Why "music with her silver
sound"? What say you, Simon Catling?[56]   125

FIRST MUSICIAN

Marry, sir, because silver hath a sweet sound.

PETER

Pretty![57] What say you, Hugh Rebeck?

---

51 *you note us* – "you mark us with
   musical notes". To *note* was to mark
   a book of music with the musical
   notes.
52 *put up . . . your wit* – "put away your
   dagger and put out the light of your
   wit". Peter takes *put out* in its other
   sense, "bring out".
53 *have at you with my wit!* "I shall attack
   you with my wit".
54 *dry-beat* – "beat without drawing
   blood".
55 *iron wit* – "dull wit".

56 *Catling*. The names which Peter in-
   vents for the musicians are fitting ones.
   A *catling* is a string used in wind
   instruments; a *rebeck* (line 126) is a
   violin, and a *soundpost* is a piece of
   wood used in the making of violins
   to support the body of the instrument.
57 *Pretty!* – "A clever answer".
58 *sound for silver* – "play for money".
59 *I cry you mercy* – "I beg your pardon".
60 *say* – "speak".
61 *have no gold for sounding* – (a) "do not
   get gold for playing", (b) "have no
   gold for testing".
62 *stay* – "wait for".

178

SECOND MUSICIAN

I say "silver sound" because musicians sound for silver.[58]

PETER

Pretty too! What say you, James Soundpost?

THIRD MUSICIAN

Faith, I know not what to say.   130

PETER

O, I cry you mercy![59] You are the singer. I will say[60] for
you. It is "music with her silver sound" because musicians
have no gold for sounding.[61]
        Then music with her silver sound
        With speedy help doth lend redress.   135

                         [*Exit* PETER

FIRST MUSICIAN

What a pestilent knave is this same!

SECOND MUSICIAN

Hang him, Jack! Come we 'll in here, tarry for the
mourners, and stay[62] dinner.

                         [*Exeunt*

(V.i) Balthasar, Romeo's servant, reaches him in Mantua and tells him that Juliet is dead. Romeo sends him to hire horses for their journey back to Verona that night, and buys poison from an apothecary, intending to take it when he has joined Juliet in the tomb.

1 *flattering truth of sleep* – "honesty of my pleasant dreams".

2 *presage ... at hand* – "are a sign of some good news that I am about to hear (*at hand*)". The irony (see Introduction, p. xvi) here is particularly painful to the audience who know that the news which Romeo is about to hear is the reverse of *joyful*; the fact that Romeo is filled with joy at his dreams makes the blow he is about to receive all the more bitter.

3 *My bosom's ... throne* – "Love (*my bosom's lord*) reigns joyfully in my heart (*his throne*)".

4 *in* – "into".

5 *how sweet (line 10) ... in joy* – "how sweet is love itself, when mere dreams of love (*love's shadows*) are so joyful".

6 *she is well*, i.e. because she is in heaven.

7 *Capel's*, i.e. Capulet's.

8 *presently took post* – "Immediately started out with post-horses". Post-horses were changed at inns on a traveller's route, so that he could travel without delay.

9 *did leave it for my office* – "left me the duty (*office*) of bringing you any news".

180

ACT FIVE

Scene I. A street in Mantua.

Enter ROMEO

ROMEO

If I may trust the flattering truth of sleep,[1]
My dreams presage some joyful news at hand;[2]
My bosom's lord sits lightly in his throne,[3]
And all this day an unaccustomed spirit
Lifts me above the ground with cheerful thoughts.   5
I dreamt my lady came and found me dead –
Strange dream, that gives a dead man leave to think! –
And breathed such life with kisses in[4] my lips
That I revived and was an emperor.
Ah me! how sweet is love itself possessed,   10
When but love's shadows are so rich in joy![5]

Enter BALTHASAR

News from Verona! How now, Balthasar?
Dost thou not bring me letters from the Friar?
How doth my lady? Is my father well?
How fares my Juliet? That I ask again,   15
For nothing can be ill if she be well.

BALTHASAR *euphemism*

Then she is well,[6] and nothing can be ill.
Her body sleeps in Capel's[7] monument,
And her immortal part with angels lives.
I saw her laid low in her kindred's vault,   20
And presently took post[8] to tell it you.
O pardon me for bringing these ill news,
Since you did leave it for my office,[9] sir.

ROMEO

Is it e'en so? Then I defy you, stars![10]
Thou knowest my lodging. Get me ink and paper,   25
And hire post-horses. I will hence to-night.

BALTHASAR

I do beseech you, sir, have patience.
Your looks are pale and wild, and do import
Some misadventure.[11]

ROMEO

                    Tush, thou art deceived.
Leave me, and do the thing I bid thee do.   30
Hast thou no letters to me from the Friar?

BALTHASAR

No, my good lord.

ROMEO

                    No matter; get thee gone,
And hire those horses. I 'll be with thee straight.
                                   [*Exit* BALTHASAR

---

10 *I defy you, stars.* It was widely believed that certain stars ruled each person's fate. Romeo declares that he will not wait for the stars to rule his life, but will take it into his own hands.

11 *import/Some misadventure* – "suggest that some misfortune is about to happen".

12 *Let's see for means* – "Let me think how to arrange it".

13 *apothecary*, one who sold drugs and medicines.

14 *which late I noted* – "whom I recently noticed".

15 *weeds* – "clothes".

16 *overwhelming* – "overhanging".

17 *Culling of simples* – "gathering herbs used in medicine (*simples*)".

18 *account* – "number".

19 *cakes of roses*, i.e. roses pressed into the form of cakes and used as a perfume.

20 *thinly . . . a show* – "spread out thinly to look more impressive".

21 *Whose sale . . . in Mantua* – "the sale of which (i.e. *poison*) in Mantua is punished by immediate death".

22 *caitiff* – "miserable".

23 *forerun my need* – "expressed my need before it arose". Note the play on *need* and *needy* (line 54).

24 *ducats*, gold or silver coins worth about one-third of a pound sterling.

25 *soon-speeding gear* – "stuff which will work quickly".

He doesn't waste in asking what & why, he wants action

Well, Juliet, I will lie with thee to-night. *being with her in death*
Let's see for means.[12] O mischief, thou art swift   35
To enter in the thoughts of desperate men!
I do remember an apothecary,[13]
And hereabouts 'a dwells, which late I noted[14]
In tattered weeds,[15] with overwhelming[16] brows,   *He was thin*
Culling of simples.[17] Meagre were his looks: *wearing tattered* 40
Sharp misery had worn him to the bones;   *clothes gathering*
And in his needy shop a tortoise hung,   *herbs*
An alligator stuffed, and other skins
Of ill-shaped fishes; and about his shelves
A beggarly account[18] of empty boxes,   45
Green earthen pots, bladders, and musty seeds,
Remnants of packthread, and old cakes of roses,[19]
Were thinly scattered to make up a show.[20]
Noting this penury, to myself I said:
"An if a man did need a poison now,   50
Whose sale is present death in Mantua,[21]
Here lives a caitiff[22] wretch would sell it him."
O this same thought did but forerun my need,[23]
And this same needy man must sell it me.
As I remember, this should be the house.   55
Being holiday, the beggar's shop is shut.
What ho! apothecary!

Enter APOTHECARY

APOTHECARY

Who calls so loud?

ROMEO

Come hither, man. I see that thou art poor.
[*He shows him a bag of money*] Hold, there is forty
    ducats:[24] let me have
A dram of poison, such soon-speeding gear[25]   60

183

As will disperse itself through all the veins,
That the life-weary taker may fall dead,
And that the trunk may be discharged of breath
As violently as hasty powder fired[26]
Doth hurry from the fatal cannon's womb.   65

APOTHECARY

Such mortal drugs I have, but Mantua's law
Is death to any he[27] that utters[28] them.

ROMEO

Art thou so bare and full of wretchedness,
And fear'st to die? Famine is in thy cheeks;
Need and oppression[29] starveth in thy eyes,[30]   70
Contempt and beggary[31] hangs upon thy back.
The world is not thy friend, nor the world's law:
The world affords no law to make thee rich;
Then be not poor, but break it[32] and take this.

APOTHECARY

[*Taking the money*] My poverty, but not my will,
consents.   75

---

26 *hasty powder fired* – "gunpowder which explodes quickly when lighted".

27 *any he* – "any man".

28 *utters* – "offers for sale".

29 *oppression* – "distress".

30 *starveth in thy eyes* – "show in the hungry look in your eyes".

31 *Contempt and beggary* – "contemptible beggary". He refers to the ragged clothes of the apothecary.

32 *it*, i.e. the law.

33 *I sell thee poison*, i.e. in giving him gold.

34 *get thyself in flesh* – "grow fat".

35 *cordial*, a medicine for the heart.

(V.ii) Friar John, whom Friar Lawrence had sent to Mantua to tell Romeo of the plans for Juliet's escape, comes to report that, because of a plague in the city, he has not been able to leave Verona to deliver his message. Friar Lawrence plans to release Juliet from the tomb and hide her in his cell until the arrival of Romeo, to whom he will send another letter.

1 *if his mind be writ* – "if he has written down what is in his mind".

184

ROMEO

I pay thy poverty and not thy will.

APOTHECARY

[*Giving him the poison*] Put this in any liquid thing you
will
And drink it off, and if you had the strength
Of twenty men, it would dispatch you straight.

ROMEO

There is thy gold: worse poison to men's souls,   80
Doing more murder in this loathsome world,
Than these poor compounds that thou may'st not sell.
I sell thee poison:³³ thou hast sold me none.
Farewell; buy food, and get thyself in flesh.³⁴
                                            [*Exit* APOTHECARY
Come, cordial³⁵ and not poison, go with me   85
To Juliet's grave, for there must I use thee.
                                                          [*Exit*

Scene II. Friar Lawrence's cell.

Enter FRIAR JOHN

FRIAR JOHN

Holy Franciscan! Friar! brother, ho!

Enter FRIAR LAWRENCE *from his inner room*

FRIAR LAWRENCE

This same should be the voice of Friar John.
Welcome from Mantua. What says Romeo?
Or, if his mind be writ,¹ give me his letter.

FRIAR JOHN

Going to find a barefoot brother out,   5
One of our order, to associate me[2]
Here in this city visiting the sick,
And finding him, the searchers of the town,[3]
Suspecting that we both were in a house[4]
Where the infectious pestilence did reign,   10
Sealed up the doors, and would not let us forth,
So that my speed to Mantua there was stayed.[5]

FRIAR LAWRENCE

Who bare[6] my letter then to Romeo?

2 *associate me* – "go with me". Friars usually had to travel in pairs.
3 *searchers of the town* – "officials responsible for the town's health".
4 *a house*, i.e. a friary, where the brothers lived.
5 *stayed* – "hindered". The authorities in Shakespeare's London locked the doors of houses of those suffering from the plague, in order to prevent the spread of the disease.

6 *bare* – "carried".
7 *nice* – "unimportant".
8 *charge/ Of dear import* – "instructions of great importance".
9 *iron crow* – a bar of iron used for bending, breaking or moving objects.
10 *beshrew me much* – "scold me severely".
11 *accidents* – "events".

(V.iii) Paris comes to visit Juliet's tomb. His page, hiding in the churchyard, whistles to warn him of the approach of Romeo and Balthasar, and he, too, hides. Romeo gives Balthasar a letter to deliver to his father, and tells him to go right away from the vault, but Balthasar suspects Romeo's intentions and hides in the churchyard to see what happens. As Romeo breaks open the gate of the vault, Paris comes forward and tries to arrest him, ignoring Romeo's appeals that he should go away. They fight and Paris is killed, and at his request Romeo lays him beside Juliet's tomb. Romeo kisses Juliet for the last time, drinks the poison, and dies, just before Friar Lawrence reaches the vault. He enters just as Juliet wakes and discovers the bodies of Romeo and Paris. They hear the voices of the watch, who have been summoned from the city by the page, but Juliet refuses to leave, and Friar Lawrence hurries away alone. Juliet kisses Romeo, hoping that the poison

continued on page 188

1 *stand aloof* – "keep at a distance".
2 *I would not* – "I do not want".

FRIAR JOHN

I could not send it – here it is again –
Nor get a messenger to bring it thee,   15
So fearful were they of infection.

FRIAR LAWRENCE

Unhappy fortune! By my brotherhood,
The letter was not nice,[7] but full of charge
Of dear import,[8] and the neglecting it
May do much danger. Friar John, go hence;   20
Get me an iron crow,[9] and bring it straight
Unto my cell.

FRIAR JOHN

Brother, I 'll go and bring it thee.

[*Exit* FRIAR JOHN

FRIAR LAWRENCE

Now must I to the monument alone.
Within this three hours will fair Juliet wake.   25
She will beshrew me much[10] that Romeo
Hath had no notice of these accidents.[11]
But I will write again to Mantua,
And keep her at my cell till Romeo come.
Poor living corse, closed in a dead man's tomb!   30

[*Exit*

Scene III. The Capulets' vault.

Enter PARIS *and his* Page *at the entrance*

PARIS

Give me thy torch, boy. Hence, and stand aloof.[1]
Yet put it out for I would not[2] be seen.

Under yond yew trees lay thee all along,[3]
Holding thy ear close to the hollow ground,[4]
So shall no foot upon the churchyard tread,   5
Being loose, unfirm with digging up of graves,
But thou shalt hear it. Whistle then to me,
As signal that thou hear'st some thing approach.
Give me those flowers. Do as I bid thee, go.

PAGE

[*Aside*] I am almost afraid to stand[5] alone   10
Here in the churchyard, yet I will adventure.
                              [*He hides behind the trees*

PARIS

[*To* JULIET] Sweet flower, with flowers thy bridal bed
   I strew –
O woe, thy canopy[6] is dust and stones –   ·

---

on his lips will kill her, but as the voices come near she stabs herself with
Romeo's dagger, and dies beside him. The watch arrive, search the churchyard, and arrest the Friar and Balthasar. The Prince enters the vault, closely
followed by the Capulets and Montagues. Friar Lawrence tells the story of
the lovers, and the truth of his account is proved by Romeo's letter. The
Prince traces the source of these tragic events to the hatred between the two
families, and at last the Montagues and Capulets are reconciled, and determine to build golden statues to the memory of Romeo and Juliet.

3/ *Under yond yew trees . . . along* – "Lie
   down at full length (*lay thee all along*)
   under those yew trees". Wooden
   constructions to represent trees would
   be placed at the side of the stage for
   this scene.
4/ *hollow ground*, i.e. because of the holes
   made in it by graves and tombs.
5/ *stand* – "remain".
6/ *thy canopy* – "the curtain over your
   bed". In Shakespeare's time beds
   often had upright posts at each corner,
   supporting a *canopy*.

7 *sweet* – "perfumed".
8/ *wanting* – "lacking".
9/ *dear employment* – "an important business".
10/ *jealous* – "suspicious". By telling this
    lie about the ring, Romeo makes
    Balthasar more suspicious.
11/ *hungry churchyard*, i.e. greedy for
    bodies.
12 *more inexorable far* – "much more de-
    termined".

Which with sweet[7] water nightly I will dew,
Or, wanting[8] that, with tears distilled by moans.   15
The obsequies that I for thee will keep,
Nightly shall be to strew thy grave and weep.
                              [*The* Page *whistles*
The boy gives warning; something doth approach.
What cursèd foot wanders this way to-night,
To cross my obsequies and true love's rite?   20
What, with a torch? Muffle me, night, a while.
                              [*He hides in the churchyard*

Enter ROMEO *and* BALTHASAR *with a torch,*
                mattock and crowbar

ROMEO

Give me that mattock and the wrenching iron.
Hold, take this letter; early in the morning
See thou deliver it to my lord and father.
Give me the light. Upon thy life I charge thee,   25
Whate'er thou hear'st or seest, stand all aloof,
And do not interrupt me in my course.
Why I descend into this bed of death
Is partly to behold my lady's face,
But chiefly to take thence from her dead finger   30
A precious ring, a ring that I must use
In dear employment.[9] Therefore hence, be gone.
But if thou, jealous,[10] dost return to pry
In what I farther shall intend to do,
By heaven, I will tear thee joint by joint,   35
And strew this hungry churchyard[11] with thy limbs.
The time and my intents are savage, wild,
More fierce and more inexorable far[12]
Than empty tigers or the roaring sea.

BALTHASAR

I will be gone, sir, and not trouble ye.   40

The setting is indicative

ROMEO

So[13] shalt thou show me friendship. [*Gives him money*]
   Take thou that.
Live and be prosperous; and farewell, good fellow.

BALTHASAR

[*Aside*] For all this same,[14] I 'll hide me hereabout.
His looks I fear, and his intents I doubt.
   [*He withdraws and hides in the churchyard*

ROMEO

[*He smashes at the gate with the crowbar*] Thou
   detestable maw,[15] thou womb of death,   — *strong express* 45
Gorged with the dearest morsel of the earth;
Thus I enforce thy rotten jaws to open,   *force tomb to open*
And in despite[16] I 'll cram thee with more food.[17]   *clearly shows*
                                                      us Romeo's intentio

PARIS

This is that banished haughty Montague
That murdered my love's cousin, with which grief   *He thinks Juliet* 50
It is supposed the fair creature died,   *died " of brother-love for Tybalt*
And here is come to do some villainous shame   *He thinks Romeo*
To the dead bodies. I will apprehend him.   *comes to deverse thi*
                                   [*He comes forward*
Stop thy unhallowed toil, vile Montague!
   unholy

---

13 *So* – "In that way".
14 *For all this same* – "Despite all he says".
15 *maw* – "stomach", i.e. the vault.
16 *in despite* – "in defiance".
17 *more food*, i.e. his own body.
18 *Can vengeance . . . death?* He means,
   "What further vengeance can you
   take, having killed Tybalt?"
19 *thou must die*. Paris refers to the Prince's
   order that Romeo will be put to death
   if he returns to Verona.

20 *these gone* – "the people buried here".
   He is warning Paris that he may join
   them if he does not go away.
21 *affright* – "frighten".
22 *armed against myself*, i.e. with the
   poison.
23 *defy thy conjurations* – "reject your
   appeals".
24 *for a felon* – "as a law-breaker".
   felony – breaking a law

Can vengeance be pursued further than death?[18]   55
Condemnéd villain, I do apprehend thee.
Obey, and go with me, for thou must die.[19]

ROMEO

I must indeed, and therefore came I hither.
Good gentle youth, tempt not a desperate man.
Fly hence and leave me. Think upon these gone;[20]   60
Let them affright[21] thee. I beseech thee, youth,
Put not another sin upon my head
By urging me to fury. O be gone!
By heaven, I love thee better than myself,
For I come hither armed against myself.[22]   65
Stay not; be gone; live, and hereafter say
A madman's mercy bid thee run away.

PARIS

I do defy thy conjurations[23]
And apprehend thee for a felon[24] here.

ROMEO

Wilt thou provoke me? Then have at thee, boy!   70

[*They fight*

PAGE

O Lord, they fight! I will go call the watch.

[*Exit* PAGE

PARIS

[*Falling*] O I am slain! If thou be merciful,
Open the tomb; lay me with Juliet.

ROMEO

In faith, I will. Let me peruse this face.
Mercutio's kinsman, noble County Paris!   75
What said my man when my betosséd soul

191

He shows compassion by fulfilling Paris' offer to lay him next to Juliet

Did not attend him²⁵ as we rode? I think
He told me Paris should have married Juliet.
Said he not so? Or did I dream it so?
Or am I mad, hearing him talk of Juliet,   80
To think it was so? O give me thy hand,
One writ with me in sour misfortune's book.²⁶
I'll bury thee in a triumphant²⁷ grave.
A grave? O no, a lantern,²⁸ slaughtered youth;
For here lies Juliet, and her beauty makes   85
This vault a feasting presence²⁹ full of light.
Death, lie thou there, by a dead man³⁰ interred.

This shows Romeo's confusion & state of mind. He can't see reality clearly.

Personification

    [*He lays* PARIS *beside* JULIET'S *tomb*]

How oft when men are at the point of death
Have they been merry, which their keepers³¹ call
A lightning³² before death! O, how may I   90
Call this a lightning? O my love, my wife!
Death, that hath sucked the honey of thy breath,

25 *betosséd* (line 76) . . . *attend him* – "my disturbed mind did not pay attention to him".

26 *one writ . . . misfortune's book.* Romeo imagines a book in which the names of those who suffer misfortune are written.

27 *triumphant* – "splendid".

28 *lantern*, the windowed tower at the top of a building to admit light.

29 *a feasting presence* – "a royal room of state (*presence*) set out for a feast".

30 *a dead man.* Romeo is referring to himself.

31 *keepers* – either nurses at sick-beds, or keepers of condemned prisoners.

32 *lightning.* Flashes of lightning were thought to foretell death. There is also play on *lightening*, a raising of the spirits which some people feel when they are about to die.

33 *his*, i.e. Romeo's own youth.

34 *Why art thou yet so fair?* There is cruel dramatic irony in Romeo's unaware-ness that Juliet, who looks as beautiful to him as she always did, is really alive.

35 *unsubstantial* – "bodiless".

36 *pallet* – "bed".

37 *set up my everlasting rest* – (a) "rest for ever", (b) "stake everything". Compare IV.v.6 and the note to it.

38 *shake the yoke . . . stars* – "shake off the burden which my unfavourable (*inauspicious*) stars place upon me".

39 *dateless* – "endless".

40 *engrossing Death* – (a) "Death who copies out the bargain in legal handwriting", (b) "Death who gains complete possession".

41 *conduct* – "guide".

42 *unsavoury* – "hateful".

43 *dashing rocks* – "rocks which break (*dash*) his bark (i.e. his life) to pieces".

44 *seasick* – "sick of the sea (of life)".

45 *speed* – "assistance".

46 *stumbled at graves.* To stumble when on an important journey was thought to bring bad luck.

SCENE III]

Hath had no power yet upon thy beauty.
Thou art not conquered, beauty's ensign yet *by death*
Is crimson in thy lips and in thy cheeks,   95
And death's pale flag is not advancéd there. *She looks as if she is not dead*
vast Tybalt, liest thou there in thy bloody sheet? → *violent death like Paris*
O, what more favour can I do to thee
Than with that hand that cut thy youth in twain
To sunder his[33] that was thine enemy?   100
Forgive me, cousin. Ah, dear Juliet, *He has killed Juliet by killing Tybalt, he*
Why art thou yet so fair?[34] Shall I believe *killed her indirectly*
That unsubstantial[35] Death is amorous, *and the best thing he can do is to kill himself.*
And that the lean abhorréd monster keeps *Death wants you*
Thee here in dark to be his paramour? *for himself*   105
For fear of that I still will stay with thee,
And never from this pallet[36] of dim night
Depart again. Here, here will I remain,
With worms that are thy chambermaids. O, here *Inadds wher tidy up the room*
Will I set up my everlasting rest,[37] *euphemism ⇒ death* 110
And shake the yoke of inauspicious stars[38]
From this world-wearied flesh. Eyes, look your last;
Arms take your last embrace; and lips, O you,
The doors of breath, seal with a righteous kiss
A dateless[39] bargain to engrossing Death.[40]   115
Come, bitter conduct;[41] come, unsavoury[42] guide,
Thou desperate pilot, now at once run on *pilot of his life, end*
winning The dashing rocks[43] thy seasick[44] weary bark. *his life*
tossed Here 's to my love. [*Drinks the poison*] O true
  one apothecary!
Thy drugs are quick. Thus with a kiss I die. *romantic, dramatic* 120

[*He dies*

Enter FRIAR LAWRENCE *at the gate of the vault,
with a lantern, crowbar and spade*

FRIAR LAWRENCE

Saint Francis be my speed![45] How oft to-night
Have my old feet stumbled at graves![46] Who's there?

he has been there so often

193

BALTHASAR

Here's one, a friend, and one that knows you well.

FRIAR LAWRENCE

Bliss be upon you. Tell me, good my friend,
What torch is yond that vainly[47] lends his light   125
To grubs and eyeless skulls? As I discern
It burneth in the Capels' monument.

BALTHASAR

It doth so, holy sir; and there 's my master,
One that you love.

FRIAR LAWRENCE

Who is it?

BALTHASAR

Romeo.

FRIAR LAWRENCE

How long hath he been there?

BALTHASAR

Full half an hour.   130

FRIAR LAWRENCE

Go with me to the vault.

BALTHASAR

I dare not, sir.
My master knows not but I am gone hence,[48]

---

47 *vainly* – "uselessly".
48 *knows not but I am gone hence* –
   "believes that I have gone away".
49 *unthrifty* – "unfortunate".
50 *masterless* – "without their owners".

51 *discoloured* – "stained with blood".
52 *comfortable* – "comforting".
53 *unnatural sleep*, i.e. because there is no
   waking from it.

194

And fearfully did menace me with death
If I did stay to look on his intents.

FRIAR LAWRENCE

Stay then; I 'll go alone. Fear comes upon me.   135
O much I fear some ill unthrifty[49] thing.

BALTHASAR

As I did sleep under this yew tree here,
I dreamt my master and another fought,
And that my master slew him.

FRIAR LAWRENCE
                                        Romeo!
Alack, alack, what blood is this which stains   140
The stony entrance of this sepulchre?
What mean these masterless[50] and gory swords
To lie discoloured[51] by this place of peace?
                                [*He enters the vault*

Romeo! O pale! Who else? What, Paris, too?
And steeped in blood? Ah, what an unkind hour   145
Is guilty of this lamentable chance!
                                [JULIET *wakes*
The lady stirs.

JULIET

O comfortable[52] Friar, where is my lord?
I do remember well where I should be,
And there I am. Where is my Romeo?   150
                [*Approaching voices are heard*

FRIAR LAWRENCE

I hear some noise, lady. Come from that nest
Of death, contagion, and unnatural sleep.[53]

195

A greater power[54] than we can contradict
Hath thwarted our intents. Come, come away.
Thy husband in thy bosom there lies dead,   155
And Paris too. Come, I 'll dispose of thee
Among a sisterhood of holy nuns.
Stay not to question, for the watch is coming.
Come, go, good Juliet; I dare no longer stay.

JULIET

Go, get thee hence, for I will not away.   160

[*Exit* FRIAR LAWRENCE

What 's here? A cup closed in my true love's hand?
Poison, I see, hath been his timeless[55] end.
O churl![56] drunk all, and left no friendly drop
To help me after? I will kiss thy lips:
Haply[57] some poison yet doth hang on them   165
To make me die with a restorative[58]
[*Kisses him*] Thy lips are warm.

The Page *and the* Watch *approach the vault*

FIRST WATCHMAN

Lead, boy. Which way?

---

54 *A greater power*, i.e. God.
55 *timeless* – (a) "eternal"; (b) "coming
   before its proper time".
56 *churl* – "mean fellow". Juliet uses the
   word affectionately.
57 *Haply* – "perhaps".
58 *a restorative* – (a) "a healing medicine",
   i.e. the kiss; (b) "a medicine which
   brings me back (restores me) to
   Romeo again".

59 *This*, i.e. her breast.
60 *attach* – "arrest".
61 *ground whereon ... lie* – "earth on
   which these woes (i.e. the dead
   bodies) lie". In line 180 *ground* means
   "cause".
62 *circumstance* – "detailed knowledge".

196

JULIET

Yea, noise? Then I'll be brief. [*She takes* ROMEO'S *dagger*]
   O happy dagger!
This[59] is thy sheath; there rust, and let me die.   170
   [*She stabs herself, falls on* ROMEO'S *body and dies*

The Page *and the* Watch *enter the vault*

PAGE

This is the place; there, where the torch doth burn.

FIRST WATCHMAN

The ground is bloody. Search about the churchyard.
Go, some of you: whoe'er you find, attach.[60]
                    [*Some* Watchmen *go out*
Pitiful sight! Here lies the County slain,
And Juliet bleeding, warm and newly dead,   175
Who here hath lain this two days buriéd.
Go, tell the Prince, run to the Capulets,
Raise up the Montagues. Some others search.
                    [*More* Watchmen *go out*
We see the ground whereon these woes do lie,[61]
But the true ground of all these piteous woes   180
We cannot without circumstance[62] descry.

Re-enter some of the Watch *with* BALTHASAR

SECOND WATCHMAN

Here's Romeo's man; we found him in the churchyard.

FIRST WATCHMAN

Hold him in safety till the Prince come hither.

Re-enter another Watchman *with* FRIAR LAWRENCE

197

THIRD WATCHMAN

Here is a Friar that trembles, sighs, and weeps.
We took this mattock and this spade from him,   185
As he was coming from this churchyard's side.[63]

FIRST WATCHMAN

A great suspicion! Stay[64] the Friar too.

Enter PRINCE ESCALUS *and* Attendants

PRINCE

What misadventure is so early up,
That calls our person from our morning rest?

Enter CAPULET *and* LADY CAPULET

CAPULET

What should it be[65] that is so shrieked abroad?   190

LADY CAPULET

O, the people in the streets cry "Romeo",
Some "Juliet", and some "Paris", and all run
With open outcry toward our monument.

PRINCE

What fear is this which startles in your ears?[66]

---

63 *this churchyard's side* – "this side of the churchyard".
64 *Stay* – "Detain".
65 *What should it be* – "What can it be".
66 *startles in your ears* – "alarms you".
67 *instruments* – "tools".
68 *mista'en* – (*mistaken*) "taken the wrong turning".

69 *house*, i.e. the sheath of Romeo's dagger, worn at his back.
70 *warns* – "summons".
71 *tonight* – "last night". Compare I.iv.50 and the note to it.

198

FIRST WATCHMAN

Sovereign, here lies the County Paris slain;   195
And Romeo dead; and Juliet, dead before,
Warm and new killed.

PRINCE

Search, seek, and know how this foul murder comes.

FIRST WATCHMAN

Here is a Friar, and slaughtered Romeo's man,
With instruments[67] upon them fit to open   200
These dead men's tombs.

CAPULET

O heavens! O wife, look how our daughter bleeds!
This dagger has mista'en,[68] for lo, his house[69]
Is empty on the back of Montague,
And is mis-sheathéd in my daughter's bosom.   205

LADY CAPULET

O me! this sight of death is as a bell
That warns[70] my old age to a sepulchre.

Enter MONTAGUE

PRINCE

Come, Montague; for thou art early up
To see thy son and heir more early down.

MONTAGUE

Alas, my liege, my wife is dead to-night;[71]   210
Grief of my son's exile hath stopped her breath.
What further woe conspires against mine age?

PRINCE

Look, and thou shalt see.

MONTAGUE

[*Seeing* ROMEO] O thou untaught![72] what manners is in
    this,
To press before thy father to a grave?   215

PRINCE

Seal up the mouth of outrage[73] for a while,
Till we can clear these ambiguities,[74]
And know their spring, their head, their true descent,[75]
And then will I be general of your woes,
And lead you even to death.[76] Meantime forbear,   220

---

72 *untaught* – "ignorant fellow". Romeo
has not observed the rule that youth
should allow age to go first. Montague does not mean this seriously.

73 *the mouth of outrage* – "the expression
of your violent grief".

74 *clear these ambiguities* – "explain these
uncertainties".

75 *their spring, their head, their true descent.*
All these terms suggest origin or
source. They are used of water, which
from its *spring* or *head*, *descends* to its
mouth (line 216); they are also used of
a family and its relationships. Since
the trouble has been the quarrel of two
families, descending down through
time, and growing greater, as a river
does as it gets further from its source,
we see how fitting this complicated
imagery is here.

76 *then will I (line 219) . . . death* – "then
I will lead you (*be general*) in the expression of your grief, even as far as
death". In this military metaphor the
Prince suggests that they will all die of
grief.

77 *let mischance be slave to patience* –
"patiently control your grief at this
misfortune".

78 *the parties of suspicion* – "those suspected".

79 *I am . . . do*·*least* – "I am the chief
suspect, though least powerful".

80 *make against me* – "tell against me, are
unfavourable to me".

81 *to impeach and purge* – "to accuse and
clear myself" (from suspicion).

82 *Myself condemnéd and myself excused* –
"condemned by myself and found
innocent by myself".

83 *my short date of breath* – "the short time
I have to live".

84 *You*, i.e. Capulet.

85 *perforce* – "by force".

86 *wrought* – "produced".

87 *writ* – "wrote".

88 *as* – "on".

200

And let mischance be slave to patience.[77]
Bring forth the parties of suspicion.[78]

FRIAR LAWRENCE *and* BALTHASAR *are brought forward*

FRIAR LAWRENCE

I am the greatest; able to do least,[79]
Yet most suspected, as the time and place
Doth make against me,[80] of this direful murder;   225
And here I stand, both to impeach and purge,[81]
Myself condemnéd and myself excused.[82]

PRINCE

Then say at once what thou dost know in this.

FRIAR LAWRENCE

I will be brief, for my short date of bréath[83]
Is not so long as is a tedious tale.   230
Romeo there dead, was husband to that Juliet;
And she, there dead, that Romeo's faithful wife.
I married them; and their stolen marriage day
Was Tybalt's doomsday, whose untimely death
Banished the new-made bridegroom from this city;   235
For whom, and not for Tybalt, Juliet pined.
You,[84] to remove that siege of grief from her,
Betrothed and would have married her perforce[85]
To County Paris. Then comes she to me,
And with wild looks bid me devise some mean   240
To rid her from this second marriage,
Or in my cell there would she kill herself.
Then gave I her, so tutored by my art,
A sleeping potion, which so took effect
As I intended, for it wrought[86] on her   245
The form of death. Meantime I writ[87] to Romeo
That he should hither come as [88] this dire night

To help to take her from her ~~borrowed~~ *temporary* grave,
Being the time the potion's force should cease.
But he which bore my letter, Friar John, 250
Was stayed[89] by accident, and yesternight[90]
Returned my letter back. Then all alone,
At the prefixéd[91] hour of her waking,
Came I to take her from her kindred's vault,
Meaning to keep her closely[92] at my cell 255
Till I conveniently could send to[93] Romeo.
But when I came, some minute ere the time
Of her awakening, here untimely lay
The noble Paris and true Romeo dead.
She wakes, and I entreated her come forth 260
And bear this work of heaven with patience; *accept what has happen*
But then a noise did scare me from the tomb,
And she, too desperate, would not go with me,
But, as it seems, did violence on herself.
All this I know, and to the marriage 265
Her Nurse is privy,[94] and if aught[95] in this
Miscarried by my fault, let my old life
Be sacrificed some hour before his[96] time
Unto the rigour of severest law.

---

89 *stayed* – "delayed".
90 *yesternight* – "last night".
91 *prefixed* – "arranged beforehand".
92 *closely* – "secretly".
93 *could send to* – "could send a message to".
94 *to the marriage* (line *265*) . . . *privy* – "her Nurse has knowledge of the marriage".
95 *aught* – "anything".
96 *his* – "its".
97 *still* – "always".
98 *in post* – "in haste", by means of post-horses. See note to V.i.21.
99 *This letter he early bid me give* – "He told me to give this letter early to".
100 *going* – "as he was going".

101 *what made your master* – "what was your master doing".
102 *by and by* – "very soon".
103 *make good* – "prove the truth of".
104 *therewithal* – "with it".
105 *See what* (line *292*) . . . *with love* – "See what a whip (*scourge*) lashes (*is laid on*) your hatred, in that heaven finds a way (*finds means*) to kill your joys by means of love" (i.e. the love between Romeo and Juliet).
106 *winking at* – "closing my eyes to". Prince Escalus thinks that he too has been punished for not taking firm action to stop their *discords*.
107 *a brace of kinsmen*, Mercutio and Paris.

202

PRINCE *doesn't blame Friar Lawrence*

We still[97] have known thee for a holy man.   270
Where 's Romeo's man? What can he say to this?

BALTHASAR

I brought my master news of Juliet's death,
And then in post[98] he came from Mantua
To this same place, to this same monument.
This letter he early bid me give[99] his father,   275
And threatened me with death, going[100] in the vault,
If I departed not and left him there.

PRINCE

Give me the letter; I will look on it.
Where is the County's page that raised the watch?
                        [Page *comes forward*
Sirrah, what made your master[101] in this place?   280

PAGE

He came with flowers to strew his lady's grave,
And bid me stand aloof, and so I did.
Anon comes one with light to ope the tomb,
And by and by[102] my master drew on him,
And then I ran away to call the watch.   285

PRINCE

This letter doth make good[103] the Friar's words,
Their course of love, the tidings of her death;
And here he writes that he did buy a poison
Of a poor 'pothecary, and therewithal[104]
Came to this vault, to die and lie with Juliet.   290
Where be these enemies, Capulet, Montague?
See what a scourge is laid upon your hate,
That heaven finds means to kill your joys with love.[105]
And I, for winking at[106] your discords too,
Have lost a brace of kinsmen.[107] All are punished.   295

CAPULET

O brother Montague, give me thy hand. *a sign of friendship*
This[108] is my daughter's jointure,[109] for no more
Can I demand.

MONTAGUE

But I can give thee more,
For I will raise her statue in pure gold,
That whiles[110] Verona by that name is known,   300
There shall no figure at such rate be set
As that of true and faithful Juliet.

*A bit late
but at least
made up*

CAPULET

As rich shall Romeo's[111] by his lady's lie –
Poor sacrifices of our enmity.[112]

PRINCE

A glooming[113] peace this morning with it brings;   305
The sun for sorrow will not show his head.
Go hence, to have more talk of these sad things.
Some shall be pardoned, and some punishéd;
For never was a story of more woe
Than this of Juliet and her Romeo.   310

The final end of this feud but gloomy ": R+J [*Exeunt*
were sacrifice.

---

108 *This*, i.e. the handshake.
109 *jointure*, the possessions settled by the husband upon his wife at marriage.
110 *whiles* – "while".
111 *Romeo's*, i.e. his statue. Capulet will pay for a statue in gold of Romeo.

112 *Poor sacrifices of our enmity* – Either (a) "poor offerings to pay for our hatred", referring to the statues, or (b) "unfortunate sacrificial victims of our hatred" referring to Romeo and Juliet.
113 *glooming* – "gloomy".

204

HINTS TO EXAMINATION CANDIDATES
(Prepared by H. M. Hulme, M.A., Ph.D.)

This section is intended to offer some help to candidates who are studying *Romeo and Juliet* for such examinations as the School Certificate or G.C.E., Ordinary Level, and who are working alone. Actual questions from Cambridge papers are used as examples to show the kinds of question that may be found on most papers for examinations at this stage.

You will see first that you must know the story of the play in some detail. Secondly, you must give yourself practice in reading the questions carefully and answering exactly what is asked; *do not expect to find on any paper a question that you have already answered.* Thirdly, you must train yourself to write quickly enough to finish the work in the time allowed (30 minutes for each of these sample questions). Do not waste time, for example, in copying out the question.

See to it that you know beforehand which kinds of question you *must* do and which you *may* do. For some examinations (e.g. London) you must do one "context" question and you may also do an essay question on the set play; for others (e.g. Cambridge) you may have some choice between "context" and essay questions.

"CONTEXT" QUESTIONS

1. Sample question from Cambridge University General Certificate of Education, Ordinary Level, English Literature, Summer 1963. Choose **three** of the passages (*a*) to (*d*), and answer *briefly* the questions which follow:

(*a*) *Servant*. Now I'll tell you without asking: my master is the great rich Capulet; and if you be not of the house of Montagues, I pray come and crush a cup of wine.

  (i) On what errand has the servant been sent? What difficulty has he found in fulfilling the errand, and how has he overcome it?

 (ii) Describe the mood Romeo was in when he met the servant.

(iii) What does Benvolio now persuade Romeo to do, and why does Romeo consent? What is Benvolio's real purpose in seeking to persuade him?

205

(b) *Mercutio.* No, 'tis not so deep as a well, nor so wide as a church
door, but 'tis enough, 'twill serve. Ask for me tomorrow, and
you shall find me a grave man. I am peppered, I warrant, for this
world. A plague o' both your houses! Zounds, a dog, a rat, a
mouse, a cat, to scratch a man to death! A braggart, a rogue, a
villain, that fights by the book of arithmetic! Why the devil
came you between us? I was hurt under your arm.
Romeo. I thought all for the best.

   (i) Whom had Tybalt wished to fight, and why? Why had
       Mercutio fought Tybalt?
  (ii) Give, *in your own words*, Mercutio's impression of Tybalt's
       method of fighting, as it is conveyed in the passage.
 (iii) Give **one** reason why Romeo thought he had acted for the best.
  (iv) What impression have you gained from this passage of Mer-
       cutio's attitude to death?

(c) *Romeo.* There is thy gold – worse poison to men's souls,
     Doing more murder in this loathsome world
     Than these poor compounds that thou mayst not sell.
     I sell thee poison: thou hast sold me none.

   (i) Give **one** detail from Romeo's description of the apothecary,
       and **one** from his description of the shop.
  (ii) Re-write, in your own words, the first three lines of the passage
       (There is thy gold . . . thou mayst not sell).
 (iii) Upon what information is Romeo acting? What news should
       have reached him from Friar Lawrence, and why did it not
       reach him?

(d) *Juliet.* O comfortable friar! Where is my lord?
     I do remember well where I should be,
     And there I am. Where is my Romeo? (*Noise within*)
     Friar. I hear some noise. Lady, come from that nest
     Of death, contagion, and unnatural sleep;
     A greater power than we can contradict
     Hath thwarted our intents. Come, come away;
     Thy husband in thy bosom there lies dead.

(i) Give the meaning of "comfortable". What mistrust of the Friar's motive had Juliet expressed that had made her hesitate to take the potion he had given her?

(ii) Who are making the noise, and who has brought them to the tomb?

(iii) Explain the meaning of
"A greater power than we can contradict
Hath thwarted our intents."

NOTES ON POSSIBLE ANSWERS

(a)

(i) To invite a number of people to Capulet's house that night for supper and dancing. He cannot read, and has asked Romeo to read aloud to him the list of the guests' names.

(ii) He thought himself mad with love for Rosaline and was full of despair because she refused to love him or any other.

(iii) To go to Capulet's feast. Romeo consents because he knows that Rosaline is invited. Benvolio hopes to show Romeo that there are other girls more beautiful than Rosaline.

(b)

(i) Romeo, because Romeo had come uninvited to Capulet's feast. Because Romeo refused to fight and answered Tybalt's insults in a peaceable way.

(ii) Tybalt fought as if he had learned to fight by numbers. He tried to show his skill but was without real courage or energy.

(iii) Because the Prince had said that any further fighting between Capulets and Montagues would be punished by death.

(iv) Mercutio tries to meet death casually and with a joke, but he is really quite disgusted that he has to die because of an ancient quarrel between the two rival families.

(c)

(i) He was poor and thin with misery. On the shelves bits of rubbish and some empty boxes were "thinly scattered".

(ii) Take your money; (it is) money which in this hateful world does more harm to the souls of men than your poor drugs, which you are not allowed to sell, can do to their bodies.

207

(iii) News of Juliet's funeral brought by Romeo's servant. Romeo should have heard that Juliet would wake from her sleep after 42 hours. Friar John who was to bring this message was shut up in quarantine for fear of the plague.

2. Sample question from Cambridge University General Certificate of Education, Ordinary Level, English Literature, Summer 1962. Choose **three** of the passages (*a*) to (*d*) and answer *briefly* the questions which follow:

(*a*) *Capulet.* But Montague is bound as well as I,
  In penalty alike; and 'tis not hard, I think,
  For men so old as we to keep the peace.
Paris. Of honourable reckoning are you both,
  And pity 'tis you liv'd at odds so long.

  (i) What recent brawl has led Capulet and Montague to be "bound . . . in penalty"? Name the two people chiefly concerned in this brawl.
 (ii) What is the "penalty" and who imposed it?
(iii) Give an example, taken from a later scene, of an attempt by Capulet to keep the peace.
 (iv) What request is Paris about to make?

(*b*) *Friar Lawrence.* A pack of blessings lights upon thy back;
  Happiness courts thee in her best array;
  But, like a misbehav'd and sullen wench,
  Thou pout'st upon thy fortune and thy love.
  Take heed, take heed, for such die miserable.
  Go, get thee to thy love, as was decreed,
  Ascend her chamber, hence and comfort her.
  But look thou stay not till the watch be set.

  (i) Say briefly why Romeo is hiding in Friar Lawrence's cell. What news has the Friar just given him?
 (ii) What is the immediate cause of the Friar's rebuke of Romeo?
(iii) State briefly **two** of the "blessings" the Friar has just mentioned.
 (iv) Explain the point of the warning in the last line of the passage.

(c) *Juliet.* I met the youthful lord at Lawrence' cell,
And gave him what becomed love I might,
Not stepping o'er the bounds of modesty.
Capulet. Why, I am glad on't; this is well – stand up –
This is as't should be. Let me see the County;
Ay, marry, go, I say, and fetch him hither.
Now, afore God, this reverend holy friar,
All our whole city is much bound to him.

(i) Who is the "youthful lord", and why has he gone to Lawrence's cell?

(ii) How did the "youthful lord" greet Juliet when she arrived at Lawrence's cell, and what was her reply?

(iii) Why does Capulet tell Juliet to "stand up"? What does he mean by "This is as't should be"?

(iv) What does Capulet do next and why?

(d) *Romeo.*   I beseech thee, youth,
Put not another sin upon my head
By urging me to fury; O, be gone!
By heaven, I love thee better than myself,
For I come hither arm'd against myself.
Stay not, be gone; live, and hereafter say
A madman's mercy bid thee run away.

(i) Who is the "youth"? For what purpose has he come to Juliet's tomb?

(ii) To what conclusion has the "youth" jumped to explain Romeo's presence? Why is Romeo there, and what does he mean by "arm'd against myself"?

(iii) To what earlier incident does Romeo refer when he says: "Put not another sin upon my head By urging me to fury"?

(iv) What is the reaction of the "youth" to Romeo's advice: "Stay not, be gone", and what briefly is the outcome?

NOTES ON POSSIBLE ANSWERS

(b)

(i) After Romeo's friend, Mercutio, has been killed by Tybalt, Romeo has challenged Tybalt and killed him. For this he expects to be condemned to death by the Prince. Instead he is banished.

(ii) Romeo wishes to kill himself.

(iii) His wife Juliet is alive and loves him. Tybalt wanted to kill Romeo, but Romeo was victorious.

(iv) Romeo has been sentenced to immediate banishment. If he is found within the city, his life is forfeit.

(c)

(i) Paris. He has gone to tell the Friar that he is to marry Juliet in two days' time.

(ii) Paris wished happiness to his wife. Juliet answered that when she was indeed a wife she would then be happy.

(iii) She is kneeling to ask pardon for her disobedience. The husband he has chosen for her is worthy of her love.

(iv) He goes to find Paris to tell him that the wedding is to be on the next day.

(d)

(i) Paris. To bring flowers and to mourn her death.

(ii) That Romeo of the Montagues has come to dishonour the dead bodies of Juliet and Tybalt who are Capulets. Romeo has brought with him the poison with which, as if it were a weapon, he will end his own life.

(iii) When Tybalt tried to provoke Romeo, Mercutio took the fight upon himself and was mortally wounded. Hearing that Mercutio had died, Romeo, in furious anger, killed Tybalt.

(iv) Paris tries to arrest Romeo; they fight and Paris is killed. Romeo places him, as he asks, beside Juliet's tomb.

(*Notes:* A good deal of accurate information is necessary here. Write as simply and shortly as possible. Number the sections carefully. See that you have not left out any of the "bits", e.g. 1(*a*) (iii) Benvolio's real purpose. For 1(*c*) (ii) and similar questions, try out your attempt in pencil first. Notice that it is often clearer to use names rather than pronouns: for 2(*d*) (iv) it is better to write "Paris tries to arrest Romeo" rather than "He tries to arrest him.")

ESSAY QUESTIONS

3. "The death of the lovers is brought about by the feud between the great families, but the effect of their death is to heal the feud."

(i) Show how Shakespeare introduces the feud, by giving a lively account of the street brawl in the first scene, including the intervention by the Prince;

AND

(ii) *Briefly* describe the ending of the feud when the Prince and the rival parties gather in the graveyard.

4. Give an account of the services rendered to Juliet by the Nurse, and show how the Nurse's own qualities present a striking contrast to those of Juliet. (Both questions are taken from Cambridge, G.C.E., O Level, English Literature, Summer 1963.)

Jot down *brief notes* before you begin to write. Remember that you will certainly not have time to write out the whole essay in rough and then copy it out later. Plan carefully; the way in which the question is arranged will tell you how to plan your answer.

Any quotations given should be short; do not waste time on long quotations of ten or twenty lines; it is more important to show that you yourself can write simply and clearly. When quoting poetry, quote in lines and begin the quotation about one inch from the left-hand margin. The quotations given should fit grammatically into your own sentences.

Hints on Question 3

Plan: Notice that you are not asked to write about the quotation itself, but since it has been given, you could well use some part of it to begin or end your answer. Write your answer in 2 sections, (i) and (ii). Give two-thirds of your time to (i) because this requires "a lively account", and one-third to (ii) which asks for brief description.

Material: Be careful to begin and end exactly where you are asked.

(i) The first scene from the beginning until the Prince leaves the stage.

(ii) The last scene from the time when the Prince comes into the graveyard until the end of the play.

211

Arrangement: The difficulty here is to know in advance how much detail you have time for. (How many minutes can you give to (i)?)

First paragraph: Use the words of the question and of the quotation to begin, e.g.

> In the feud between the two great families of the Capulets and Montagues, two of the Capulets' servants (give their names if you know them, and are sure of the spelling) are ready to pick a quarrel the very moment they meet with two of the Montagues' men. They insult each other like children (say how, if you can spare the time). Sampson tells Abraham that he serves as good a master as Abraham, but changes this word "good" to (what?) when they see (whom?), a Capulet, of fiery temper, approaching. (In one brief sentence say why they begin to fight, and with what weapons.) B——, a noble Montague, draws his sword and tries (give one phrase); T—— refuses to believe (what?), calls B—— (one word) and forces him to defend himself. As the fighting continues, an officer and some of the citizens try in vain to stop the uproar. Old Capulet rushes out, wearing ——, and calls for ——, but his wife tells him that a —— would be better for such an old man. (Complete this paragraph with one similar sentence about Lady Montague and her husband.)

Second paragraph: (This must be kept quite short to make up for the time taken by the first paragraph.)

> Prince Escalus now (form a verb from the noun "intervention"). He is very (one simple adjective) and commands all those who are fighting to (complete the phrase in 4 words) on pain of ——. There have now been (how many?) street battles between the Capulets and the Montagues and he will punish with —— any future ——.

(ii) (You have now little time left and must write very briefly. Leave out altogether the story of how the deaths came about. Give as many as you can of the following points.)

The Prince is shown the three bodies (give names). Lady Capulet is ready to die of sorrow as she sees her daughter newly dead. Montague's wife has died (when?) in grieving for (3 words, including "son"). The Prince points out what punishment has come upon Capulet and Montague. Their children, who should have been the joy of their old age, lie dead. Capulet takes the —— of Montague, as he would gladly have joined Juliet's hand to Romeo's. Montague promises (what?), and Capulet also will make a splendid effigy of (whom?). So, at last, the feud is healed.

Hints on Question 4

Plan: Give two-thirds of your time to "services rendered" and one-third to the "striking contrast". (You have probably prepared "character sketches" of Juliet and her nurse, but remember that you can earn marks here only for some points of difference between them.)

Material: Scenes in which the nurse appears up to the time when she chooses "ornaments" for Juliet's marriage to Paris.

Arrangement: Write two paragraphs on "services rendered" and one or two paragraphs on "contrast".

First paragraph: Begin at once without any introduction. You will earn marks only for information given.

Juliet's nurse has looked after her and loved her since Juliet was a tiny child. She remembers how Juliet first (finish the sentence in 3 words). It is the nurse who first tells Romeo (what?) and she finds out (what?) for Juliet as —— is leaving the feast. After the balcony scene Juliet sends her nurse to bring back Romeo's message: that they are to be married (when and by whom?). The nurse is to bring into the house the rope-ladder by which ——.

Second paragraph:

The nurse brings the news of Tybalt's —— and Romeo's ——. (Do not be misled into telling any more of this part of the story. You have no time to spare.) She then goes to Friar Lawrence's cell, taking Juliet's —— to Romeo. Next morning she warns Juliet that ——. The end of her influence over Juliet comes about when she advises her to marry ——, saying (quote a phrase or sentence). Here we see (one sentence of comment, that when Juliet most needs help, the nurse ——). She helps to choose the ornaments for Juliet's wedding to —— and it is she who finds Juliet apparently dead.

Third paragraph: (Give 3 or 4 points of contrast with examples from the play.)

Juliet can express herself very simply and directly, as when ——. The nurse, by contrast, often (do not say "always") talks too much. (Give one instance in one sentence.)

Juliet is very trusting. (Give one or two very brief instances.) The nurse, on the other hand, is rather suspicious (see what she says of Romeo's man). Juliet thinks that true love is sufficient reason for marriage, but the nurse tells Romeo that the man who marries Capulet's daughter will (quote the three words). Juliet is constant in love, but the nurse thinks it better for her to take a second husband since Romeo is banished.

ADDITIONAL ESSAY QUESTIONS

5. With close reference and brief quotation, illustrate Shakespeare's presentation through his poetry of (i) *beauty*, in the scene in which Romeo leaves Juliet to go to Mantua, and (ii) *horror*, in Juliet's soliloquy when she takes the potion. (Cambridge, G.C.E., O Level, English Literature, Summer 1963)

6. Give an account of the part played by Friar Lawrence, showing his importance in the play.

7. "We strongly sympathise with Juliet because she receives little help and guidance at home – father, mother, and nurse, all fail her." By careful reference to the play show how far you consider this statement to be true.

8. "Romeo's misfortunes and final tragedy are caused by circumstances outside his control." By careful reference to the play show how far you agree with this statement. (Cambridge, G.C.E., O Level, English Literature, Summer 1962)

GLOSSARY

This glossary explains all those words in the play which are used in Modern English as they were in Shakespeare's day, but are not among the 3,000 most-used words in the language.

The notes opposite the text explain the words which are *not* used in Modern English. In these notes it has been necessary to use a very few words which are also outside the 3,000-word list; these are included in the glossary.

Explanations in the glossary are given almost entirely within the chosen list of words; the few exceptions will be found explained elsewhere in the glossary.

Only the meaning of the word as used in the text or notes is normally given.

n. = "noun"; v. = "verb"; adj. = "adjective"; adv. = "adverb"; p.t. = "past tense".

A

abate, to grow less, make less.

abbey, place where religious men and women live apart, giving their lives to God.

abhor, to hate.

abound, to be abundant, plentiful.

absolve, to set free from blame.

abuse (v.), to use badly, ill-treat; (n.) a wrong use, offence.

access, way in, entrance.

accursed, lying under a curse, hateful.

accustom, to make used to.

addled, empty, infertile.

adieu, good-bye (French).

adjacent, lying near.

ado, trouble and excitement.

adversary, enemy.

adversity, misfortune.

afflict, to cause pain (to).

affliction, pain, sorrow.

afire, on fire.

agate, a hard, precious stone.

agile, quick-moving.

alas, exclamation of sorrow or regret.

alderman, one of the group of men who govern a city.

alliance, the joining of families by marriage.

alligator, a large, man-eating river creature.

aloof, at a distance.

ambiguity, uncertainty, something which can have two meanings.

amen, may it be so (a word used at the end of a prayer).

amend, to make better.

amorous, inclined to love.

anatomy, body.

anguish, great pain or sorrow.

apace, swiftly.

apparel (v.), to clothe; (n.) clothes.

appertain, to belong (to).

215

apprehend, to seize, arrest.

apt, (1) ready; (2) well-suited.

arbitrate, to decide who, or what, is right or wrong.

arithmetic, the science of numbers.

ashes, fine dust left after something has been burnt.

aside, words spoken by an actor which the other actors on the stage are not supposed to hear.

assail, to attack.

asunder, apart, in pieces.

atmosphere, a surrounding air or feeling.

augment, to increase.

B

baggage, a good-for-nothing girl or woman.

bait, food put on a hook to catch fish.

baleful, harmful.

bandy, (1) to throw about; (2) to exchange blows.

bankrupt, one who is unable to pay his debts.

baptize, to make someone a Christian by putting water on him as a sign.

bark, ship.

battlement, defensive wall on the top of a castle.

bawd, an immoral woman, a go-between.

befit, to be proper for.

beget, to produce, cause to be born.

begot, p.t. of *beget*.

beguile, to cheat, deceive.

behest, a command.

behold, to look upon, see.

beloved, loved.

bench, a long seat.

bent, intention, inclination of the mind.

beseech, to beg for, ask earnestly.

bestride, (1) to sit or stand with one leg on either side of; (2) to stride across.

betrothed, engaged to be married.

bewitch, to charm, have a magic effect on.

bier, wooden carrier for a dead body.

bladder, a bag of skin or leather used to contain liquid.

blade, sword.

blazon, to describe.

blessing, that which brings happiness, favour.

blister, a small swelling on the skin, filled with a liquid like water.

blubber, to weep noisily.

blush, to become red in the face.

bode, to be a sign of what will happen, especially evil.

boisterous, rough, wild.

bondage, slavery.

bonjour, good day (French).

borne, p.t. of *bear*, to carry.

bosom, the human breast.

brace, *a b. of*, two.

brag, to boast.

braggart, a boaster.

brawl, noisy quarrel.

breach, (1) an opening; (2) a break in a defending wall.

bride, a woman about to be married, or newly married.

bridegroom, a man about to be married, or newly married.

bridal, relating to a wedding.

brief, short; *briefly*, shortly, quickly.

brine, salt water.

brisk, quick, active.

bud, a flower before it has opened.

budge, to move.

bump, a swelling caused by a blow.

216

C

calamity, a great misfortune or evil.

cancel, to strike out, put an end to.

canker, (1) a worm or disease which eats away plants; (2) *cankered,* diseased, eaten away.

cannon, a large gun.

canopy, a curtain hung over a bed.

carrion, (1) dead body; (2) feeding on dead bodies.

cast (off), to throw away, or aside.

celibacy, the unmarried state.

challenge, an invitation or call to fight.

chamber, room of a house.

chambermaid, woman who takes care of a chamber (q.v.).

chaos, confusion, absence of order.

charge, to command.

chase, pursuit, running after.

chaste, (1) virtuous or pure in matters of love; (2) unmarried.

chastity, (1) virtue, purity; (2) the unmarried state.

chat, a friendly, unimportant talk.

checker, to mark with spots or streaks of different colour.

cherish, to care for, protect.

chide, to scold, find fault with; p.t. *chid.*

choice, (1) the act of choosing; (2) what has been chosen.

chorus, words said, or a song sung, usually by a number of people at the same time, but in this play by one person only.

Christian, a follower of Jesus Christ.

cleft, split.

climax, (1) the most exciting event in a series of events; (2) the highest point.

cloak, a sleeveless outer garment.

closet, a small private room, often used for hanging clothes.

clown, (1) man employed to amuse others by tricks and jokes; (2) the fool in a play.

club, heavy stick.

coachmaker, one who makes large, four-wheeled carriages.

cockatrice, imaginary serpent, said to cause death by looking at a person.

cockerel, a young cock.

collier, one who carries coal.

comic (adj.), making people laugh.

comment, to speak about.

compass, area, limits.

compliment, an expression of praise or admiration.

compound, a mixture.

conceal, to hide.

conduit, a water-pipe.

confession, the telling of one's sins (q.v.) to a priest.

confessor, a priest who hears confession.

conjure, to call up a spirit from the dead.

consent (v.), to agree; (n.) agreement.

consort (with), to go about in the company of.

conspire, to plot, make a secret plan to do something unlawful.

constable, an official whose job it was to keep the peace.

constrain, to compel.

contagion, disease which can be passed on by touch.

content, (1) satisfaction; (2) matter contained in a book, speech, etc.

contradict, to say the opposite.

convert, to change from one state to another.

cope (with), to encounter, struggle with.

217

cordial, a medicine for the heart; a pleasant drink made from fruit.

corn, hard thick skin on the foot, caused by the rubbing of the shoe.

corpse, dead body of a human being.

couch, to lie down.

counterfeit (v.), imitate in order to deceive, pretend; (n.) an imitation, a false copy.

couple, to put together to make a pair.

court, to woo.

courteous, polite; *courtesy*, politeness, good manners.

courtier, one who attends at a court.

covert, a secret, hidden part of a wood.

cram, to stuff full.

cross, to hinder, oppose.

crotchet, (1) a very short note in music; (2) a strange notion.

crutch, a stick to help one walk.

cull, to select, gather.

curfew, a bell rung to warn people to stay indoors and put out their lights and fires; here in the play, a bell rung at 3 or 4 a.m.

curtsy, a polite greeting made by bending the knees and bowing.

D

dagger, a pointed knife used as a weapon.

damn, to condemn to everlasting punishment after death.

dank, very damp.

dash, to knock to pieces.

deadly, causing death, mortal.

deceased, dead.

deck, to adorn, dress in fine clothes or ornaments.

decree, a command.

dedicate, to devote, or set apart for some special purpose.

deflower, spoil, destroy.

deformity, ugliness.

demesne, (1) area, (2) estate.

denote, to mean, indicate.

depart, to go away.

deprive, to prevent from using.

deputy, one who is given power to act for another.

descry, to be able to see something a long way off.

desperate, wild, rash.

despise, to scorn, have contempt for.

detest, to hate.

devise, to imagine, plan.

devout, religious, devoted in service.

dexterity, skill with the hands.

dial, clock-face.

dignified, stately, worthy of honour.

digress, to turn aside from.

dine, to eat dinner (the main meal of the day).

dire, *direful*, terrible, horrible.

dirge, sad funeral song.

discord, notes of music which do not sound well together.

discourse, speech.

discreet, wise.

dismember, to cut into pieces.

disparagement, the dishonouring of a person by speaking of him as of little value.

dispatch, to kill.

displant, to root up and plant elsewhere.

displeasure, feeling of annoyance or anger.

disposition, one's natural way of feeling or acting.

dissembler, deceiver, pretender.

distil, to draw drops of liquid from.

distraught, violently distressed.

divers, various, different.

divine (adj.), god-like; (n.) parson.

doleful, sad.

doomsday, day of judgement at the end of the world.

dote, to love foolishly or excessively.

downright (adv.), strongly.

dram, small measure of drink.

drama, the branch of literature concerned with plays for the theatre.

dramatis personae (Latin), "the people of the drama", a list of the characters in the play.

dramatist, a writer of plays.

dreadful, causing fear, horrible.

drivel, (1) to talk nonsense, (2) to run at the mouth.

drizzle, to fall in small drops.

drudge, one who does hard, unpleasant work for little reward.

drunkard, one who has lost control of himself through taking too much strong drink.

duellist, one who engages in a fight with another person conducted according to fixed rules.

dumps, low spirits.

E

Easter, feast day in memory of Christ's rising from the dead.

ebb, to flow back.

economy, the careful use of what one has so that nothing is wasted.

effeminate, (used of men), womanish, lacking in courage.

e.g., for example.

elf (pl. *elves*), a small fairy imagined as living in woods.

eloquence, ability to make effective speeches.

emperor, ruler of an empire.

enamoured (*of*), in love with.

encamp, to make a camp.

enforce, to compel.

enjoin, to command.

enmity, the feeling of hatred between enemies.

enrich, to make rich.

ensign, flag.

entertain (an idea), to have in mind.

entreat, to ask or beg earnestly.

episode, one event in a set of events.

environed, surrounded.

errand, a journey to carry a message.

evermore, for all time.

excel, to be better than others.

execution, performance, carrying out.

exeunt (Latin), they go off (the stage).

exit (Latin), he or she goes off (the stage).

exposition, explanation.

expressly, in clear terms.

exquisite, excellent, very beautiful.

F

fall out with, quarrel.

famine, extreme shortage of food.

fantasy, imagination.

fathom, a measure of six feet in length, used in measuring the depth of water.

fearful, (1) terrible; (2) full of fear.

feign, to pretend.

fellowship, company.

felon, a law-breaker.

fencing, the sport of sword-fighting.

fester, to rot, decay.

fetch, to bring from another place.

feud, a long-continued family quarrel.

fickle, (1) changeable; (2) favouring first one and then another; not faithful to one.

fiddlestick, a stick used to play a violin.

fiend, a cruel-spirited person, a devil.

flint, hard, sharp stone.

folks, people.

forbear, to pause, keep oneself from doing something.

forebode, to foretell or be a sign of some future event, usually evil.

forefather, a person from whom one is descended.

forefinger, the finger next to the thumb.

forfeit, payment which has to be made as a punishment.

forswear, (1) to break one's pledge; (2) to swear to give up.

fortnight, two weeks.

fountain, a spring or stream.

fray, fight.

friar, a brother, member of a religious group.

friary, the place where a group of friars (q.v.) lives.

frost, the act or state of freezing.

fume, smoke.

function, particular work or duty.

furious, very angry.

furnish, to supply.

G

gad, to wander about looking for amusement.

gall, (1) bitter liquid; (2) bitterness.

gamble, to play cards or other games for money.

gape, to have the mouth wide open.

garish, too bright, showy.

giddy, feeling as if the head were turning round.

gipsy, member of a wandering race that lives in covered carts.

glossary, list of difficult words with notes explaining them.

glove, covering for the hand.

gnat, small flying insect which bites and draws blood.

gorge, to eat greedily.

gory, bloody.

gossamer, fine silky thread.

gossip, one who engages in worthless talk.

grandsire, grandfather.

grasshopper, a jumping insect.

gravity, seriousness.

grievance, (1) cause for complaint; (2) distress.

grievous, very serious.

griping, painful.

grove, a small group of trees.

grub, worm.

grudge, ill-will; anger against someone for something in the past.

gyves, chains or bars fixed on a prisoner's feet.

H

hag, an ugly old woman.

handsome, good-looking.

harlot, an immoral woman.

haunt, a favourite place which one frequently visits.

hazel, a reddish-brown colour.

hazel-nut, the nut of the hazel tree.

headstrong, strongly self-willed.

health, *to drink someone's health*, to raise one's glass and wish him good health.

henceforth, from now on.

herald, a person or thing which announces some future event.

hereabouts, near here.

hereafter, after this.

heretic, one who holds a teaching which is against the general belief.

herring, a fish.

hideous, very ugly or unpleasant.

hist! silence! listen!

hoar, grey or white with age.

hoarse, rough in sound (of the voice).

holy, devout (q.v.), devoted to the service of God.

homely, simple.

hoodwink, to cover the eyes.

household, all those living in one house, family.

huge, very large.

I

idolatry, the worship of an idol.

i.e., that is.

illiterate, unable to read or write.

impeach, to accuse.

impel, to urge, push on.

importune, to question closely.

impute, to consider as belonging to.

inauspicious, promising bad fortune.

inconstant, changeable, fickle (q.v.).

incorporate, unite in one body.

inexorable, unchangeable.

infection, disease.

inter, to bury.

intercession, the act of asking a favour for someone.

interchange, exchange, putting each in place of the other.

intrusion, uninvited entry.

inundation, flood.

invocation, a prayer calling for help.

issue, result.

itch, feeling on the skin which causes a desire to scratch.

J

jocund, merry.

jolly, happy, merry.

K

kin, family.

kinsman, a male relative.

knave, a tricky, dishonest fellow.

knight, a man of noble character.

L

lace, to mark with streaks (lines).

lady-bird, a small red or yellow insect with black spots.

lash, to hit with a whip.

last, the wooden or iron shape of a foot on which shoes are made.

lath, thin slip of wood.

leisure, time free from work or duty.

lengthen, to make longer.

lenity, mercy.

Lent, a period of forty days from Ash Wednesday to Easter.

lenten, having to do with Lent.

lest, for fear that.

liege, a lord to whom service is owed.

light upon, to find unexpectedly.

likeness, form.

limp, to walk lamely.

lisp, to speak, saying the *s* sound as *th*.

lively, full of life.

livery, special dress worn by the servants of a rich man.

loathe, hate; *loathsome*, hateful, foul.

lock, a curl of hair.

logic, art of reasoning; *logical*, according to reason.

looks, appearance (of a person).

lour, to look threatening, angry.

lure, to draw a person on by promises.

lusty, young and strong.

221

M

madam, title given to a lady.

maidenhood, the unmarried state (of a girl).

maintain, to assert as true, support.

mandrake, a plant used as a drug to cause sleep.

mane, long hair on a horse's neck.

mangle, cut, spoil.

manslaughter, the unlawful killing of anyone.

mar, spoil.

margin, border round the printed page of a book.

martial, warlike.

martyr, (1) to kill someone for his beliefs; (2) to cause great pain to.

Mass, the central act of worship in the Catholic Church.

matron, married woman.

mattock, tool used for breaking up the ground.

meagre, thin, starved.

meantime, the time between two events.

meddle, interfere.

medlar, a small brown fruit.

melancholy, feeling of sadness.

menace, to threaten.

merchandise, goods bought and sold.

meteor, a falling star.

metre, the fixed arrangement of light and heavy syllables in poetry.

midwife, a woman who helps at childbirth.

minim, a short musical note.

minister, to serve, supply.

minstrel, a singing musician.

mire, mud.

misadventure, an unfortunate event.

miscarry, to go wrong.

mischance, a piece of bad luck.

misshapen, badly shaped.

morsel, small piece.

mourner, one who grieves for a dead person.

muffle, to wrap, cover.

mumble, to speak indistinctly.

musty, stale, mouldy.

N

natural (n.), a born fool.

nickname, a name used by friends instead of one's real name.

nimble, quick and active (in body and mind).

nipple, that part of the breast through which a baby gets its mother's milk.

nourish, to nurse, give food to.

nun, a woman living with a group of other women a life devoted to God.

O

oath, (1) a statement one swears to be true; (2) a promise made to God.

obscure, to make difficult to understand.

obsequies, funeral ceremonies.

occupy, take and hold possession of, to fill a space.

odds, *at odds with*, opposed to.

oft, often.

orchard, garden of fruit trees.

osier (adj.), made of willow twigs.

outcry, show of anger by the people.

outrage, (1) outcry (q.v.); (2) wrongful act which causes great anger.

overhear, to hear something said to another person which one is not intended to hear.

P

pace, to step, walk.

packthread, strong thread.

paramour, lover.

parts, personal qualities, abilities.

pate, head.

peevish, bad-tempered, hard to please.

pen, to shut in.

penalty, punishment.

Pentecost, Whit Sunday.

penury, extreme poverty.

perforce, by force, of necessity.

perjure, to swear falsely.

pernicious, wicked, harmful.

peruse, to read carefully.

perverse, wilfully doing what a person wishes one not to.

pestilence, disease which spreads quickly, plague; *pestilent*, troublesome.

physic, medicine.

pie, dish of fruit or meat with pastry (q.v.) covering.

pilot, a person who guides a ship.

pine, waste away through grief.

pinion, wing of a bird.

pink (n.), a kind of flower; *the pink*, the height of perfection; (v.) to adorn cloth or leather by cutting holes in it.

plait, to join three or more strings, threads or bands together by turning each over the other in turn.

plantain, plant with broad leaves.

pluck, to pull (off, out).

pomegranate, large fruit containing many red seeds.

portent, a sign of some future event, usually unfavourable.

posterity, descendants.

potion, a drink of medicine or poison.

poultice, mass of hot material put on skin as a medicine.

prate, to talk foolishly and excessively.

predicament, difficult situation.

predominant, superior.

presage, to foretell.

prick, to make a small hole, pierce.

privy (*to*), having special knowledge of.

proceedings, events.

profane, to put something to an evil use.

prolixity, wordiness.

prologue, a speech introducing a play.

promotion, advancement to a higher position.

prompter, one who helps an actor who has forgotten his words.

propagate, to multiply, increase.

prose, language without rhyme or metre (q.v.).

prostrate, lying stretched out.

proverb, short wise saying, usually well-known.

provoke, to make angry, excite.

prudence, carefulness, wisdom.

pry, to look into something which is not one's business.

pule, to cry like a child.

pump, light dancing shoe.

pun, a play on words in which one word is used in two senses at the same time, or in which words with the same sound and different meanings are used.

purgatory, place in which souls are purified after death and made fit for heaven.

purge, to get rid of.

Q

quench, to put out (a fire) with liquid.

quince, a hard fruit.

223

R

rail, to use violent language.
rancour, deep hatred.
rank, foul.
rapier, long thin sword, sharpened only at the point, used in practising sword-play.
rate, scold, speak angrily to.
raven, a large black bird.
ravening, greedily seeking food.
receipt, a receiving.
receptacle, a space which contains or holds something.
reclaim, to bring back.
redress, the setting right of a wrong.
region, space.
repent, be sorry for, regret.
repetition, the saying or doing again of something.
resolution, decision.
retain, to keep.
retire, to go away.
retort, to turn back (a blow).
revel (n.), merry-making, entertainment; (v.) to make merry.
reverend, worthy of great respect.
righteous, just and good.
rigour, severity.
rind, skin.
rite, ceremony.
roe, (1) female deer, (2) eggs of a fish.
rogue, dishonest fellow.
rosemary, sweet-smelling evergreen bush.
rote, memory.
rouse, to wake up.
rude, rough, violent.
runaway, one who runs away from something.
rush, tall grass-like plant growing in wet places.

S

sack, to attack a town or building and carry off everything of value.
sallow, of a pale, yellow colour (of the face).
salutation, greeting.
saucy, rude, disrespectful.
save, except.
scare, frighten.
scope, field of action, area.
scurvy, low, foul.
season, to preserve food by adding salt, herbs etc.
seduce, to lead into wrong-doing.
sepulchre, tomb.
sever, to cut, separate.
shank, leg.
sharp, a note in music half a tone above the true pitch.
sheath, a case for a sword or dagger.
shed, to let fall, make flow (tears, blood etc.).
shin, front bone of leg below the knee.
show (n.), a display.
shower, to rain.
shrink, to draw back from.
shroud, the cloth in which a dead body is wrapped for burial.
shun, to avoid meeting, keep away from.
siege, attack, assault on a fortress or town.
sigh, deep breath.
signify, to make known; *significance*, meaning, importance.
sin (v.), to break the laws of God; (n.) an act which does this.
sire, father.
skull, the bony framework of the head.
slack, to go slowly or lazily.

slander, false statement made to harm someone's reputation.

sluttish, dirty.

smock, loose, ornamented outer garment.

soar, to fly high in the air.

sociable, fond of company.

sojourn, to stay for a time in a place.

sound, (1) to measure the depth of (water); (2) to make music; (3) to express.

soundly, thoroughly.

sparkle, to give off sparks, flash light.

spear, sharp metal point fixed to a long stick and used as a weapon.

spit, to fix on the point of a weapon.

spite, hatred, anger.

spleen, ill-temper.

spoke, bar joining the outer part of a wheel to the centre.

spy, to see at a distance.

squirrel, a small grey or reddish animal with a bushy tail that lives in trees.

stab, to pierce or wound by sticking a knife into.

stark, stiff.

state, pomp, rich ceremony.

stealth, secrecy.

steed, horse.

steep, to make wet through.

stifle, to prevent from breathing.

strangle, to kill by pressing hard on the throat making breathing impossible.

stratagem, a trick to deceive.

streak, a long irregular line of colour.

stress, to say with special force.

strew, to scatter.

structure, the way a thing is built up.

submission, yielding.

substantial, solid, real.

subtly, cleverly, cunningly.

suicide, the act of killing oneself.

sum (v.), to add up; (n.) the result of adding all the parts.

sunder, to separate, cut apart.

sup, to eat supper.

supernatural, not capable of being explained by the ordinary laws of nature; beyond what is natural.

supple, easily bent.

surgeon, a doctor.

sweetheart, lover.

swift, quick in movement.

switch, whip or thin stick.

sycamore, a kind of tree.

syllables, the separate sound groups into which a word can be divided.

T

tackle, ropes used on a ship.

tainted, having a bad smell.

tale, story.

tallow, pale hard animal fat used in making candles.

tardy, late, slow.

tarry, delay, wait.

tattered (clothes), torn, ragged.

team, a group of two or more working together.

teat, part of the breast from which a baby draws out milk.

tedious, long and dull.

temper, (1) to mix; (2) to soften.

testify, to assert the truth solemnly.

theme, subject of thought, speech or writing.

thwart, to prevent someone from doing what he wishes.

tickle, to cause a person to laugh by light touches.

tide, time or season.

tidings, news.

tilt (at), to ride at with a spear, thrust.

225

toad, small frog-like animal.

torch, a flaming light, e.g. of burning wood soaked in oil.

torment, to cause suffering to.

tortoise, land and fresh-water animal with a hard shell.

traces, leather bands joining a horse to a carriage.

tragic, sad, distressing, as in a tragedy.

transgression, wrong-doing, going beyond the law.

transparent, (1) which can be seen through; (2) clearly understood.

treacherous, disloyal, untrustworthy.

treason, disloyalty, betrayal.

trespass, offence.

trifling, unimportant.

troop, to move in company.

truce, a period of peace.

trudge, to walk wearily.

trunk, the main part of the body.

tush, an exclamation of impatience.

tut, an exclamation expressing anger or disagreement.

tutor, to teach.

twain, two.

twinkle, to flash from time to time, like stars.

twist, to turn, change direction.

'twixt, between.

tyrannous, cruel, unjust.

U

umpire, judge.

unaccustomed, unused to.

underneath, under, below.

undertake, to take a duty upon oneself.

unfold, to reveal, make clear.

unhallowed, unholy, (v. *holy*).

unruly, disorderly, unwilling to obey.

unsavoury, unpleasant.

unseemly, unsuitable, not fitting.

unsubstantial, having no body.

untangle, to put order into something mixed or confused.

untimely, not happening at the normal time.

unwieldy, difficult to manage.

usurer, money-lender.

utter, to speak.

V

valour, courage.

vanity, emptiness.

vast, very large.

vein, one of the pipes which carry blood in the body.

vestal, pure (used of unmarried women or girls).

vex, to trouble, distress.

vial, small glass bottle.

villain, wicked man.

visage, face.

W

waddle, to walk with short steps, like a duck.

waggon, (1) a strong cart; (2) *waggoner*, one who drives a *w*.

wail, to cry out with grief.

wanton, wild, uncontrolled, immoral.

ward, young person under the control of a parent or older person.

wary, cautious, looking out for danger.

wax, to grow.

wayward, wilful, uncontrolled.

wean, to accustom a child to food other than milk.

226

weep, to cry (with tears falling).

wench, girl.

while, a short time.

whine, to make a long-drawn complaining cry.

whit, the smallest possible amount.

whore, an immoral woman who sells herself.

wield, use in the hand.

wit, (1) good sense; (2) cleverness in amusing speech.

womb, (1) part of the mother's body in which an unborn child is carried; (2) any hollow container.

wreak, to put into effect.

wrench, to pull or twist suddenly and violently.

wring, to twist.